No Road
Is Ever Straight

Andrew C. Jacobs

TABLE OF CONTENTS

ACKNOWLEDGEMENTS

Producing books like these, especially on a yearly basis, demands a level of commitment from our US team who needs to be continually recognized. Led by our head of Pre-Press, Rich Green, it is a monumental effort of which I am continually appreciative.

I also want to thank Katie Hannington, one of the finest editors I have ever had the pleasure to work with. In addition to being thorough, she has the ability to decipher my notes and communicate what I want to say.

In addition, I want to thank the entire IIUS team. Your dedication, work ethic and great ideas has helped enabled us to clear a path through the insanity of our economy and position to soar in the future.

And finally I want to thank my wife Wendy and children Ben, Alex and Kayla for being there. I am so fortunate for having them as a part of my family and always by my side.

DEDICATION

I proudly dedicate this book to my grandfather and our company founder Morris Jacobs. His courage to start his own company with no experience or prior knowledge of our industry was counterbalanced by his incredible drive and determination to succeed. I only knew him after he retired but would have liked to have seen him in his prime, he must have been formidable and I am confident he would have loved to see where we are today.

JANUARY

1/1/10
4:00 PM EST
Home, NJ

A new year; a new book begins.

We had a little more snow last night, so I shoveled this morning before walking with Uncle Dave. As always, we talked about everything in general. He said he thought my greatest attribute was my ability to sell and make deals. He has mentioned that before and since I agree with him and am moving in that direction, I began to tell him about the potential radio station idea. I received an email this morning from my partner Ben in China confirming that he now has a high level contact in Malaysia who will help with promoting our plan here if he deems it worthwhile. Ben has asked me to write out a proposal for him, which will be a modified version of what I have already sent others. The plan has morphed into what I hope will be a win/win for all of the groups involved. It must be in order to give it the best chance for success. Listed below is where we stand so far with the groups involved and their potential gains and risks.

Ideal Jacobs U.S.
Potential Financial Gains:
1. Create a radio/media network in Malaysia
2. Create a partnership with a New York Radio Station
3. Create a partnership with various independent music groups
4. Set up a QVC-like network based in radio and through the internet
5. Warehouse and distribution deal through the radio station, advertisers from both sides
6. Create additional radio stations in Malaysia and branch out to Thailand, Singapore and the rest of Asia

The New York Radio Station
1. Additional outlet for their content
2. Additional markets for their advertisers that they can charge for
3. A secondary media market from their website where they can produce programming with paying sponsors
4. Go after a completely new market area via the music of independent bands brought in through both the U.S. and Asia
5. Have a cut of the warehouse and distribution profits

6. Have the home shopping network system be part of their website to help attract and keep listeners

The Country of Malaysia
1. Revitalize a dying area: broadcasting radio shows
2. Bring in new commerce from both Malaysia and the U.S.
3. Sell Malaysian produced goods in the U.S.
4. We can bring in other companies to go public
5. They can utilize the system to promote commerce, jobs, and benefit for those starting their own businesses

Our bank in Malaysia
1. Loan us money for the project
2. Help bring other U.S. companies public in Asia

Our advertisers in the U.S. and Malaysia
1. Chances to sell goods and services in Malaysia
2. Chances to sell goods and services in the U.S.
3. Can produce their own programming and have an outlet for it
4. We can store and distribute their products for them

Independent Bands
1. Chance to be heard both in a major U.S. market and through the internet site
2. Chance to be heard on Malaysia radio and through their internet site
3. The chance to sell their music
4. The chance to produce their own programming

Conventional radio stations' market share and profits are being hurt worldwide by the burgeoning of the internet. It is common for many stations to stream their programming in the form of podcasts to try to gain listeners after the original transmission. Getting paid for this service is becoming increasingly difficult. We propose a new model, which combines the best of all aspects of conventional and satellite radio, the internet, blog streaming and the online marketplace to harvest the benefits of the programming offered.

One of the reasons for the worldwide success of satellite radio is their lack of commercials and categorized programming. Since they do not normally depend on sponsors or advertising, they can afford to have many segmented groups that do not appeal to any one defined group of products and services that would be paid for by sponsors. However, there are still the monthly charges for membership and commercials on some of the stations. Conventional radio that is theoretically free is still interrupted by commercial breaks for 15-20% of the airtime. Home shopping networks, while functioning fantastically on television, have never been attempted through a combination of radio and internet streaming.

What we propose is to tap into the following groups:

1. Those who have their radios on all day, tuned to the same stations
2. Those who listen to radio in their cars and offices
3. Those who do not have the money or access to satellite radio
4. Those who don't have regular access to the internet at home or in the office

Our radio stations in the U.S. will provide Malaysians with 30 hours of New York style, non-religious, non-political, non-sexual programming each week. For the hours of programming besides sports and weather, we will offer program blocks of independent bands from North America segmented by genre. American sponsors from the U.S. stations will have the opportunity to pay for advertising time on our Malaysian station in order to begin tapping into the Asian market. Their products will be warehoused and distributed by our company. At the same time, Malaysian sponsors will have the ability to buy time on our U.S. stations to help create markets for their products starting in the New York area. Their products will also be warehoused and distributed by our company. Once the model proves effective, other U.S. stations will be added so that Malaysian advertisers will be able to reach a much bigger market and U.S. advertisers from all of our stations would be able to advertise in Malaysia. The website of all of the stations involved would be modified to online shopping centers where all of the products and services of our advertisers will be available for discounted sale. The music of the independent bands will also be offered for downloading.

One of the limitations of free radio is that there are only 24 hours in the day for programming. Through the internet, we can offer additional broadcasting space by creating sub-networks online with much less expensive rates. This will bring on an entirely new kind of revenue flow with all of the advertisers' products and services being offered on the online shopping system. Once the online system is up and running, we will also devote programs to strictly selling the products by the advertisers, who will formulate programs of interest to listeners and promote sales. For instance, health companies would sponsor health-related programming and herbal vitamins, much like it is done now. These sub-networks will be accessible worldwide through our website, which will also spur additional sales revenues.

Once these systems are in place, the chance for creating worldwide networks will be possible and will be funded by various stations and groups of stations going public on specific exchanges. The money produced from their sales will not only be an enticement to their owners who have only seen profits drop recently, but will also give life to an entire market segment that is moving downward. Consolidation on a global scale for independent radio stations has never been done before and has no prior model in combination with online shopping. Many people in the world, especially those over 40, spend little time on the internet, especially for shopping. If they had a simple way to be directed in shopping online for products they would not normally see at discount prices, then a whole new group of people could be utilized for business. Using conventional radio to move potential customers to our sites along with the right programming and advertisers will be a driving force in who buys a particular product and where they buy it.

1/2/10
8:14 PM EST
Home, NJ

Kayla's best friend from college, Alexa, has been over for a few days. She is from Cape Cod, Massachusetts and is a total joy to have around. Besides being a loyal friend to my wonderful daughter, she is a good person with high aspirations for the future. Wendy and I took them to dinner tonight and they will probably be going out later. It snowed a little today and is now about 20°F. I won't be biking outside for a while until it warms up.

1/3/09
4:04 PM EST
Home, NJ

After tennis with my brother and working out downstairs, I had lunch and visited my parents. I heard from Vinnie, who told me that things are moving along well in Thailand. It sounds like he will have everything done by Tuesday. He has a tough job with a high degree of pressure and time constraints, but it is something he is very good at.

1/4/10
9:38 PM EST
Home, NJ

It still continues to be cold. It was tough getting up this morning, though the five alarm clocks helped. After getting to the office, playing tennis and eating my second breakfast, I spent the day in meetings for the radio and ballistic programs, doing paperwork and selling. We got the final figures for last year, which were down about 25% (not counting IJX), which made us a little better than even. It is not bad for a very tough economy, but not nearly good enough.

1/5/10
9:18 PM EST
Home, NJ

It was another day of selling and planning. Staying on the phones and email can drive me crazy, but I know my constant barrage of potential businesses will work. We also prepared documentation, food and samples for tomorrow's trip, but we are still not sure who we are seeing.

JANUARY

1/6/10
7:09 AM EST
New Jersey Turnpike

Jack, Mike and I are on our way to Washington and it has already been an adventure. Jack was stopped on his way to meet us because he had a tail-light out. When we set up together, there was a tanker truck on fire and we sat in traffic for about 90 minutes. Despite the delay, we are continuing our quest for our meeting with the attorney. I emailed John regarding our meeting and he was happy to report his morning was open and the delay would not be a problem. Whether it is planes, trains or automobiles, things happen and that is the way it goes. This is an extremely important meeting regarding our ability to export our technology, so I want to get there. By the way, Mike asked where the food was in the car and I recalled his own rule: he does not get fed until he finds a rest stop. I think he is sufficiently motivated; I know I am.

Jack has been working on finding a supplier to make panels for the water barrier project and it looks like he has one in Ohio. If so, Mike will need to drive out there to pick up the finished product. We have a conference call with our partner Trelleborg and the customer at 2:00 PM today, which we plan to make while on the road. I am hoping we can give them final pricing by this Friday and get moving soon because they need our finished prototypes within the month.

It is a cold, cloudy day here in New Jersey. It is almost daylight, but it is a heck of a lot better to be moving than to be stuck dead in traffic. I hope the guy whose truck burned got out in time. There were five traffic helicopters in the air as we passed the accident.

1/6/10
3:24 PM EST
New Jersey Turnpike

Amazingly, with Mike's incredible driving, we made it to our appointment at 10:05 AM, less than 45 minutes late. Jack and I met with three attorneys and it was apparent that these three gentlemen knew their stuff from the onset. We spoke about export licenses, areas of government, registrations, and various systems we would need and contacts that could help us. They would also act as general guides to get us where we wanted to go. We showed them our composites, drawings and new ideas and they thought they all had merit. It will mean a great deal of work on our part and probably a lot in attorney fees, but I feel it is the right path. I also feel we have no choice; as good citizens, we have to protect not only ourselves and the interests of our company, but our nation a well.

Once outside, I called a local customer but they could not see us. So it was back in the car for the conference call with Trelleborg and our potential marine barrier customer. More samples would be needed for their tests. The potential numbers of units needed have jumped so much that if the orders come in as indicated, then we will not only need multiple outside suppliers but to build our own facility. The amount of infrastructure costs could mean quite exciting and a little frightening. After that, we had some fun (I am being facetious) trying to find the parking area which housed Jack's car. Eventually, we did find it and now Mike and I are on our way to my house. Once there, I hope to go out for a walk before going to dinner with Kayla and Wendy.

1/7/10
9:24 PM EST
Home, NJ

It was one of those fantastic days filled with the potential of what could be and getting a lot of necessary work done. We are working on signing on a new rep in New Jersey and possibly a whole group in Washington DC. So far, they like what they see regarding the composite. I started working on becoming government registered for International Traffic in Arms Regulations (ITAR). It will be a big effort, but I think it is worthwhile. Knowledge is power and doing the new manual and system myself will force me to learn in the best way possible. It is like a new ISO system and I don't mind the time or the effort.

I heard from Alex, who was on a bus in Egypt going to the pyramids, and there may have been a problem with his debit card. More snow is predicted for tomorrow morning. My car was in for a checkup two days ago and today the engine light went on, which is a bit frustrating.

1/8/10
10:00 PM EST
Home, NJ

Vinnie is back from Thailand and he did a fantastic job. There are only three areas left to take care of and then all responsibilities go to IJX for maintenance, guidance and oversight. We found out that IJX is expanding again with another press line. I also found out all eight sales sites are now up and running in China.

1/9/10
3:07 PM EST
Home, NJ

This morning I was live at WOR Radio so Elana, Mike and I zoomed our way into Manhattan with no traffic. After we parked, we stopped by a local coffee shop to pick up our guest, Peter K, who is a nutritionist, physical therapist, author and trainer. It turned out to be a good show. Before we went on, I told Joe I would like a minute to talk about the economy. The unemployment rate is once again officially at 10%, so I asked our listeners to consider the possibility that now may be one of the best times to consider "going for it." I know it is rough, but only in times of extreme stress will people often be willing to try something new, listen to unusual proposals or take courses of action they would never consider in calm times. Then I introduced Peter and the rest of the time flew from there. He was an excellent guest and spoke about his life and getting his product sold on QVC, a home shopping network. Joe liked him because he went to Rutgers and played on their football team; he is an avid fan.

Peter joined us for our traditional after-show breakfast at the local delicatessen. He seemed happy with his appearance and even got some immediate feedback. The only low note was a $65 parking ticket in Manhattan, but I chalked it up to the cost of doing business and did not let Mike feel badly about it. We were home soon after and everyone went off to do their own thing. Dave Williams was at a track meet for his niece, where she had a personal best in the high jump. I worked out by myself and went back home to enjoy a glorious nap. In a little while, Wendy and Bunny, who just came from Florida, will go to Barbara and Cliff's house and back into Manhattan for dinner at the restaurant where Barry is the sous chef. Wendy's brother Buz and his wife Terry are also meeting us there, which is nice because they live near Boston and we rarely see them.

1/10/10
4:28 PM EST
Home, NJ

I met a new personal record yesterday: it is the first time I was ever in Manhattan twice in one day. Before my radio show days this would have been almost inconceivable, since I used to go into New York City an average of less than five times a year. We went over to Barbara's house and rode into the city along with Cliff and Bunny. It was an easy ride in and we got to Forge Restaurant a half hour early.

As we walked in we saw Katie, Ben's girlfriend, who works there and had waited to see us. We sat at the bar where the others had drinks and I did not, as usual. When asked by my brother-in-law Cliff why I do not drink, I told him there were two reasons. The first was that when I did drink modestly in the past, I found that alcohol loosened my ability to censor what I was saying and I had said some things that would have been better left unsaid. The other was that if I was going to splurge the calories on something it would be more like chocolate cake, which I like much better than alcohol.

Barry is the sous-chef in this establishment and the food was excellent. True, it was totally wasted on me for thinking the best parts of the meal were the dinner rolls and chocolate cake. The rest was good, but I don't get that excited about food. To me, it is mostly for fuel and I am happy as long as it tastes good and I can eat quickly. The rest of our crew did justice to the quality of the menu and a good time was had by all. The service was also excellent, so it was a very pleasant time. We were back home by 9:30, which is definitely late enough when you are up early. Especially after the pressure of being live on the radio, I was asleep before 11:00 PM. One of the reasons I will stop doing my show is that it is interfering with my sleep schedule. Getting up early on Saturday every other week to be on the air takes away an hour or two of sleep and hearing the program on Sunday nights makes my energy flow. Even though it is taped, it makes it harder to get to sleep.

After a nightmare interrupted my sleep, I got up and played tennis with Ira. He is doing well and we had a good time. From there, it was to my basement for a band workout and some time on the treadmill.

Today was the 80th birthday party for Barbara's mother-in-law Myrna and her twin Joyce and it was a wonderful affair held in a restaurant near our house. There was good food and company, so it was a nice time. At one point I was sitting with Buz and Saul, who owns a plumbing supply company and is very successful. We were talking about the economy and all of us agreed that 2010 will probably be about the same economically as 2009. I was being optimistic, since I will not be surprised if it is actually worse. I did not know that Buz was a fan of Mr. Obama and I did not get his reasons for being one. Both Saul and I plan to try to increase our sales outside the U.S. The more Mr. Obama makes it difficult to do business in this country, the more those like Saul and I will go outside the U.S. Does the president really think he can stop business and force us to do things the way he and the congress dictate? There are always options and none of us are going to sit back and accept the terms they decide we have to live under. With luck, the November elections will halt his "progress" and small business people will have the chance to succeed again.

After we returned home, I went for a walk outside. Soon I will go the office, drop off my stuff for the week, pick up some food for dinner at the diner and later listen to the Lifeguard Show. Bunny, Wendy, Kayla, Barb and Barry are downstairs trying to duplicate a recipe they saw on TV. It is very fun to hear the laughing and good times emanating from our kitchen. Bunny is being picked up soon for the airport and I am not sure if Kayla is going out tonight. Alex comes home from Israel and Egypt early tomorrow morning. I miss him and am glad he will be home.

1/11/10
9:43 PM EST
Home, NJ

Sales for IJX were a new record for 2009! This is amazing, absolutely fantastic results and even better since that is the main year to count for the multiple for going public. I spoke with Jeroen and we made plans to meet in the near future. His sale potential could be major for 2010. We actually have the potential to pay off the credit line this week. I am extremely happy considering the economic conditions and especially considering how much money we are spending on R&D.

I heard a General Motors official say how happy they were since they would definitely make money this year. It is astounding how quickly he could forget about how they actually went bankrupt and screwed their suppliers and debt holders. Suddenly, their past debts is not counted, they had a clean slate and are proud since they are now profitable. It is easy when you can change the rules as the president sees fit. No one is bailing us out and no one should have helped them. It was a big mistake and will haunt us for years.

1/12/10
7:08 PM EST
Home, NJ

It is another cold day, but mostly clear.

After tennis, it was back to the office and we all worked on more of the military and commercial projects and paperwork. We had a meeting at 11:30 with Jack, Mike, Al and John the export attorney. I am extremely happy to report that the four initial inventions I wanted to be able to export are in good shape and we will get a formal approval for them this week. It paves the way for us to move worldwide and I will breathe a big sigh of relief when we have the written record. Meanwhile, I continue to read through the mountains of ITAR related information and we hope to have our application to become an exporter ready within the week.

Wendy, Ben, Kayla and Alex should have finished dinner by now in Manhattan and all but Ben should be on their way to the theater to see "Jersey Boy." I hope they have a blast. After I came home from the office, I let Bailey out and fed him. He was happy to see me. Then I took out the recycling, had dinner and will relax for a while before I start reading more ITAR related information. I don't mind it; I actually find it interesting in short bursts. People are upset that the U.S. banks have finished a profitable year and the high office holders will be taking huge bonuses. The people in charge created the system where they could do it and I don't have a problem with capitalism working.

1/13/10
9:44 PM EST
Home, NJ

After repeated attempts by Mark from WOR to try to gain support for the Malaysian radio deal, it became apparent that it was not going to work. I killed the deal from all sides. My dream for a network will either have to wait or remain incomplete. It is not the first time a dream doesn't happen and won't be the last.

Alex and I met with Rosa the jacket designer today. We will have everything she needs by the end of next week and the jacket should be ready the first week of February; that project continues.

Once the shows and the jacket are done, my trips to New York City will probably be greatly curtailed, which is fine. It has been a fun run, but it is time to center on more, of what is possible. John the attorney continues to do a good job and we should have our written clarification of our products regarding dual usage by next week. Then we can plan our attacks on Asia and Europe. I am now scheduled to go back to Asia in mid-March and Ben and I will plan out the countries to see in order to go after customers for our new product lines. I relish the challenge. Within two weeks, both Kay and

Alex will be back at school, which is better for them. They will be happier and though I will miss seeing them every day, it will be back to the norm for Wendy and I. Alex is at a reception for the company that is sponsoring his internship for the summer. They seem genuinely happy to have him and are paying for his time. He hopes to learn a lot.

1/14/10
9:52 PM EST
Home, NJ

My serve was off in tennis, which meant the rest of my game followed and defeat was inevitable. It is good to keep my ego in check. I went back to the office with the realization that layoffs would need to take place unless something drastic happened. Mike will give me the breakeven number tomorrow, so we will see what we have to do. Once we are down to that amount for the reduced sales I am figuring for the next six months, I should be able to breathe a little easier and concentrate on growth for all parts of the world. Focusing on the positive is tough when you have to recognize reality. After we go public in July, our expenses will drop here in the U.S., but that is seven months away and too long to hold out as we are. No one said it would be easy, but the next group of good times we have will be all the sweeter from going through this.

1/15/10
10:49 PM EST
Home, NJ

It became apparent today that sales were not going to cover costs and it was time for action. I met with our VPs and told them I would give my recommendations for who would be laid off so it could be done immediately. At the same time, Mike would compile figures for the last few months to see what our monthly costs were and what we need to make in sales to break even. We had both by mid-afternoon and we decided that one of our manufacturing people and our order write-up manager would have to go, as their jobs could be taken on by others. In addition, one of our VPs was given notice that if sales were not developed by the end of next month that would cover his costs, he is out too. Sometimes people want to be laid off to take a vacation on unemployment, but this was not the case here. They are good people and we are cutting flesh and not fat, so I hope to bring them back on as soon as possible. To say the least, it was a very difficult day. I have been dreading it for over a month, but I am glad it is finally taken care of. We have a direction to follow and we will check again at the end of the month regarding sales and costs to see if more must be done. It is strange that we have the tougher of times with the economy here, but the new composite and defense/military areas look like they could be extremely good. We have the potential for giant success; it is the yin and yang at the same time.

Meanwhile, Europe and Asia look good so there is no great turmoil as long as we get control over costs here and make sure we are at least breaking even for the short term. I got an email from one of my tennis partners who had an injured shoulder. I hope he gets better and I will scramble for replacements until he can get back. Tennis with my brother this morning was very pleasant as usual and he was playing well. Temperatures have moderated here to a balmy 45°F late in the day. Uncle Dave and I are scheduled to ride outside tomorrow and it will be the first time in weeks. I look forward to it after breakfast and listening to our show. Another certain thing is I am off the air as of the middle of next month and will focus totally on sales and building the business. My troops want me to center more on the core product lines and I have been doing so with the conversion of customers' telecom panels to our plastic versions. It seems to be gaining momentum, so I will follow up everywhere else when I have the energy to attack. We are in for a wild ride.

1/16/101
1:08 PM EST
Home, NJ
On our porch

It was a treat of a day regarding weather; about 50°F outside. After making breakfast and listening to the Businessman's show on WOR this morning, Uncle Dave and I were able to bike outside. I did not even need a face mask, which made it all very pleasant. I started off by going to our meeting point, which has a stream running by where fish are visible during the warmer seasons of the year. Although the fall leaves had been swept away, the sunlight bright and conditions perfect, there was nothing swimming that I could see. The water is very cold and they are probably in the deepest area in a state of semi-hibernation. It was a very pleasant ride and we spoke about what had gone right and wrong lately.

I am tired; it has been a tough week and there is an excellent chance I will fall asleep out here, especially since I will be working on our new ITAR, reading through a mountain of government regulations. The best way to learn what is needed for any new system is to read the core documents yourself. This way, you gain your own perspective and you can hold your own in conversation with experts who are used to people just agreeing with whatever they say. I leave a lot of things for my people to take care of, but company policy, systems and new areas are not included. This is the way I keep a handle on what is needed and required in new directions for us to head toward. I am happy to be by myself for a while, not counting Bailey. The time alone is peaceful. There is a senate election this Tuesday for the seat vacated after Edward Kennedy died. Originally thought to be a democratic seat, the republican candidate has made great strides and the race is now even. If he gains the position, the healthcare initiative may die. We can hope.

1/17/10
4:47 PM EST
Home, NJ

After lunch I took Alex to the airport to go back to school in St. Louis. We were talking about his plans for the next five years. He is talented, driven and very intelligent and my bets are he will do well. Right before he got out he asked me if business trips were fun and I told him they were a blast, but a lot of work. He is anxious to get started on them when the time is right.

I went to my parents afterward and they both seem well. The conversation, as with my brother, touched on the senatorial race in Massachusetts. Tuesday will be a very big day in our country's history and it is strange that it will come down to one election. Kayla's best friend Alexa comes back home tomorrow night and will stay until they both leave on Wednesday.

1/18/10
8:58 PM EST
Home, NJ

We heard from the export attorneys regarding sending our defense information overseas. So far we are fine, but we will have to tread carefully. I sent over a proposal for a procedure to handle non-U.S. customers regarding information and when licenses would be needed. If they agree to my course then it will be relatively easy for preliminary testing and pricing so we don't lose too much time with business that won't happen. I spent the day selling and doing paperwork and read more of the export license data when I got home, compliments of the government.

I am 2 ½ pounds over my goal weight and am having trouble losing it, which is bothering me a lot. Certain times of the month are harder than others, but I will not stop until I am back. I do not like the feeling of tight pants. I spoke with my son Ben today twice. He will research possible award competitions we can get into regarding our two radio shows. If we win, the publicity may be enough to get us another show. If not, we are retired. The big election in Massachusetts is tomorrow, though the results may take a few weeks.

1/19/10
9:43 PM EST
Home, NJ

The office atmosphere is returning to normal after the layoffs. I still feel like I failed, which I did, regarding having enough profitable work to keep everyone employed. As Wendy reminded me, we did not guarantee jobs for life but I still feel like I let them down. On a happier note, we have fantastic prospects for business this year and for the near future, so I will persevere day to day selling and helping to create new product areas. We have been emailing with John the export attorney and are almost ready to lay out our attack of the non-U.S. customers and countries with our commercial based products. I look forward to that challenge. We sent in our ITAR application and if approved, we will create and install an ITAR system within Ideal Jacobs. Wendy canceled her California trip for tomorrow because they are expecting 20 inches of rain in the next week. It is fine since Kayla is leaving tomorrow for school and now it won't be just Bailey and me. Wendy has rescheduled for next month. We have been cutting down our overhead and will be close to breaking even, but I won't know for sure until the end of February. It is good to be going in the right direction and moving toward profitability.

1/20/10
7:57 PM EST
Home, NJ

The senate race in Massachusetts produced a Republican victory. It is an amazing win considering his opponent was greatly ahead just a few weeks ago. That means the senate no longer has a Democratic majority. The president, very intelligently in my view, called for a reforming of his national insurance program to get support from both sides. It is a good chance for both sides to start talking and acting sensibly for the first time in years.

We had two meetings on the ship protector project today and we are moving closer to submitting the first set of prototypes. If all works well, they will hopefully start ordering a lot of products in the spring. Sales for this month are down about 50% from last year, which is a little worse than I expected, but still roughly in line. We will stay at our reduced staff for a while. IJ Thailand is having the aches and pains of starting up, costing more than expected with no production, but I think it will be fine by this spring. It is good we have been through this before, so we have the experience to be patient.

Wendy and I had lunch with Kayla and her best friend Alexa before they went back to school. Kayla just called to tell me that she got there safely. It is sad to see her go. I miss her a lot, but Cornell is a good place for her now. I hope to see her in April. Wendy is out with her friends playing Mahjong, so Bailey and I are home alone and it is quiet and peaceful.

1/21/10
9:44 PM EST
Home, NJ

The new product lines are being readied for sale outside the U.S. My plan is to send out our revised product sheets next week, attack Asia in general to see if there is interest and then focus on Thailand and Malaysia. I love selling new things, especially stuff that is so different with our own ideas infused. Ben may not be able to come with me on the calls. The purpose of my visit is for going public and he has some related work to do after Monday. We will do as needed. At the same time, I will begin scheduling my next trip to Europe with Jeroen for early April. We will sell not only the new lines, but also the areas of new business he is working on and maybe see some new customers. It will mean a lot of traveling.

The economic news in the U.S. continues to be dark. I look forward to being back on the road. The money is out there and I want to go get it.

1/21/10
10:13 PM EST
Home, NJ

I almost just made a bad mistake and set my five alarm clocks for 6:45 AM instead of 5:45 AM. I must be really tired, so I will go to sleep soon. It was a day of lots of emailing, calls and meetings. It was grueling but necessary. We are working on a second patent for the ballistic armor and we came up with a lot of great options for it today. We will start selling it by itself early next week. If it works out well, it will mean a safe way to protect people from firearms and blasts and a way to monitor the other side of barriers even when one can't see them. It is really cool stuff and fun to work on.

1/22/10
9:59 PM EST
Home, NJ

It was an early start for a Saturday morning, but normal for a show day. I was up by 5:45 and Mike, Elana and our guest Jodi Topitz were on our way to Manhattan in the early morning daylight. There were no delays going in and we parked at our normal spot in front of the pornography store and place where we have breakfast. From there it was a quick walk to the station, a flash of my ID card and we were up in the waiting area with plenty of time to spare.

Right before we went on, I found out that Jodi and my wife were friends and have known each other for years. It is a small world. Jodi is an interior designer and artist and we spoke with Joe about the importance of design especially in tough times to achieve a calmer home. We discussed prices, how to choose what stays and what goes and working out a balance between people living together regarding design in general. It was a good show and Jodi eventually got three phone calls from listeners wanting more information. I started out the show discussing the economy and how I thought it was still going down. I said that President Bush had "mission accomplished," President Obama had "We have turned the corner," and I thought both had been wrong. I will be known for "things are not going to get better anytime soon and people should set their sights on at least a year more of trouble." It is not the happiest of messages, but the admitting the truth is better so you can plan and deal with it.

Breakfast afterward was its usual fun time. When we got back home, I ran to the office to set up a Federal Express package for IJX including some paperwork for our public offering and went out biking. It was about 40°F and a very pleasant ride. Then I went home and did little else. Wendy and I went out to dinner and watched part of the Screen Actors Guild awards. I hope to be asleep soon now.

JANUARY

1/23/10
3:44 PM EST
Home, NJ

It is an overcast Sunday afternoon here in NJ. I played tennis with my brother, worked out on the treadmill in our basement and then Wendy and I took my mom and dad out for lunch. The occasion was my Mom's 81st birthday, which is next week when I will be away. It was an enjoyable time. Wendy spoke with mom and dad and I spoke mostly about business and the world. Afterward I exercised more back home in the basement and I will soon be reading more ITAR related information. Describing what we do becomes increasingly complicated, but I must remember that, as in the past, labels are still our primary business and profit center and will remain so for the foreseeable future. Unfortunately, they are becoming more scarce in the U.S. as manufacturing leaves the country. Our plan to follow the business around the world has worked well, but we have to keep branching out. Just as our non-U.S. sales are now bigger than domestic, we have to expand our product lines to move to other profitable niches. If our new products actually function and are bought by others, then the sales potential is almost infinite. Obviously selling custom items is more profitable than commodity items and usually products from our own ideas utilizing our own IP (intellectual property) are the best. In the meantime, we will continue to patent our ideas domestically and branch out from there. If things weren't really tough, then no one would be listening to our new ideas. From that standpoint, it is the best of times. It all balances out. It is fun to think about what good things can happen.

My brother mentioned at tennis this morning that the editorials by the liberal columnists in the New York Times were all blasting Mr. Obama this week. To have a president apparently lose massive amounts of support from his base is not a great thing. I am all for governing from the middle, but if his liberal support is leaving him, it paves the way for a much more conservative, right wing government to come in. I am not for a conservative base to that degree and I think it can be as equally destructive as the liberal one we have now. Protectionism and various types of discrimination and bias can be brought back in huge amounts and I fear for what can be.

1/25/10
9:40 PM EST
Home, NJ

I got notice today that my presence was requested in San Jose next month, which means my tentative traveling schedule will be quite hectic if all comes to pass. So far, it will mean two days in Minnesota, one day in Atlanta, one week in Asia, three days in California and six days in Europe all by the second week of April. That is not so bad overall, but it is still a lot of time for me away from home. Never the less, they are all important and I do not begrudge the time. There is now a lot of potential business out there and we are going after it, even though I still think the economy is losing ground. My initial calls making appointments for my Asia trip are going well and between that and selling the new product lines to Canada and the U.S., I am busy. Once those two countries are done via phone and email, I will start on Mexico and Europe. Jack and I spoke with Jeroen today. He is working on selling the new product lines and I plan to be out with him in early April to push more. If the new business comes through, then his situation will probably be altered so that he is a stockholder in a new company we will be forming. Mr. Obama is coming under increasingly tough fire from all sides. I am afraid he will start going for even higher taxation and protectionism, which I do not think are good for anyone. We need to get to the mid-term elections so one of the houses can be shifted and he cannot have everything he wants. A gridlock is what we need, along with time for the economy to fix itself. We can all be left alone to heal the system.

My nephew Jeremy was back home this weekend after a tough bout of diverticulitis and 10 days in the hospital. It will mean a diet change for him. My mom had the same problem, but he is very young to experience it. It is a tough reminder that health is such a gigantic deal and everything is altered without it. Mike from our office and his wife had a baby boy today. He, his wife and son are all great. Birth is truly a miracle.

1/26/10
7:45 PM EST
Home, NJ

Whenever something hits me emotionally and I find myself having a very big reaction, I like to try to step back and figure out why. Often, fate has set up a reason for something to happen and if I am calm, I can see the opportunity and seize it. In this case, it was my impending trip to California. In my initial estimation, it would have been better to go to see the customer in Guadalajara where our distribution center is located so I could spend a few days with Paulina and make sales calls in addition to the meeting. But the customer was very firm in their requests, so I booked the flight today for next month. This, among other things, means Wendy and I will be traveling a lot separately and won't see each other much. As for California, when I took the time to see where I was going, I found out there were a lot of customers I had either never seen or not visited for a long time. Therefore, I decided it was a good thing that I was going.

I spent the day making more sales calls, emails and pushing our new product lines in general. I also emailed Paulina and Jeroen to use the new product files I had sent them to email every customer we have in Mexico, Europe and Scandinavia to push our new membrane switch, cut foam and composite ballistic lines. They are quite diverse in their scope, but I like branching out. I also emailed Ben to please do the same thing in Asia. I am getting replies back from my emails there and am starting to fill in the sales call appointments when I go in March. Ben had also emailed me that he wants to meet Jeroen and I when we go to Europe. That is the first full week in

April and it will be quite a trip. Right now, it will probably begin in Scotland, possibly to England, Germany and will end in the Netherlands. The energy level of the three of us together should be quite high, except of course when I pass out while Jeroen is driving.

By the time I finish going through our database, probably in the spring, I won't have to do it again for at least a year and the potential business it should produce will effectively negate the need for any salespeople here in the U.S. Our office people here, led by Al, are extremely good at working with customers and going after new business and prospects as they are offered through daily interaction. My job is to get business, create new product areas and help us expand worldwide while keeping the sales as they leave.

Wendy is out playing Mahjong with her friends and should be back around the time I plan to go to sleep so I can say goodnight. Bailey is here with me lying on the bed, quite contented. It is peaceful and the way I like to think about home when I am traveling. However, "home" is something you have to earn and playing it safe doesn't cut it. Like defenses in sports that often fail, you have to keep putting yourself out there with the knowledge that nine out of ten ideas will fail, you will lose money, time, effort and look like a fool. But it doesn't matter. You must keep moving ahead, retire or die. Those are the three choices and I like the first option best.

1/27/10
9:39 AM EST Newark/Liberty Airport
Continental Airlines Lounge
Newark, NJ

Yesterday continued with the clarity that manufacturing, as we have known, is dying in the U.S. More of our customers are demanding prices that are increasingly lower and the mass runs immediately move outside of our country. Again, the good news is we have the capacity to do that part outside the U.S., which is excellent. Our lease in Maplewood will be up in April of 2013, which means that we either change our manufacturing to fit the new structure of the world or take on different manufacturing that has more stability. Both have their advantages and we don't have to make a decision for 24 months, but that is not that long. In the meantime, we will continue as we are. I am moving toward the new product lines as quickly as possible and with that in mind, we are looking at equipment to handle the new composite plastic materials which is bulky and needs a lot of height. It is not that expensive so we could go into the short-run area without a gigantic money outlay.

The weather for today was supposed to be good, but there is a sudden snowstorm in progress and getting here was not easy. There were lots of accidents, but Mike is an excellent driver so there were no problems.

My trip to California next month is on and I have been calling potential customers to visit. I am also hoping to get into a defense manufacturer there through Jack's contact. They could order a giant amount of our new product line and I need to get in there. I emailed the Jack's contact, but he was promoted and passed me to a new man. I have not heard back from him yet, but I will push hard when I get back. I am tired and bit wired, so a few days in Florida would be good if the weather does not stop us. I will go check the board to see if we are delayed. If not, I will head to the gate.

Mr. Obama gave his State of the Union Address last night. I feel he has no touch with the reality of business. He lives in the world of theory and is surrounded by people who feel the same way. Any change will most likely be bad. How can we compete with China, which not only has amazing resources and a booming economy but a government that can make instantaneous changes? The Chinese care much less about personal rights and much more about capitalism and the chances to make money. They are formidable and I am not sure our congress' chest pounding of America being number one that I saw last night is going to do any good. In fact, I think their delusion is extremely destructive. We will try to use it to our advantage.

1/27/10
8:09 PM EST
Lake Worth, Florida

Even though there was an unanticipated snowstorm, our plane left without much delay. I sat next to two very nice people and I mentioned my shows on WOR to them. A woman in front of us overheard me and mentioned she had listened to me. What a thrill to find a fan!

My wonderful mother-in-law was waiting for me at the airport and we zoomed off to their apartment at the Fountains Development. It was exactly as I remembered it with beautiful golf courses and pretty buildings. It is good to be back. A couple of my in-laws' friends are interested in renting our house in the Berkshires. I had already checked our homeowners insurance and we were fine to rent, so my wife had left it up to me to negotiate. They were very nice people and after a few minutes of talking, we closed the deal. They will be there July, which means Wendy and I need to get up there in June to move some of our stuff into the basement to make room for them. It was a compromise for us. I wanted to sell it because we use it so infrequently and she wanted to stay. This will help to offset some of the costs.

I went swimming later. The pool water was warm and even though the air was getting cooler, it was a beautiful time. Then I took a shower, got dressed and talked to my son Ben. He has a chance at a great sounding job and I hope he gets it. Dinner was at their country club and was very good. I brought my dessert of chocolate cake back here and put it in the freezer. I have always liked frozen desserts, which probably stems from my youth when my mom used to freeze everything in an attempt to hide it from us kids. It has been a good long day. I am tired and hope to be asleep soon.

JANUARY

1/28/10
9:22 AM EST
Lake Worth, FL
My in-laws' apartment

I have come to the conclusion that I am really bad at being on vacation. I don't know what to do. I got up early, played tennis with one of the club pros Hans, who by the way is extremely competent. We had a great time and the early morning weather was cool and clear. I did not have much trouble adapting to the slower Hard Tru surface, but Hans, as always, could put the ball anyplace he wanted. I did not mind; that is why he is the pro. Besides, I could hit the ball as hard as I liked. He got me so tired that I could barely walk by the time we finished and I felt great.

I took a shower back at the apartment and had five hard-boiled eggs and watermelon for second breakfast. Then I got bored. Amazingly, it took almost no time so I began trying to figure out what to do with myself. I guess it takes a day or two to wind down and it doesn't help that it is still Friday and a workday. Everyone else gets to be working and I am supposed to be relaxing. That is the point I think, but I am missing out on the fun of working. To me, that is where the excitement is. It is where the game is played and I don't like to be out of it. However, I could tell yesterday that I was near the edge of being a little out of it emotionally, so it is good to pull back a little. I will go to lunch soon with my in-laws and maybe I can get my father in law, who has not been feeling well, to come out to drive the golf cart while I play nine holes of golf. It would be good for him to be outside and I rarely get a chance to play or spend time with him alone. In the meantime, I am still thinking about work. I will go through my emails and make some notes to try to make sure I don't miss anything while I am away. I really want to see that defense company when I go to California next month, so I plan to start pressing for an appointment later today. Since we do no business there or with any of their other divisions currently, I have nothing to lose being as aggressive as I feel necessary to get in there. I can apologize for being too pushy once I am there, but first I have to get the appointment. It is like the difference between asking permission and asking forgiveness. One stops you and the other at least affords you a chance. I was reading the local newspaper here this morning and the sentiment seems the same everywhere. Our government is frozen into two camps of Democrats and Republicans, who hate each other and are willing to see the country go down before working together. It is a sad state of affairs for all of us, but I will have to figure it will continue and base our marketing and world movements on that. Business will get continually tougher here in the U.S., which means that we have to focus only on niche areas and move the rest of the easier mass run products out to our other companies in order to survive and prosper. It may take a year or two to be able to refocus everything necessary, but in the end I think we can still manufacture here as well as abroad and be very profitable in all.

I will waste no time on wishing for what I want in our government and economy and focus instead on how to benefit what is there. Reality is the key. We have little time to get into and solidify our position.

1/28/10
8:35 PM EST
Lake Worth, FL
My in-laws' apartment

After multiple calls to my office and hanging out by the pool, Bunny, Jeff and I had a delicious lunch. Then it was more office work, editing and trying to think of new inventions. I look forward to being in Florida to play golf with my father-in-law, but his health has not been great and he informed me before I came down that we would not play. Not playing, however, did not mean he could not drive the golf cart while I played, so after some not so gentle prodding we were out on the course in the mid afternoon. The weather was amazing; partly sunny, about 80°F (no worries; I had on a hat and sunscreen). I generally play with one club, a five iron, so I don't have to try to get used to a bunch when I haven't played recently. Jeff, unfortunately, did not have one. I settled on a six iron instead and by the third hole I was starting to hit pretty well. By the end of six holes, the fatigue from the morning tennis workout had set in, so we went back to the clubhouse and had some soft drinks.

I have not been drinking much soda lately and having a diet soda and pretzels was one of the best snacks I have had in a while. The discussion that ensued between Jeff and another local homeowner eventually evolved to politics and when I came back in from calling the office, they had begun a discussion on the worst U.S. president in history. They had been centering on the second President Bush, but I came back with President Carter, which did not help to quiet the conversation down. Luckily, Bunny called to say that we had to get back to prepare for dinner, so the discussion ended there. Dinner was at a local fish restaurant and I fully admit I ate last night's frozen chocolate cake in the freezer with a bunch of blueberries afterward. It was wonderful. Tomorrow I will begin the journey back home.

1/29/10
1:28 PM EST
West Palm Beach Airport

I got a lot of sleep last night, had a big breakfast in anticipation of the calorie usage I would need to play tennis with Hans again, worked out with my bands and was out on the court by 9:00 AM. Yesterday was much different than today in that it was about 10 degrees warmer with faster winds. Since Hans had the wind to his front, his balls were coming in much lower, which meant I had to get them earlier. It took a lot more effort. That, combined with the effects of yesterday's tennis and golf playing and this morning's band workout, meant my energy levels were used up rather quickly. This left me with the decision to bear with the pain, keep hitting the ball with my usual force and stop trying to run down every point or take it a little easier and go to a spin, softer shot game. Eventually, even after we changed sides so I had the wind coming at me, my body gave me no choice and I had to slow down.

My neck felt like it was in vice and the soreness in my body, which usually comes at the end or after I play, set in much sooner than usual. It was still a lot of fun, but I was not upset when it was over. I bid Hans a fond farewell until my return next year and I got back to the apartment, changed my clothes and went to the pool. The warm water was therapeutic and I felt much better by the time I finished. Afterward I packed, had lunch and relaxed until it was time to say goodbye to Jeffrey, who was very happy I had come. Bunny took me to the airport. I am extremely fortunate to have my in-laws. I will see them again when they come up for the summer to the Berkshires, which is not too long from now.

So far, the plane is on time and I have food, water and gum. Wendy is going to pick me up at the airport and I imagine we will go to dinner from there. I miss her and look forward to being back home. I was working on the water barrier project last night regarding putting together a pricing matrix. The customer wants some budget prices and I want to send them soon, so if there is a problem with the cost or the weight of our parts, which need to float, it is better we know now. Brett has been working on the test holder for the collision tests due for this customer at the end of February. He should have all the information ready on Monday. If the customer has a problem with that price, doesn't want to pay it or is late paying, then it will give us a good indicator of what their demeanor will be like when we do millions of dollars in business together. I am not sure if they know they are being tested as we are, but this is a group effort and if there are problems of any kind, I want to know now rather than later.

Even though the government says the economy grew at a good rate last quarter, I don't believe the numbers are real. The worst is not over; we may have hit bottom, but we are not going up yet. Mr. Obama met with the Republican leadership this week. I hope they can start working together to do something positive that won't make our economic situation worse, especially for small businesses.

1/29/10
10:26 PM EST
Home, NJ

The plane was roughly on time and I have mostly finished the first edit of my latest book; both good things. My wonderful wife was there to pick me up and after dinner and some food shopping for my office, it was back home.

February

2/1/10
6:47 PM EST
Home, NJ

Yesterday was a normal, happy Sunday. It was good to be home.

It was a day of catching up and working on new projects and sales. January is over and we will find out within a few weeks if the cutbacks we made were enough. We are supplying more information for the stock offering. It is amazing how much they want from us here, let alone from our people in Malaysia. There is so much to do, especially when sales are slower. Of course, I am spending a great deal of time on new projects, which often takes more time than doing the work on hand. The efforts will produce results.

2/2/10
7:20 PM EST
Home, NJ

I have been trying to book my flights to Asia for March and have not been having much success with my usual flight discounter. I tried two new groups today. One had a good flight, but they lied about their rates on their website. The other had the same flight and I will probably book with them tomorrow. I will leave on a Friday and get back on a Saturday. It will be a long trip, but should give me a lot of time in Malaysia and Thailand to go after new customers and try to sell the new and current product lines to people we have already dealt with. That first meeting on Monday is with the people taking us public, so that will be a grueling day. It is always great getting the flights done for the longest part of the trip. I can begin to fill in the rest from there.

We have been working on a large water barrier project with our new material and the product is going into a test phase. However, the customer is having some problems with the formal testing facility regarding price. We have already offered to make part of the test units and today we also offered to conduct the tests themselves by arranging the 75-foot drop test with special photography and sensor readings. We should be able to give them a price tomorrow. I don't want the project held up because of this, so we are pushing to help. This one piece of business could be a giant deal for us and I want to help it along the best we can.

We are considering a new distribution center in Belgium. Igor Gomes wants to move there permanently and is already learning Dutch. It could be a good way to assist Jeroen in channeling the business into a company that we control. In addition to being an excellent graphic artist, he can also run the inside of the center including writing up orders, packing and shipping, which should help keep overhead costs down. It will be a long process to get everyone to agree.

Jack helped to get me an appointment with a large defense contractor in California when I go out there later this month. I will now try to fill in more calls between that company and Flextronics. I will ship samples ahead because I am hoping the defense people will want to test them at their firing range while I am there. If not, we may test them beforehand so they can see the results.

We are helping to move more business to IJX as it leaves the U.S. My feeling is it is much better to get them the business than lose it altogether, however, our team here sometimes thinks we should try to hold on to it longer. We have to appear like a seamless global entity and if that means the business has to go to Europe, Asia and Mexico and out of the U.S., then I will not try to stop it from happening. We have to change our model here and go back to our roots, which is little or no commodity work, strictly difficult jobs needed quickly, and covering more unusual areas like the new composites. Regardless of what is happening in the world, I feel we are moving in the right direction and that it will bear fruit. We have to do everything at the same time, which is difficult but definitely doable.

My son Ben started a new job yesterday and so far so good. It holds a lot of potential and I hope it works out well.

2/3/10
9:36 PM EST
Home, NJ

It snowed last night so I started the day off by shoveling about two inches of snow. It was a pleasant experience; the weather cold but beautiful. Then it was off to the office. After breakfast number one, tennis and breakfast number two, it was a day of meetings, sales, paperwork and finalizing my long trips to Asia in March. Brett has been working on hurricane resistant walls for builders and he may have found a new niche. We will know more next week. More information is needed for Malaysia and going public and it must be driving Ben nuts.

We are working on putting in our ITAR system in anticipation of being accepted later this month. I will have it checked by our attorney before implementation. I woke up early this morning. Maybe I felt the snow was coming, but I know I heard the snowplows once I woke up, which meant it was deep enough for the driveway to need tending. It is time for sleep.

2/4/10
9:44 PM EST
Home, NJ

When I got to the office this morning, I knew something was wrong. It was nothing major, but something was not quite right. I had been tired, as usual, during my morning routine and I had forgotten to shave, as happens once in a while. The only problem with this is that even with the razor and shaving cream I keep in the office I still manage to cut myself a lot. It is a small price to pay to be able to get right back on schedule.

We had a lot of good things happen today. A set of tests for a department of energy project turned out successfully. I hope this paves the way for us to work on a big project.

2/5/10
10:00 PM EST
Home, NJ

A big snowstorm is expected for tonight, so Elana is sleeping over and Mike is picking us up early if the snow permits. Otherwise, Joe will run a taped show and we will record another one on Tuesday for next weekend. Elana, Wendy, Al and I have been pondering the offer from WOR for extending my show and we are working on a counter offer.

It was a very good day. A group from Washington that is highly connected to the defense and military establishment wants to represent our new product line. We are working on the agreement. Brett is scheduled to visit a potential composite supplier Monday and I am hopeful they can be our first primary source for the new lines. We have some interest in our products at Picatinny. The head man has told some of his staff to contact us. The repeated mailing of our ideas seemed to have piqued their interest. Eric seems to be able to take my drawings and make renderings of what I want and it is amazing he can do it with such accuracy and speed. The unemployment rate dropped to 9.7%, some say because of the large numbers who have given up looking. We are not out of the woods yet. I am learning a lot about our new plastic materials. It is fun and exhilarating to be on the cusp of a new niche area.

Joe Bartlett is sleeping in the city tonight so he can definitely make it to the show. It would have probably meant no sleep for me if I had stayed there. I am looking forward to the morning to see what the weather conditions are.

2/6/10
4:39 PM EST
Home, NJ

The giant snowstorm did indeed come, but when I got up this morning and checked outside, not much had fallen here. It had mainly occurred down south so I contacted Mike and we were on our way. I had no idea if we had skirted the storm entirely, but if there was any chance, we were going forward. Elana was already up and by the time Mike got to pick us up, both Wendy and Bailey were also awake. The ride in was swift with no problems; it seems the storm had kept many people off the roads.

When we got into Manhattan there was even a parking spot in front of the studio building. The snow was falling, but even less had accumulated in the city. Joe had stayed locally last night so he was on the air when we got there. I always try to think of something topical to talk about before we get started with our invited guest. Today, it was the art of cleaning snow from a driveway, the need for planning and the correct execution for maximum efficiency and pleasure of the experience. Joe asked me if I would discuss Mayor Bloomberg's comment that the police and firefighters of the city should march on Wall Street, saying the stock brokers and bankers should get their big bonuses. It was the trickle down theory that unless they got their money, paid their share of taxes and also spent it on city-related services, then Manhattan would be even worse off than it already was. I definitely agreed with the mayor. Joe favored the other side of the argument, that the "big guys" were benefiting from ill-gotten gains since they were the cause of the original economic problem. Then we had a brain surgeon on as a guest, who was excellent, and the time flew by rapidly as usual.

Afterward Mike, Elana and I all decided that even though there was not much snow falling, we had better get out of Manhattan as fast as possible. We were back at the house by 9:30 AM. Elana stayed for breakfast and Wendy, she and I had a nice time talking and eating until about 10:00 AM. I shoveled snow and went down to the basement for a band workout and some walking on the treadmill. Meanwhile, Elana had left and Wendy and I went to have lunch. It is rare that we can share three meals in a day together, even when we are on a vacation, so it will be an extra treat to have dinner together tonight. I got an email from a fan who really liked the doctor on the show today, which was nice, so I forwarded it to Elana. She mentioned the physician had a great time and if we stay on the show we may designate him as our medical expert and utilize him when talking about health care related issues. Soon I will get back to work on the ITAR system and then go out to dinner with friends. Parts of New Jersey had a blizzard yesterday and I hope they shovel out without too many problems.

2/8/10
8:52 PM EST
Home, NJ

It was a frustrating day on multiple counts. We had a chance at taking over all of the label work for a large customer. Right now, we probably have about 5% of the total work and I offered an overall price reduction to get the balance. We would redo all of their artwork, tooling and color matching at no charge and we could set up to distribute in the U.S., Europe and Asia. We also would not cherry pick, but would take all of the orders regardless of how small they were. This represented probably 100K of no charge tooling. The head man was with me, but his second in command wanted to commoditize everything and slow things down so he could get multiple quotes on about 700 items. This will not only draw out the whole process and result in a gigantic amount of work for them, but in the end the profit will have been sucked out. It will be worth very little to me and they will still end up paying more since they will have to pay for set ups, artwork and tooling, which I would have given away for nothing. It is frustrating since I think the head man would have grabbed the reduction, allowing us to set up a worldwide system for them and leaving him to reap the praise. After that, the second in command began sending me labels to quote that others had already done. I'm not sure what makes him think I have an interest in beating a dead horse until there is no profit left. It will rapidly become a waste of my time, which is too bad. He could have looked like a star and now he is just another cog in a corporate wheel who will probably go rightfully unnoticed until he is either fired, laid off or drifts into oblivion.

It is now 9:39 PM the same evening. In retrospect, things are very good, great in fact. Sometimes all that is needed is a good night's sleep, a hug and a smile from your wife or the wagging tail of your dog greeting you. It is the little things that can often turn the tide.

2/9/10
8:21 PM EST
Home, NJ

More work was needed for going public, but I think we are nearing the end, at least until I go back to Asia next month. Our people there are setting up calls for the new material and I am hopeful for huge potential here and around the world. A big snowstorm is expected to start tonight, so tennis is probably canceled tomorrow. I will shovel; it is not a problem.

2/10/10
9:49 PM EST
Home, NJ

The predicted precipitation did indeed occur and I woke up this morning to a small amount of snow with much more predicted later. I shoveled, went to work and exercised there. Tennis was canceled because of the weather. We got the first purchase order from the sea wall people and it was good to receive it because we can now move on with the test rig.

I had a meeting with our export attorney John and all seems clear for us to export our new commercial based composite inventions. We can also manufacture them in non-U.S. plants. He is checking if manufacturing in China will work. Otherwise, we have to start in Thailand. It is good to have some solid information on the subject and I feel much better about selling it on my future trips.

The snow got worse during the day but I made it home without incident and began shoveling the approximately seven inches of snow that had fallen. Eventually, I got too tired to keep going. I ate a very large dinner and couldn't seem to drink enough water. I must have used more energy shoveling than I thought.

FEBRUARY

2/11/10
9:08 PM EST
Home, NJ

I got up this morning and shoveled the driveway again. I did not finish, but I could tell by the way my back felt that I was done. At the office, I exercised with the bands, stretched and answered my email. Today was to be a big potential day and I needed to be mentally and physically ready. At 10:00 AM, I had a conference call with Brett and two other men about the composite matreial. One was an entrepreneur, who seemed very successful and had lots of business including some military related areas. The other worked for one of the man's companies and was a metallurgist. Brett had showed them our new line and our inventions and they were interested. We spoke for a while to get a feel for one another and the vibe felt good. We promised to get them samples for testing and they showed Brett their various operations.

Wendy and Barb should be on the plane to Florida to see Jeff and Nanny. It is very quiet here. I shoveled again when I got home, but still didn't finish everything. Bailey knows Wendy is not here and does not like it, but he is next to me and has accepted the situation. I will attempt to get back here to see him after tennis tomorrow so he won't be by himself for very long. It is lonely here without her.

2/12/10
10:13 PM EST
Home, NJ

I sent in the form today to set up my cremation when I die. It is strange to have finally taken care of it. The place where Wendy and I are to be buried above ground was established a few years ago. Since Wendy is not being cremated, I will have some extra space in my area where I will store some of my stuff. I know it sounds crazy, but I would like to bring a few of my favorite books, some CDs, a laptop if there are no environmental problems with that, a bottle of water and probably some granola bars. Of course, I will also bring our dogs' ashes and some dirt from the backyard where we spread Hershey's ashes, figuring she might want to come. It is a bit surreal to plan your own funeral. Since I believe in reincarnation, where I am buried means less, but it is comforting to know I will have some familiar things around me.

It was a good day. Wendy and her sister got to Bunny's in Florida and they were all having a good time when I spoke to her this afternoon. We are moving ahead with changing IJN from a sales company to a full scale Dutch entity. There are a lot of details to work out, but it needs to be done since we are going public.

It was good playing tennis again this morning. I have been shoveling snow instead for the last two days and the rib injury I sustained has been acting up. I still have more cleaning to do tomorrow, but at least I won't be under any time pressure. I miss Wendy. It is very quiet around here, though it is good to have Bailey.

No Road Is Ever Straight

2/13/10
9:14 AM EST
Home, NJ

It is amazing what nine hours of sleep will do, but I am still a bit tired. This is not unusual for the end of the week. I got word from Jeroen this morning that he has accepted our plan to create the new IJN company. I emailed Ben, who is on vacation in Malaysia for the Chinese New Year holiday, about what was going on.

The Saturday radio show this morning was good; the cohesiveness between Joe and I is improving. Tomorrow is the last Lifeguard show and next Saturday is the last Businessman show. I was emailing with Elana, whose car is going into the shop, so I will need to pick her up. We will do a band work out together, which means I am probably in for a lot of pain. Once we finish (and assuming I can still move), I still have shoveling to do. Other than that, it is probably an afternoon of paperwork. I have a lot to do and it is a good time to catch up since Wendy is away. She called me this morning and told me their fancy dinner was unfortunately canceled last night due to a very heavy rainstorm.

2/14/10
1:54 PM EST
Home, NJ
Valentine's Day

I just got a text from Wendy, who has landed at Newark/Liberty Airport and should be home soon. I missed her.

It is a pretty and cold winter day here and the temperature is a little above freezing so some of the snow is melting. More snow is possible this week. I have been reading a lot over the last few days, which is part of my research whenever I move into new areas. In the military area, I am reading two books by retired Colonel Douglas Macgregor, whose firm we are negotiating with to represent various defense and military companies. He is famous for his service in the army and his views on tactics and military structure. I can see why he is so highly regarded and viewed suspiciously for his unconventional views of how our military should change and function. I will send him our game and a copy of the interview I did with the retired Israeli military general for the Lifeguards show who was also the number two officer on the Israeli Entebbe raid in Uganda. That interview seems to be of major interest to most officers in our military and I am happy to share it.

2/15/10
9:44 PM EST
Home, NJ

Dr. Bittner came in today from Nebraska to go over the hand washing monitor we are making for his Veterans Administration hospital. So far so good and we should have a working prototype from Don by April. If it

28

works, it could go nationwide and be a big seller for us. I will contain my enthusiasm until it happens. I just received an email from my partner Ben that IJX had a banner month in January. They are doing extremely well. I feel like we are not keeping up here in North America, but the new product lines seem to be moving so I have great hopes for this year. We have been working on the testing unit for the water barrier project. The idea of using springs to simulate water resistance after the striking of our test panels with a metal smasher looks like it might be dangerous. Jack and Brett had the idea of using an airbag, which appears to be much safer. We will broach the idea with the customer tomorrow.

We are getting strung out with finances and we have to spend more money up front. Our R&D costs are zooming, which means we have to access the credit line. We can't stop now; we are too close to finishing. I hope I am right in where we are going.

2/16/10
9:43 PM EST
Home, NJ

My birthday was a good day.

I heard from WOR that there is no chance for a one hour version of our Saturday show and syndication at this time. My radio/media career is over, at least for now.

We heard from the water barrier people and it seems that the combined prices of our and partners materials were way over their budget. We will work on a modified plan.

Meanwhile, Brett, Jack and Vinnie have been doing a great job with the test rig and are getting ready for the process itself.

It snowed again last night and today, but I got most of it shoveled this morning. There has been a lot of snow lately. I hope it is not a problem while I am away.

2/17/10
7:17 PM EST
Home, NJ

A good part of the day was spent in meetings regarding the water barrier project. Our two tier pricing structure seems to be acceptable, but the size and materials keep changing and fixing costs is like shooting at a moving target. Still, tomorrow I hope to be ready for the first round of prototype pricing to give to our partner, who will add their part and forward it to the customer. The customer agreed to our test system today and we hope the first round will be the first week of March. If it is successful enough, then the prototypes should be ready to test in early May. If those tests go well, I hope to be ready for orders by this summer. I am finding the process very interesting and I am learning a lot about a new area. My dad used to refer to the process as "going to school." Meanwhile, I am still selling whenever there is time and working on other projects.

Wendy should be on her way to California. She left me happy little notes around the house saying she already misses me, as I do her. I hope she has a blast seeing one of her best friends for a few days. The house is lonely without her. Bailey knows she is away again and is not happy about it.

2/18/10
7:34 PM EST
Home, NJ

Wendy is in California with her friend Diane and it sounds like she is having a great time. I also got a chance to talk to Alex and Kayla, and those three conversations alone are enough to spread good cheer.

We are closer to signing on with the Potomac League. They will represent our products to the military and defense contractors and will be on commission. They have a potent force of contacts, expertise and experience and I look forward to working with them. By the way, one of their members, a former colonel in the army, emailed me about another company that harnesses the motion of the wind and body movements to create electricity. He thought it might go well with the new military uniform we are designing. It turns out that Jack had already been speaking with them and their boss called me. After explaining our proposal, he agreed to review it next week. We may venture together and have the Potomac League represent us both. I had shots of adrenaline flying through my body a good part of the day. It is an amazing feeling; a true natural high.

2/19/10
9:04 PM EST
Home, NJ

I played tennis with my brother this morning. It was a normal Friday; we were both exhausted and our tennis playing showed it. Keeping the correct score was virtually impossible and needless, since neither of us cared. The companionship and camaraderie was all I sought and that was fulfilled. My body must be changing with the new exercise system because my pants are tight and today I punished myself by wearing an extra snug pair to make sure I did not overeat. Curiously, when I weighed in I was only one pound over goal weight, which meant it was definitely a body change. I will attempt to modify my eating to get my clothes to fit easily again. It will be a massive mental fight for me if I have to get my clothes altered. I have been wearing the same size for decades.

We did get the purchase order from the barrier people, which meant we are full scale ahead again. Negotiations with the Potomac League are completed and we have an agreement. I am working on some new inventions again. I am dealing with the same emotions, but it is such a great feeling to create something new that it is a joy to continue. I heard from Wendy today.

She sounds good and is having a wonderful time. When she gets back we will have to decide if she is coming to meet me in Europe when I go in April. We will probably meet in the Netherlands for a long weekend. Eric, our fantastic industrial designer, is taking a new job and will stay with us part time. I did not want to stop him since I can't use him full time right now. Things change and you have to accept them and move forward.

My crew here in the U.S. is a little beaten down and battle weary from the last year. We need a big score of business, not only for the profit itself, but for the emotional lift it will bring. I am most of the way through our database in the U.S. and Canada following up where it is needed. I should be done within the next month. After that, it will not be necessary again for at least a year, which will give me more time to work on new sales, product lines, inventions and other areas. It is early for a Friday night, but I am going to try to go to sleep soon. Since Bailey already appears to be asleep, I don't think he will mind.

2/20/10
6:41 PM EST
Home, NJ

Today was our last IJ Businessman show. I had prepared the script including the goodbyes I planned for the end. We got to WOR with plenty of time, thanks to Mike's able driving. We went on the air and it was a bittersweet time. I spoke about my mentor Jean Shepherd, who had once been on this station, and Mike spoke about his company and my mentoring there. Then Ray Foley, a bartender, talked about how he took what many consider a dead end job and made it into a wonderful career. In a short time, we were at the end and I gave my thanks to Elana, Wendy and Joe. Just like that, it was over. Our usual place for breakfast was too crowded, so Elana, Mike and I ended up next door. It had been a great last show.

We went home and Elana and I did a band workout, which may not have been the smartest thing since I later went for a long bike ride with Uncle Dave. It was a calm journey, but my body was really hurting and I was very hungry by the time I got back. After a huge lunch I continued reading Warrior's Rage by Doug Macgregor. Since we had signed an agreement with his company and would be working together, I wanted to try to get through at least one of his books as quickly as possible.

I have a lot going on and not doing radio is probably the best thing. Still, the adrenaline rush of being on the air is hard to pass by. Maybe some day I will be there again.

2/21/10
3:47 PM EST
Home, NJ

The snow has melted a lot, but more stormy weather is predicted for later in the week. Hopefully it will be rain. I was going to see my parents, but they were not home. I decided to go shopping for a new piece of luggage, as mine got bashed up a lot while traveling, but I did not find a suitable replacement. From there it was off to the natural foods supermarket for supplies and then back home. Bailey and I sat out on the porch and I finished Doug Macgregor's book. You learn a lot about a person by reading his work; unintended things often come through. I hope I have learned a lot about how he thinks as well as what he believes in. Both will be of big help in us guiding him and his company to market and sell our products.

2/22/10
8:48 PM EST
Home, NJ

I got a call from Wendy at about 5:05 AM this morning; she had just landed! It is good to have her back in the state of New Jersey. I went on with my usual day; was destroyed in tennis and tried to eat high protein to go with my new diet, at least until dessert at dinner. It was a good day. We found out we got our ITAR registration, which means we can officially export approved military/defense rated items. This is a very big deal for us and another step in moving our ideas from concepts to actual products. I spent part of the day selling and part getting ready for this weeks sales trip. I came home to my wonderful wife, which was a great treat, but I will have to leave her again on Wednesday morning. After I get back on Saturday, I will be home for almost two weeks before leaving for Asia. Going public is taking a lot of time and money, but I hope it will be worth it by the time we finish.

2/23/10
4:17 AM EST
Newark Liberty Airport

I just sneezed and erased everything I had typed this morning; I hope that is not a precursor of the day to come.

I spent yesterday getting ready for this trip to California, which involved lots of odds and ends including some information for going public in Asia. Eric finished the rendering for the new Ideal Suit, our version of a combat uniform that includes a new type of flexible armor we have not built yet. I got up at 2:45 AM and Mike took me to the airport. There may be a snowstorm coming later in the week while I am gone. He said he will shovel for us; he is a good man. Airports are lonely places, especially early in the morning or late at night. I am looking forward to being on the plane and beginning work on the finalization of our ITAR system. It is mostly done but still needs to be combined with our quality/environmental health and safety system. I think it will be easier for everyone if they only have one system to learn. Since I have no sales calls planned for this afternoon, I have the whole day and night if we need to preliminarily finish it and have the system put into effect immediately. I will also have it checked later by our export attorney for any needed changes. I never wish for delays, but I would rather have them like this when I don't have to be anywhere than on a day with close connections and sales calls or when I am trying to get home. Things tend to even out and I try to keep that in mind. The gate was not marked on the departure board; I will need to confirm I am in the right place.

2/24/10
10:44 AM PST, 1:44 PM EST
In flight

I am glad I checked because I was at the wrong gate. Happily, it did not matter and we were off on time. Word has it that there is a major snowstorm expected in our area tomorrow and Friday. I am sorry I won't be there to battle it in person. I spent a lot of the first trip working on the general format to integrate the ITAR system into our ISO system. I am spending the balance of this flight to San Jose actually melding the two systems together. It is a lot of work, but I am making good progress. I am also happy I have no appointment today since I am already tired. Once I land and get to the hotel, I will probably work out and then go back to work on the systems. The two flights took more than seven hours, the same amount of time it takes to fly to Europe. No complaints though; they have been on time and I have gotten a lot done. It would be nice if the hotel had an indoor pool where I am going. It will help get my mind rejuvenated for more systems work later. I will try to nap.

2/24/10
6:02 PM PST, 9:02 PM EST
Fairfield Inn and Suites, San Jose

Both flights were great and we landed right on time. It was a beautiful day here in San Jose, which only added to my guilt for not being home during the impending snowstorm. I wanted to hit the storm head to head and try to shovel my way out, or use the snow blower if necessary. I suppose it was not meant to be, but still the guilt is there.

After working on both plane rides for the ITAR system, I realized it would need more time. I got to the hotel, worked out for awhile and decided to get some dinner. I did not want to sit in a restaurant alone, so I went to a nearby Subway restaurant and got a salad and soup. I wanted a little more protein and there was a Mexican restaurant nearby. I normally do not like spicy food, but there was a sign for grilled chicken so I went in. The man behind the counter was very nice. I ordered my first burrito with just chicken, rice and cheese and it was delicious. It was so good that I plan to go back there tomorrow night and for the same meal.

I figure that if I keep working like this, the ITAR system should be fully integrated with our quality, environmental health and safety system by the time I get back. I will have Mike fix the formatting and check it quickly so we can get it to the export attorney for review and full implementation of the system. I know we don't have any ITAR products being produced right now, but I want the system in place right away.

I called home; I miss Wendy and Bailey, but I will be better tomorrow. The second day away is usually better than the first, especially if I have no calls. I will get acclimated. Back home they are predicting anywhere from 6 to 14 inches of snow depending on the path of the storm. It should be passable by the time I return and I can dedicate some of Sunday to cleaning up any of the snow that Mike was not able to handle. I am going to try to stay on NJ time, which means I will go to sleep soon.

2/25/10
7:28 PM PST, 10:28 PM EST
Fairfield Inn and Suites, San Jose

I have been feeling guilty all day. A major storm has hit New Jersey and I am not there to take care of it. Happily, we have fantastic neighbors who are helping Wendy, but I still feel badly for her. The storm should end tomorrow and I am hoping I can get home without too much delay on Saturday. After a lot of sleep last night, which I greatly needed, I worked out in my room this morning and forgot that my jumping on the floor can make a lot of noise. Wendy has mentioned this to me before. I realized it after hearing someone banging from underneath me. I felt terrible and finished my workout in the gym and outside. Feeling badly, I made a donation to Haitian Relief in the unknown name of the person I awakened. I hope they forgive me and I hope not to repeat the same mistake again. After a good breakfast of seven hard boiled eggs, cereal and a partial banana, I watched part of the President's health summit with the Republicans. I don't think it will accomplish much.

Then I was off to Foxconn, where the people were extremely nice. There may be a chance of more business and I was very glad I went. Afterward I went back to the hotel to work on merging the ISO and ITAR systems. It is a lot more work than I thought. I got some lunch at the Mexican restaurant before going to Flextronics. The meeting went well with one buyer from Mexico. She and her superior, who has a lot of experience with the company, have all of North America. We spoke back and forth and I told them how I thought they could best use us.

On my way back to the hotel, I found a local supermarket. Luckily there was also a FedEx store there. I may send some of my stuff back so I can easily carry my bags on the plane. I bought some food and was back at the hotel for some more working out, eating and work.

2/26/10
4:42 PM PST, 7:42 PM EST
Fairfield Inn and Suites, San Jose

My call this morning was to BAE, a world defense contractor who has the ability to buy a lot of our new product line if they so choose. I got there with plenty of time and the nice receptionist promptly took both my cell phone, which has a camera, and my car keys. She said taking car keys stopped people from forgetting to pick up their cell phones. I immediately felt naked without both, but persevered. The people in the meeting were both knowledgeable and pleasant. Actually, they seemed to know more about the chemical makeups of our products than I did, which is not unusual since they were long time pros. As always, I promised to get them the necessary data and they were interested in the samples I left with them for testing. I am hoping to get some feedback within two weeks. Well, that is when I will start bothering the head guy for information. We should have a non-disclosure in place by next week. I took a chance leaving the plaques without a signed testing agreement, but if they are going to take our products I might as well find out early. It was a good meeting and I was happy with the results.

Back at the hotel, I got my lunch at the Mexican restaurant for the last time before heading over to Hitachi Cable for the last call of the day. The headman there was very nice. Their business was centered on U.S. automakers so they are also hoping for a better year. It started raining as I was leaving and I resolved to get back to the hotel so I could get my boarding pass. My flights were not canceled due to the snowstorm. I have been in touch with the office and Wendy and the worst weather will be over. I packed some of my clothes and things into a box and went to the FedEx store to send them back and lighten my load for tomorrow. I bought my dinner and food for tomorrow, printed my boarding passes and finished the first pass of the Quality/Environmental/OSHA/ITAR manual. I will get it printed at the main desk and go through it tomorrow to make the next set of edits. In the meantime, I asked Mike to email me the quality manual so I could edit that for ITAR. I ran into some technical problems, but I think we are now okay. I will work for a while longer, maybe go for a walk outside as the rain seems to have let up, eat dinner and then take it easy. I just got our quality manual with Mike's help; onward for more editing.

2/27/10
4:71 AM California time, 7:51 PM EST
San Jose Airport

I kept working until I finished the procedures manual revisions and went back to FedEx to print it out along with the quality manual. I picked up dinner and by the time I got back to the room I was pretty tired. I spent the rest of the evening getting ready to leave and called Wendy, who is fine. I got up at 2:30 AM this morning and worked out for awhile. No one was at the National Car Rental counter when I got to the airport, so I left my GPS, keys and documents at the desk and hoped for the best. So far my plane is on time and since I have a lot to do I am looking forward to being in the air and being productive. We are on time to leave here to get to Houston, though I have no word about the plane home. I bought some chocolates and got some Starbucks cards for our neighbors across the street as a thank you to their kids who shoveled our driveway twice. They are great neighbors and have been a joy to live by for almost twenty years. It is amazing that we have been on our street this long; it is a quiet, beautiful place that I look forward to coming home to. Wendy says there is a lot more for me to shovel when I get home and I hope that starts tomorrow morning.

2/27/10
4:45 PM EST
In flight

With all of the worry, we got into Houston on time and I found out we were only an hour late for home, which was fantastic considering the weather. I got most of the revised procedures manual done. I wrote in the changes for the quality manual but could not put them into the file I have, so I think I am going to try to relax for a while. It has been a very productive trip.

There was an earthquake in Chile today which has led to a tsunami warning for Hawaii. The weather seems to be getting unstable. I don't think Mr. Obama's latest initiative to get health care moving will go very far. It sounds like both political parties are just posturing to place blame, which is a pity because there is a lot that needs to be fixed.

2/28/10
Aprox. 4:00 PM EST
Home, NJ

I landed yesterday about an hour late, which was nothing considering the potential for long delays and cancellations, and my wonderful wife was there to meet me. We went home, had dinner, I shoveled a little snow and got a long night of sleep. It was great to be back to my normal routine this morning. I played tennis with my brother and shoveled. The snow had begun to melt and was very heavy, but it was a great workout. I finished in time to have lunch before heading to the office. I have some new inventions I am working on, so I sketched them to send out to our VPs and got ready for the week in general.

MARCH

3/1/10
7:18 PM EST
Home, NJ

Dinner last night was very nice. We dined with a couple we met when we were at a resort in Arizona. He is with an investment group and she is president of the U.S. operations for a large upscale jewelry maker. They are both interesting, intelligent and a lot of fun. We rarely go out on Sunday nights, but this exception was definitely worth it.

I had a strange night of sleep. I have been working on two new maritime inventions and I kept waking up throughout the night about every two hours to make notes. It is strange how my mind works sometimes. I had a great day today; very productive and a lot of fun. Mike is working on the final version of implementing the ITAR system and we will meet tomorrow. I was working on various projects in addition to going to get my teeth checked. For many people a visit to the dentist is a foreboding experience, but Dr. Browne and his wonderful staff make it a joy. It is a place I not only look forward to visiting, but can actually relax and laugh while I am there. My fantastic in-laws are buying me a new iPod for my birthday. It will be able to hold all of my songs, a few movies and my Jean Shepherd taped radio show. I count on him to relax and to help me fall asleep quickly when I am far from home. He passed away a few years ago, but his talent lives on.

3/2/10
8:03 PM EST
Home, NJ

The large amount of snow we had is continuing to melt, which is a very good thing since more is expected tonight. It is not supposed to be much, so I will probably shovel when I wake up and that should do it for the day. I am paying for being off from tennis a few days last week. My stamina was not where I needed it to be and I was breathing heavier than normal. I also lost, which is not unusual. Still, my new band exercises are giving me more upper body strength and I can hit the ball harder. It was a good day with more potential for the composites. We are having a lot of fun trying to market them everywhere. I got confirmation from Wendy that she can come meet me in the Netherlands in April so I will book the flights soon. She is very excited, which makes me happy we can do it. Eric is moving on to another full time job next week but is still supposed to work 15-20 hours for us. If not, he will train one of our guys, maybe sooner rather than later. He is extremely talented and I hope he stays a part of our team. We have a lot riding on this new business being successful and I hope I have gambled correctly.

I went to see Dr. Mesnard for my semi-annual physical today. So far everything is good. He took blood to get a PSA reading to send to the urologist. I am in good shape with the dentist and the doctor. There is one checkup left and that will be it for another six to seven months.

3/3/10
7:32 PM EST
Home, NJ

It was a good day. We got the results back for some testing on our rifle plaques that had no metal strike face in them and they did extremely well. I hope it will be good enough to turn some heads regarding our materials.

Alex called earlier; he has a cold and has been overworking at school, but he will be finished with his midterm work this Friday and will come back home. He leaves on Saturday for Spain to see his best friend, so life should get progressively better for him as the week moves on.

We are pushing our defense and military contacts and we will either get results or be told to go away, but we need to get some answers soon. The cost of this effort is very high. It is a fantastic adventure; very interesting, stimulating and a lot of fun. However, the money and time outlay is so great we can't continue forever without money coming in. I got a new iPod today, courtesy of my fabulous in-laws. Rich began uploading my files to it and it has enough capacity for everything. Rich told me he also uploaded my WOR programs to it along with my various CDs.

3/4/10
9:01 PM EST
Home, NJ

Today was potentially very big day. Brett had a contact regarding selling our storm panels. After hearing their conversations, I got the feeling that they wanted not only an exclusive on our material, but also a potential partnership for a plant. I wrote out a proposal, which will still have to be checked for the equipment costs before we submit it. If everything checks out, we will wait to submit it on the 15th when Brett goes to see their operation in New Hampshire. We may set up a partnership, they will help finance. The new plant could also handle the maritime project if it comes through. It is a very exciting prospect. The rest of the day was spent marketing, selling and designing. We are working on the new ballistic cocoon concept to protect ships that are being repaired, renovated, built or stored. We received word from the export attorney that the concept can be sold outside the U.S.

MARCH

3/5/10
10:18 PM EST
Home, NJ

Alex came home tonight! He looks wonderful, though a bit tired. I have been working on new inventions, selling and marketing. I had lunch with John Rudder who is a good man and straight with his advice. Gary was in with our tax returns. I made less money this year than last, so I am getting a tax refund. If that is a common occurrence, the treasury will be in even more trouble with reduced receipts. The unemployment rate stayed the same as last month, which is a lot better than an increase. I still have hopes that we have seen the bottom. Ben is meeting us in Amsterdam and he, Jeroen and I will make sales calls, though I am not sure where yet. Igor from our office, our new liaison to the Netherlands, will also meet us for a morning of meetings so everyone can get acquainted. I need sleep.

3/6/10
5:38 PM EST
Home, NJ

After breakfast it was off to the office to meet Elana for a "band" workout. She put me through the paces, but it was not as painful as last time. Eric is working on my next idea and we should have his rendering by Tuesday. He starts a full time job on Monday and I hope he still has time for us. If not, I will send one of our MAC guys to him for rendering training. We will keep sending out ideas until they start breaking and bringing in business. I went home from the office to change for a bike ride with Uncle Dave. It was a beautiful day here; about 50°F and a cobalt blue sky. I was tired from the first workout and wiped out by the second.

After a huge lunch, I visited my parents and went back home. Alex, Wendy and I have been catching up. We will drive him to the airport soon; he is off for a week in Madrid. I won't see him on his return, as I will be leaving for Asia. I am very proud of him; he is working hard and looking great. It is always strange for me when someone else is leaving here. I am both sad and excited when it is my turn. But, no worries. I will be traveling a lot (even for me) until June, so I will be ready to stay around home then.

3/7/10
9:05 PM EST
Home, NJ

It was another gorgeous early spring day and hit about 60°F. It brought back thoughts of playing outside as my brother and I played indoors. Afterward, I went home, had a snack and headed over to Barb and Cliff's. They drove us into New York City for brunch at Barry's restaurant, Forge. It was a very pleasant time with good food and conversation and we even got to see Ben and Katie. From there, it was off on my bike Stella on a wondrous two-hour journey filled with fresh air and lots of thinking. We brought in dinner and Wendy and I watched the Academy Awards pre-show. I was working on some new inventions and an idea Brett had that I have expanded on. I will send them out for review tomorrow. My mind is already going into travel mode for this Friday. I will probably start packing tomorrow to be ready by Thursday night. I hope I sleep tonight.

3/8/10
5:25 PM EST
My office, NJ

We have spent the day getting ready for the big seawall impact tests on Wednesday. Brett will be coming down tomorrow with his van loaded with testing gear and we will go over everything here. We did more work on the potential hurricane business, getting samples ready for my trip to Asia, the trip to Europe and all basic paperwork and sales. I had lunch with Wendy and Elana today, which was a fun break. Now I am tired and will be going home soon. I just checked the weather for both Kuala Lumpur and Bangkok and it looks like low 90°s F.

3/9/10
5:20 PM EST
My office, NJ

It always amazes me that at about 3:00 PM I am tired and dragging and always want to pack it in to go home. But if I hold out until 4:00 or 4:30, I usually get a second wind and often a lot of good stuff happens.

It has been quite a day. The preparations for the big water barrier tests tomorrow are completed, Brett is on his way down with the test gear and Mike has already prepped the slow motion camera for pictures. There is a high level of excitement and caution amongst our troops. We don't know how the test equipment will work and how our samples will perform, but we are optimistic. Tomorrow after tennis I will be here to get any last minute tools and will head up to the test site. Everyone else should be there already.

We received good news from our export attorney. The preliminary look at our procedures manual with ITAR regulations included is going well, we have the information on how to certify our sub-contractors regarding ITAR and we have information we can send overseas regarding our new antenna covering material that will allow signals to pass through. I also hope to confirm a sales call in England for my European trip that will mean not needing to go to Amsterdam first.

3/10/10
4:37 PM EST
My office, NJ

Today was the day for the big seawall tests.

From the beginning this morning, it was apparent that a huge team effort would be needed and it happened. We ran the first test at a 30-foot drop and everything worked perfectly. Unfortunately, the next two drops at 68 feet did not go so smoothly and the falling weight actually bent the unit holding the test plaques. Faced with a grave problem, not to mention a time restraint, we abandoned the finished fixture that Brett had so ably built and created a temporary base out of wood that worked perfectly. Test after test had the 50-pound weight dropping 70 feet and smashing down on our various types of composite and Trelleborg materials, simulating a six-ton boat speeding 50 miles per hour into our barrier design. All of our panels functioned and the results were much better than we had hoped for. After a very tiring, productive and happy day, we all left around 2:30.

The data, including still pictures, slow motion video and regular video, will be processed over the next few days and will give all of our companies valuable information regarding what our material can do. The next stop for the customer is to pay for the work we have done and enlist us to make full-scale prototypes. From what we saw today, we believe our panels can do what is needed; a very welcomed conclusion to a lot of planning. Special thanks today go to Brett for creating the wonderful tests units, which were not only functional but also very stylish; to Vinnie for being up in the 70-foot tower for hours; Mike for running the slow motion video; and Dave for being there to help fix all the things that needed modifying. We have a new "ship skin" invention, which is actually a new type of armor, which we intend to start marketing immediately.

3/11/10
5:25 PM EST
My office, NJ

Today was spent getting ready to go away, which meant a lot of paperwork intermixed with selling. By the time I leave for the airport midday tomorrow, virtually everything for the trip should be ready and I should be able to relax when we takeoff. I am waiting now for the download information for our website for the test data from yesterday. Mike created a fantastic video covering most of what happened and I think the customer and other potential customers will like it. I am also sending a new invention along with it. Jack is due in tomorrow morning to bring me the last batch of samples for the trip and he and Brett will work on our next patent application next week. I am also hoping that last group of information I sent to our bank people in Malaysia is all that is needed from our side to go public. I can only imagine how much time Ben has spent on it. The chances of our trip to Thailand are looking increasingly bleaker due to the violent demonstrations there and I am already emailing with Ben about an alternative trip to IJX and speaking with the government officials there about our hurricane plaques and other commercial products. It may end up being for the best in the end and I will not be upset if I don't make it to Bangkok. The thought of a million protestors with the real chance of violence is not appealing. My mind constantly wanders to preparation and alternative plans when a trip is imminent, especially while playing tennis. I have learned how to download songs from Kayla's iTunes account, though it is a dangerous habit because I find myself adding songs all the time. There is nothing like having the right music on the road whether for exercising, trying to stay calm or easing homesickness. The music, movies, Jean Shepherd and my CDs are very important to my mental well-being for the trip, so I try to be very careful regarding power supplies, adapters and keeping my devices in good condition.

3/12/10
2:11 PM EST
JFK Airport, NY
Korean Air Lounge

Darn it! I just remembered I packed my pretzels in my large suitcase that is now on its way to the bottom of the plane. I suppose I can always buy some before boarding. It has been a wild day already.

After playing tennis with my wonderful brother, it was back to the office where I spent the morning finalizing all plans and getting the various composite materials ready for IJX and IJT. I have them in my suitcase and will leave them with Ben. Thailand is no longer a destination since there are rumors of a possible revolution tomorrow, so I am going to Kuala Lumpur, Penang and then probably to IJX in China. That is not necessarily a bad thing. Change is normal and often turns out well, so I will ride along for a while and see what happens.

Mike the driver was on time to pick me up for the airport and as always I was very sad to leave Wendy and my home. I am due back next Saturday. The ride to the airport was uneventful and I even got a chance to nap a little along the way. The plane is on time so far and the airlines appear to be well run. This is my first time with Turkish Air and so far all seems well. The video that Mike made has now been distributed to some of our customers, partners and various other potential contacts. I look forward to the reaction; we think the test results were awesome. While I am gone, Jack will be working on a new type of composite and Brett will be working on our next patent application. I look forward to being up in the plane.

3/13/10
3:36 AM Istanbul time, 8:56 PM EST
In flight

I have become a great fan of Turkish Air. The flight has been well-run, with a great staff, delicious food and a really good seat. Our arrival time is a little more than six hours from now and then I have a layover until I catch my next flight. It looks like we were delayed less than an hour in take off, which, considering the rainy weather and construction on one airstrip, I am very happy about. I have been doing the final edit on the first quarter of last year's book. Katie finished her part and now has another job, so I resolved to get the last edits done on that so at least a quarter would be done soon.

MARCH

3/13/10
7:52 AM Istanbul time, 12:52 AM EST

Approximately 1:40 until we land. We are going 955 KL/hour.

I got between three and four hours of sleep, which was excellent, and I am slowly converting over to Asian time. We are currently crossing over the German Alps, but I can't really see them since I don't have a seat with a window. I always try for aisle seats for better restroom access.

This trip has a few purposes; the main one is to meet again with various advisers and bankers regarding going public in Asia. It has been an extremely long and complicated road for Ben and his crew, but it seems to be nearing an end. When I land, he and I will meet and he will prep me as to more of what to say and what not to say in front of them.

The market and manufacturing in Asia for the commercial products are huge for our new products, so there is a lot to talk about. The third part, now that we are not going to Thailand is to go to IJX and let our people there see me in person, know that everything is well and that we are growing as an international company. I joke that they need to see me breathing and walking around, but it is really true. They want me around in case of emergencies and to help engineer world growth, but otherwise they want to be left alone, which is fine with me. I will visit, we may or may not take some of the team out to dinner and I will spend the bulk of the visit there in the conference room working on my own. Since we are not going to Thailand, we may go to Penang in Malaysia. Ben has a target, a small printing company, that he may want to take over and wants to check them out. Finally, we are also making sales calls both for the new materials and our standard lines and I hope to have a positive impact in those areas. Things are often in flux and what I expect will happen can completely change. That is fine; I will go with what happens and try to be flexible.

While over there, I will also talk to Ben about IJ Netherlands being converted to a fully Netherlands-based company and then give IJ Malaysia the option to buy them. It is hard for our individual teams not to be in competition with each other and part of my job is to push for profitable growth while keeping the worldwide team spirit thriving. One way to do this is to have IJ US spur the innovation into new products and then spread them worldwide, as in the case of the composite plastics. It has been an amazing adventure and we will keep throwing as much of our financial resources and manpower into it as we can afford.

My tax return for 2009 reflected what I am sure is a similar tale for the rest of our country. I made a great deal less in 2009 than 2008 or 2007. I put a huge percentage of our profits back into the company for research and development and I do not begrudge the money or the massive amounts of my time. Of course, it will be great if this new area takes off, but it is all a huge gamble. If I can't take the constant pressure, then it is time to get out of the game. Along with the pressure, however, comes enormous amounts of adrenaline that surge through my body enabling me to keep going at times when I would normally assume it to be impossible. I have not seen the potential for huge growth like I do now in all of the years I have been in business. This is one of those times in our history when the planets may be aligned and our profitable sales can increase by factors of 5 or 10 times. I will worry about financing the raw materials and production later if the business comes through. That is a whole different kind of pressure, but one I would like to bring on.

3/13/10
11:09 AM Istanbul time, 4:09 AM EST
Istanbul Airport

My plan was simple. I would check in at the transit desk, get my next boarding pass for Kuala Lumpur and then go outside to the baggage area and make sure my bag was not there and on its way to Malaysia. Unfortunately, the transit desk people could not get me a boarding pass for two hours and since I was worried about my suitcase I got a 30 day Visa and went out side the secured area. I figured that I could go outside and walk around in the fresh air for a little while. I checked that my bag was not there, and once satisfied that it was not, I went outside. Unfortunately, the combination of the noise and pollution negated the benefits of being outdoors, so I made my way back inside. It was not easy finding my way, but I am now waiting for the Malaysian Air desk to open so I can get my boarding pass and get back inside. In retrospect, it was a good plan and I would do it again. Maybe there will be an observation deck once I get inside again. Airports are very lonely places when you have to wait; this one is filled with lots of exotic looking people some of whom look lost and frustrated. I hear snippets of various languages and you can read peoples life histories on their faces; how they move, their clothes and their baggage.

I wonder how many hundreds of thousands of people have sat in this airport seat I am occupying; not a great thought for someone who is germo-phobic. On the other hand, a woman is sitting down next to me who emits a pleasant fragrance, so I guess it all works out. It is good I won't be playing tennis for 10 days. My elbow has been bothering me and I could use a rest from the pounding on my body. I wonder if I will have time to go swimming in Malaysia today. That could be fun and a great way to loosen up my body. For that trip I am now flying into London and will meet a new prospect I got from Paul at Trelleborg. Then I plan to fly to Munich the same day and sleep there. I am hoping that Ben and Jeroen can meet me either the night before or early the next morning. I like Munich, so it will be good to go back there. Sleep deprivation is starting to kick in, but I have to be careful where I doze off. Some of my stuff could be taken or I could miss the next flight. Alex is back home from Madrid and I heard he had a great time. I am glad he is there now to keep Wendy company since I am away. I am not sure when he leaves to go back to school.

MARCH

3/13/11
12:01 AM Malaysia time, 11:01 AM EST
In flight 6:41 TO GO 36,997 FT. Altitude, -72°F outside
Passing over Iran

I eventually got checked in and through security by about 12:30 PM Turkish time. What little I saw of Turkey I found interesting. Maybe we can do business here one day so I can look around.

Once inside, I met a man named George who had been born in Latvia and emigrated to Melbourne, Australia two decades ago. He conducts some type of business I was not clear about and seems to have a rich love of life. He is a pleasant flying partner. Sleep deprivation has definitely crept in because I almost cried twice while watching a movie and I am not sure if that would have been my normal reaction. I will try to get three or four hours of sleep after I finish writing here and editing some more. I am making great progress with the final edit for the first quarter of my next book. If I can do that then I should be fine for the meetings that will happen as soon as I arrive. I am listening to music I downloaded myself off of iTunes. Since I am technologically inept, I will brag about the fact I did it. Of course I did have Rich's help the whole way and he did show me how to sync it to my iPod and then make playlists. Oh yes, he did download iTunes to my computer in the office, so in retrospect I have virtually nothing to be proud of and will move on.

It was interesting talking with George about his perception of Mr. Obama and the economic meltdown of a year ago. Did I think if the President had done nothing we would have gone into a world depression? I said I did not think bailing out Chrysler, GM and the banks was a good idea and I think letting the chips fall might have been harder at first, but would have led to a quicker recovery. Even more interesting is that I am editing the same time period last year so I have a fresh retrospective from my own writing. Some of the things I predicted came true and others not but the overall thrust that the economy was going to need time to recover was right. I think people outside the U.S. have a much better image of the president than many of us do in the U.S. They only see the ten second sound bites that come through the news channels, they don't see the results of his core policies. He is still trying to get a health care bill through. He makes it sound like he knows better than the people and we should shut up and trust him. He, however, has virtually no experience in business or economics (or politics for that matter) and my initial hesitancy about him being elected has unfortunately been justified. No matter; I have no influence in this, especially since I left WOR. The best I can do is be as successful as I can, create as many good jobs as I can and safeguard my team as much as possible worldwide.

3/13/10
5:36 AM Malaysian time, 4:36 PM EST
In flight

We are about an hour away from landing. I find at least one interesting occurrence in most long flights. Right after breakfast is served, there are usually about 90 minutes left and the entire atmosphere of the plane changes. The calmness is gone and people are once again emerging from their position in "timelessness" to rejoin the world. I will now fill out my entry documents; I asked for two since I usually mess one up. I hope I have no problem getting my suitcase back since I lost my baggage claim ticket. Titan from IJ Malaysia should be outside waiting for me and then we will be to the hotel. I do not know if I have a room or need to wait for one this afternoon. A shower would be nice and so would an hour to workout first, but I am not sure if I will get either. No matter; I should be able to workout sometime later in the day. Both flights have been very good and I look forward to being outside in the fresh air again. It will be hot in Malaysia; I hope our meeting is in the hotel.

3/15/10
9:17 AM Malaysian time, 9:17 PM EST
Malaysia Industrial Development Finance Building Kuala Lumpur

We landed roughly on schedule yesterday and Titan was there to pick me up. Happily, I had no trouble getting my suitcase without the baggage claim ticket. It took less than an hour to get to our hotel and then I had about 90 minutes to relax a little, get changed and shower before the meeting. The gathering was to go over our final offering for going public and some of our consultant advisors were there along with Ben and a few of our people from IJX and IJ Malaysia. What I thought would be a two-hour meeting turned into an all-day affair excluding lunch. This was difficult, as I had to focus on a lot of details and go over things as well as stay awake, which was very tough considering jet lag. But I made it. I also showed the guys the new composite samples and they were extremely happy with the prospect, not to mention the new video we had made last week. We warned them about the possible problems with information and materials regarding ITAR regulations, everyone understood and we were prepared for the set of meetings today.

(Continued 5:01 PM Malaysian time at my hotel)

After that, it was back to my room for a band workout and then down to the gym for the treadmill. Unfortunately, by this time I did not have a full hour, as I like to do, because dinner was at 7:00, so I ran and walked for about 30 minutes hoping I would get about the same amount of exercise. I had given up running years ago because of the pounding on my legs, so I was hopeful there would not be any damage from what I did. I went back to the room and showered again and met Ben and the rest of the IJX people here for dinner. I was periodically nodding off during dinner and toward the end was just trying to make it through so I could get back to the room. Ben made dinner a brief and fun activity and I was asleep in my room by 9:45. I got up at 5:30 so I would have time to work out, although I probably could have used a few more hours of sleep. I did most of the band workout in my room and ran on the treadmill in the gym. So far my legs have been sore, but not unbearable, so I might continue adding on some roadwork when I am traveling. After a very hearty breakfast of seven eggs, cereal, fruit and two small pancakes, I was dressed and ready to meet Ben and Hing, two close advisors for going public, for our meeting. Once again, there were a bunch of people and as I said to Wendy this morning, it has finally sunk in that we are doing this and it is a real thing. It is a very big deal, probably before I did not want to admit it to myself so I did not get too nervous, but that attempt at self-deception is now gone. We had various speakers about what was required for the process and what was needed from us. The requirements for the level of the Malaysian Exchange we are entering have gotten much stricter so we have to be careful to make sure we fully disclose and everything is clear. Our consults, including lawyers and accountants, wanted everything perfect both so the government would have few questions in their review of our application and to make sure we did not break any laws. They kept reminding us about the fines and jail terms if we messed up. Two men were there who were going to be on our board of directors, and both seemed competent. There is still more information they need from us and it will take some time to get it squared away. I think the June timetable is a little too optimistic for the actual day of the IPO; I figure it will be more toward the end of July. Ben also mentioned I will be needed here every month for the next few months, so I will probably put off my trip to Mexico until after this is done.

After that, it was back to the hotel for a quick lunch then Hing, Ben and I went to a local military installation regarding the new material. After the advice of our export attorney, I was very careful with what I said about our new composites and what they could do. I spoke about commercial applications and then they asked about some military variation. I told them I would have to check and get back to them. In the meantime, they gave us the name of a former colonel who owns a company that makes many products that could be useful for us and we are trying to see them later in the week. I got back around 4:00, had the hotel send up a man to open the room's safe, which I locked by mistake, and then went down to the pool for a swim. The water was warm and the weather perfect. I am pretty tired and done exercising for the rest of the day. I have until 6:30 for dinner with Ben, Hing and another man, Charles, who I believe is an apparel manufacturer and might be interested in our composite.

3/16/10
7:45 PM Malaysian time, 7:45 AM EST
Crowne Plaza Hotel Kuala Lumpur

Dinner was indeed very interesting last night. Charles has a big business importing various types of sportswear and sports-related equipment. He brought along a pro swimming coach named YY and the two of them discussed the marketplace and what could be possible regarding our products. They were interested in the "band" package we had set up for Peter K. I mentioned they could market the packages and his program over here and we could probably get Peter to come over to help promote it. He seemed interested. Dinner was a wide array of very unusual dishes, a good portion of which I would not try. We also spoke about sports and it turns out that Charles is a good badminton player. He asked me to play before I left on Friday. I am under no illusions that my tennis playing will help me (in fact, it may hurt), but it doesn't matter. He is a very pleasant and I look forward to an adventure.

Today we visited two generals and a few majors regarding our new composite material. They were enthused about the possibilities, even though I could not go into much detail. Abul, our host and liaison, paved the way for my talk this afternoon and I think it went pretty well. They said they don't do the actual buying, but they have to know us if we are to move forward. It was a little intimidating standing up before the military people, but they were pleasant and I felt comfortably prepared. After lunch, we left town to go to the Malaysian equivalent of our West Point and their military research center. The composites were a big hit there too and we are hopeful they will include us on their journey to make things lighter, do a better job and cut down on cost. The afternoon meeting was with two research people; one a former Colonel and the other a two star general. It was a lot of fun and I think we made some headway into getting our products recognized, then it was back to the hotel where I explained my new invention for Charles to Ben. We can market it under his own brand. It is a lock box for valuables when you are working out and if they move more than ten feet without being shut off then an alarm will be triggered. Ben and Al liked the idea, so I will sketch it by Friday when I see Charles.

3/17/10
12:45 AM Malaysian time, 12:45 PM EST
In flight from Penang to Kuala Lumpur

I got good night's sleep and was up at 4:45 to get ready to meet Ben and embark on our trip to Penang. Once at the airport, our CFO of IJ Malaysia, PK, met us. We had one purpose and that was to visit a company we might want to buy once we go public. The taxi ride and trip down there all went without incident and P.K.'s very nice wife picked us up at the airport and took us to the plant, a label manufacturer something like us. They have about 18,000 square feet and are run by a man and his wife. The man is an engineer and very well connected to many of the telecomm companies where we were not. It would be a good fit concerning marketing, but we needed to meet them both to get a feel of whether it would work. We sat for a while and seemed to speak the same language, not only in terms of business, but in general philosophy and marketing thrust. They too wanted niche areas of higher profitable business. We started to speak about money when they took us on a plant tour. We had to leave shortly thereafter with the promise that they would send us more information and we would send a proposal. Once back in the car, we began researching how much their building was worth and the value of their equipment. I will put together a proposal.

MARCH

3/17/10
3:40 PM Malaysian time, 3:40 AM EST
Crowne Plaza Hotel Kuala Lumpur

I got back to the hotel, finished the proposal and emailed it to Ben. He just emailed back some comments and it needs some tweaking, which is expected. As soon as I finish emailing back to him, it is off to the gym. Who knows, maybe I will be daring and take another swim. I am yearning for some home style food, so I may venture out afterward and look for dinner. I have lots of paperwork to do later.

3/18/10
1:46 PM Malaysian time, 1:46 AM EST

I was planning to sleep later this morning, but that did not happen. I was up at 5:00 and went downstairs to the gym. Then I realized they did not open to 6:00, so I went to the pool and walked around the perimeter while I spoke to Al and Brett. Catching up with Al is always an adventure and things at the office are busy. Afterward I called Brett regarding the new potential composite plant and also branding our two new product lines. We have a commercial and military/defense area, so we are running a company contest for good names. I offered my suggestions, but they are rarely selected by our team, so I will not hold my breath. After breakfast I answered emails and called Ben to discuss an offer for the company in Penang we visited yesterday. We agreed on the plan and I emailed it this morning. There has been no word back from them yet. I was down in the lobby at about 10:50, to meet Hing and prepare for our call with one of the major defense/military manufacturers in Malaysia. Ben went home last night after we got back from Penang. Having the drop test video has been wonderful and after I showed the two gentlemen our radome material, jacket and other samples, they seemed upbeat about the prospect of doing business. It will probably take a while unless there is an immediate application. I was really happy when they asked me to see their plant tomorrow, which is about 90 minutes away. They are going to pick me up at 12:30, so I should have plenty of time to get back from badminton. I will go to their facility and then they will get me back to the airport. I am not flying until after midnight, so I have ample time. Hing and I both felt it went well. It was good to be able to speak about the potential of working together on a larger scale. The imagination soars when potential is unlimited and I like that.

Hing and I had lunch. I wanted to get some background information on him. He has an interesting past; coming from a small, local village and being sent to Singapore and London by his dad to study law. His father gave him no choice, but Hing calmly followed the path. He is very successful now and one of two main advisors for our going public. I am glad he is on our team.

It was confirmed that I have to be back here in late April, so I am checking flights now. I have an overnight on May 1st to see Alex, so I will plan around that. After lunch I went back to my room, but am now sitting in the lobby because housekeeping is cleaning. I will go back now, book my trip to see Alex and probably change to go out for a walk. The rest of the day will be spent in paperwork, email, eating and packing for tomorrow.

3/19/10
1:05 PM Malaysian time, 1:05 AM EST
In transit to go see Malaysian defense and aerospace contractor

I went walking yesterday after lunch with Hing. I thought about going up the Twin Towers and crossing their connecting bridge, but after I walked a while in the high heat and humidity and saw the security at the site, I decided to forget about it. Kuala Lumpur has its own look to it, as does every big city. This one seems prosperous and its 3,000,000 people generally happy. I got back to the hotel by late afternoon and went to the pool to read some more of the manual regarding going public. It is very thick with a lot of legal terms but I am getting through it. I bought two salads for dinner and some sandwiches for today. Around 7:30 I got really sleepy, so I decided to turn in. Mission accomplished; I slept from about 8:00 until 4:30 this morning. I went walking by the pool since I needed to call Al, who told me the office is doing well. After breakfast, I taxied over to Charles' Country Club. I spoke to Brett on the way. I am going to finalize my flights to and from Boston next Wednesday to meet with the man we may partner with for a composites plant. I also spoke to Wendy; Bailey is not getting better and surgery is probably a necessity. She was not happy that I was going to go away again at the end of April and might prefer that I go as soon as we finish in Amsterdam. I will try to do whatever works best for her. I'll know better this weekend.

The country club was supposed to be an hour away and Charles said that he was coming early because he knew I had a call this afternoon and I did not want to be late. There was virtually no traffic and we made it in about 30 minutes. I wandered around the area looking for the badminton courts and found Charles signing us in. I have not played badminton in about forty years so I did not know what to expect. We went into this large room with many courts, we were alone and he explained the rules. Badminton is a mixture of tennis, table tennis and squash. The basics are to use a rubber nosed part with feathers to make it fly. The idea is to use your wrist as much as possible. This, of course, goes directly against all tennis ideals but as we started I slowly got the hang of it. That is my forehand and swerve were okay but my backhand was a mess. We played for over an hour and the workout was wonderfully extreme, just what I wanted considering the traveling I was embarking on. Afterward we had a drink and relaxed for a little while. Charles is an amazing man. He is self-made with a calm exterior and a driving force pulsating inside him. His business is expanding and he seems at peace with the world. After showering, he drove me back to the hotel where I got packed and did some emailing.

A man named Gunny, who is very pleasant, picked me up for my call. We are on our way to his plant and it is very hot outside, about 36°C or 96 degrees F. We should have about an hour and a quarter to go before getting there. My stomach rebelled as badminton was finishing. I have food with me but I am not sure if and when I can eat it. No worries; I should be fine through my meeting and can worry about that afterward. Gunny suggested I take a nap, a suggestion that I will try to follow.

3/19/10
2:09 PM Malaysian time, 2:09 AM EST
En route to Melaka

The two most incongruous things I have seen so far: While walking in Kuala Lumpur yesterday, I saw a hotel sign advertising that Elvis Presley would be there that night. The second was a sign I saw on this road trip, which advertised a western resort with cowboys and Indians. It is strange what leaves the United States.

Gunny says that the town of Melaka, which we are passing, has a lot of historical sites and offered to show me on the way back to the airport if there is time. I might actually do some sight seeing (by car of course) and on our general route anyway. There are miles and miles of gorgeous palm tree groves; they are harvested for the palm oil. Gunny pointed out a rubber tree, but I am not sure I actually saw it. It is amazing to think that rubber does actually grow on trees; not like money.

3/19/10
5:37 PM Malaysian time, 5:37 AM EST
En route to Kuala Lumpur Airport

I met with the head of new business for CTRM, one of the people from yesterday. He gave me a rundown of their company history and product lines. They are doing very well in commercial aerospace and the military areas and I see potential for working together. He will send a non-disclosure agreement to us next week, so I can send him some test results and some radome samples for testing. Afterward he nicely asked Gunny to take me sight-seeing in the town of Melaka. This area was once settled by the Dutch and the British before their independence. It is a fascinating place filled with multiple architectural styles. Now on to the airport through rush hour traffic.

3/19/10
9:52 PM Malaysian time, 9:52 AM EST
Kuala Lumpur Airport Lounge

Gunny got me to the airport in plenty of time. I ate two sandwiches and the insides of another I had been carrying, which gave me the needed space in my secondary carry-on for my clothes to change into later. I was able to check in early and make my way to one of the best airport lounges in the world, Malaysia Air, here in their hub. I have been editing the first quarter of my new book and will be done in the next few days. I am starting to lose it and don't know how much longer I can focus but I will go as far as I am comfortable and then stop. I have about two and a half hours before I head to the gate. It is calm here and pleasant. I will call the office soon.

3/19/10
3:27 PM EST
In flight to Istanbul, Turkey

The flight is in good shape and we appear to be running ahead of schedule about eight hours to go. After a very good dinner, the cabin lights went out and most people seem to be sleeping. Since it is 3:27 AM from where I left, I should be out cold right now. I suppose I did have a short nap and a can of Pepsi, so I will probably be up for at least a little while. I changed from my suit pants to my spares and I am feeling pretty good. We are currently flying over the Bay of Bengal on our way toward Madras, India. As is normal, time seem to have stopped and I can do whatever I like. It has been a really good trip and I am excited to get back and move on with everything. I know I am incredibly fortunate to be able to go after the things I want and to have a great worldwide team behind me. I will not take anything for granted. For now, I will do some more editing and probably sleep for a while. Some rest sounds good.

3/19/10
8:30 PM EST
In flight to Istanbul, Turkey
Approximately 3 hours to go.

I am officially bored, so I decided to review the presentation of CTRM, the company I visited yesterday. After reviewing the presentation,, I can see a few applications both commercial and military, where we can work together. The more we talk between companies the stronger trust can build, the faster things will move and the greater the chance for actual business. We need the ability to translate my ideas into actual applications via renderings quickly and we can't take the risk of being slowed down. It is time to go back to the "old school," which means pen and paper, to start sketching.

I do love this business; the creativity it allows us and the ability to soar is limitless. Maybe I will have our art department take a shot at the two ideas for Charles' sports equipment and clothing business and see what they come up with. They love a creative challenge.

3/20/10
7:03 AM Turkish time, 1:03 AM EST
Istanbul Airport Air Turkey Lounge

We arrived early and when I went to the transfer desk to get my next ticket for JFK, I found out I needed to go through three different areas. It did not matter since I had plenty of time, but I need to remember in the future that at least 90 minutes are needed between flights. As it is, I have about three and a half hours before takeoff so I am fine. I will hang out here for awhile and then walk and try to get myself tired enough to get three to four more hours of sleep on the next leg. I hope to be okay to sleep tonight at home. This is a nice, smaller airport so there is not a lot of stuff to see, but I always like going through the food courts to see what local foods are offered. Since I still have provisions with me I will pass on it here and eat the airplane food, which was excellent last time on Turkish Air. I am getting really tired, but will try to work some more before I get home. Mike the driver will be a welcome sight when he comes to pick me up. I came up with a few variations on some of our current inventions. I will check them with the export attorney before offering them outside the U.S.

3/20/10
9:32 AM Turkish time, 3:32 AM EST
Istanbul Airport

This airport takes the prize for most security checks. I had three from my transfer and then another four getting inside the gate. I wonder if the threat level has been raised? There is a strike at British Air; maybe that has something do with it. No matter; I am through and I am glad I got here early. I can see that my computer power pack is just about empty, but I have a spare. My two cell phone batteries, however, are just about gone. I think I can power them on the flight over. I watched a movie, "Goodbye Columbus," on my iPod. The first time I saw it was with my sister during one of the summers we were down at the Jersey Shore. I must have been about 11 years old. It was a long time ago. It is nice how some things can be frozen in time so the look, feel and sound of a movie can be like a trip in a time machine. I finished editing the first quarter of my book. It is now ready for the final. Igor Gomes from our office designed the new cover, which I like it a lot. I dozed a little before, but still hope to get some sleep on this flight. My ability to work may be about tapped. I yearn to be home.

3/20/10
1:25 PM EST
In flight

We have 2:15 hours until we arrive in New York, which should put us at sometime around 3:42. That would be great, as by the time I get through customs and immigration, get my luggage, find Mike the driver and get home, I still might see Ben and Katie if they are still there for dinner. It has been a calm flight with an excellent crew and food and I would not hesitate to recommend both Turkish and Malaysian Airlines. I will now go through this log so I can update my VPs before Monday morning's meeting. The only minor problem I have is that both my cell phone batteries are nearly empty and the outlet I counted on in this plane did not fit my plugs. I hope I have enough to get in contact with Mike. Tomorrow will be a normal day and back on schedule. Wendy said the weather should be good for an afternoon ride after tennis, which will be a great way to spend a Sunday.

No Road Is Ever Straight

3/22/10
9:44 PM EST
Home, NJ

Sunday was spent playing tennis, biking, going to the office and catching up. It was a beautiful spring day. I also did some paperwork at home and relaxed with my wonderful wife. It was tough getting up this morning and I ate an extra big first breakfast knowing I could be in for trouble with my Monday tennis game. Sure enough my partner was out for blood, but after being blown out in the first set, I held my own in the second. The rest of the day was spent in catching up, meetings and lots of emails. Things were good and I wanted to keep them moving. We are now talking about bringing back one of the people we laid off, which is a very good sign. The big projects are moving here and to Asia and I am preparing for calls in Europe next month. I am working on some new inventions and will check with our export attorney to see what can go overseas. I am glad he is on our team. Being away made it much easier to adjust to Daylight Savings time. Now we get more daylight later in the day; a very nice thing.

3/23/10
9:10 AM EST
Home, NJ

We saw the water barrier people in today. There was a lot of discussion regarding design of the unit, how our parts and Trelleborg's would or would not mold together and our overall capabilities. There is potential for a massive order, but the customer needs to set up a program to evaluate the needs of their customers. I suggested another round of samples. They wanted to get the design of our panel and how it attaches to their finished unit so we are doing both. We have not been paid for the work we have done yet and the invoice is overdue. This is not a good sign. In the meantime, we spoke about adding defensive and offensive capabilities to the seawall making it a "living" barrier. One of the customers looked through our book of renderings and likes some of our ideas. We will offer suggestions on how to make the barrier a weapon. I have no trouble taking care of terrorists. However, hurting innocent people is not something I want to live with. Therefore, I want to make the barrier as recognizable as possible as a place to stay away. The health care bill was signed today. The democrats are dancing in the aisles. Their political futures are riding on it being accepted.

3/24/10
5:47 AM EST
Newark/Liberty Airport

Great news: Kayla came home last night – a day early! I had gone to sleep, but heard her get in and got a hug before I went back to bed. I am on my way to meet with the men from New England regarding a joint venture for a composites plant. I am not sure what to expect, though sometimes it is good not to have expectations. I emailed Ben this morning to contact Abul, the telecom broker we know from Malaysia, and one of the military groups we had met with. I have an idea for an anti-pirate device and we need a written agreement in place before we can share the information. I have a real problem with pirates and groups that imprison others, most governments would rather not kill, so our inventions will be designed to disarm, immobilize and track. After repeated changes with our export attorney, I think we are in a good place regarding what information we can share and what will need to be checked for export licenses.

I have my breakfast of oatmeal, bananas, cinnamon and raisins with me. I am already hungry, so I will prepare it with a small amount of water creating a log that I can eat like a loaf of bread on the flight. I almost did not make it through security with my larger bottle of mouthwash. I will probably use what I need and throw it before coming back; I do not want to risk delay. We will email Vincent, the Penang plant owner Ben and I visited last week. He turned down our offer to buy his facility, but wants to be a supplier and research partner. Ben and I are in agreement with this; the email will start the adventure.

3/24/10
12:06 PM EST
In flight

We arrived about 8:00 AM but there was traffic and Brett and our two guests took about 30 minutes to pick me up. We went to a nearby hotel restaurant and laid all of our cards on the table there. The two men had a potential location for a plant in New Hampshire and lots of contacts that might be able to use the composite materials we would plan to build there. They had strong engineering, design and plant experience as well as extremely good political and banking connections. We had the material itself, the various processes for new products, the ability to invent new applications, plant creation and running experience and the joint willingness to take some big chances. We met for about two hours covering our respective backgrounds and what we wanted to accomplish. I was dropped off at the airport afterward, where I rushed to try to get an earlier flight. I was fortunate in that even though it took a while to get through security, there was a delayed flight back home and I was able to catch it. Mike is scheduled take me from the airport to home, where I will get my car and go to the office. I hope to get there by 2:00 PM. This was an extremely good, fast trip and we have a lot of work to do to get the next round of test materials created and tested. We will make a video of those new tests like the last one and I am hoping it will have the same positive impact on those who see it.

No Road Is Ever Straight

3/25/10
9:48 PM EST
Home, NJ

Business is getting better. Receivables are growing, but money is coming in slow, which means our credit line with the bank is getting higher. I am not stopping and I will just have to live with the debt. I did lots of paperwork today, some dealing with our public offering in Asia. I want to be a good chairman of the board so I am studying the materials they gave us and beginning to ask a lot of questions. There is no word yet as to our next meeting there. Kayla is home and she looks wonderful, except for a cold. She is a joy to have around.

3/27/10
9:26 AM EST
Home, NJ

It is a cold morning with temperatures around freezing right now, but my flowers seem okay. I am scheduled to go biking at about 11:00 AM and I may need a mask and thermal boots. I slept about 9 ½ hours last night and I needed it. I had a strange set of dreams as usual, but nothing disturbing. I am having some trouble with my right elbow. I am hitting the ball harder in tennis, and this combined with the band workout is putting more strain there. I may go for a cortisone shot. I suppose I could back off on the exercise, but that will probably not happen. As my wife has asked, what will happen when I can't play tennis anymore is that I will probably turn to swimming. I do not think I can make the transition from all-out tennis to a more laid back version and will probably have to change sports. It is part of my obsessive personality and something I accept; change is possible but modification of effort may not be.

I have almost everything ready for what happens when I die. I know that may sound strange, but being the type of person who needs to be prepared, it was something I needed to do. In the event that I go into a coma or become brain dead, I have left instructions to keep me on life support for one week, in case of a miracle, then let me go. I do not want to bankrupt my family nor be a vegetable for any amount of time. Once any organs are donated, the rest will be cremated and I will go to the place Wendy and I picked. The only thing I have not done is pick the urn. Kayla suggested a nice wooden box and I may or may not leave that up to my loved ones. Having the conversation with Wendy and Kayla was good. Since I believe in reincarnation and the spirit continually moving on, I am not that concerned, but I do like to be prepared. I visited a person who could see into other worlds for awhile, just long enough to prove to myself it existed. I cut myself off to make sure I was not unduly influenced by those who had passed before me.

I have been doing a lot of reading for our public offering in Malaysia. I am extremely thankful it is a former British colony, as all of their documentation is in English and based on British law. Even so, it is very complicated.

MARCH

When I send over questions, I sometimes get the feeling that I may be stepping over boundaries of the culture there, so I don't push too hard. I still want to know what is going on since I am responsible for at least some of what goes on. Malaysia is a much different place than China; much less direct, more polite and less pressured. I like them both.

A lot of things are at a critical juncture right now; going public, potential joint ventures and partnerships, new inventions and patents. I know that only one out of ten new things will work and therefore failure is a necessary part of moving ahead. I can't have one without the other. By definition I must fail, potentially look bad and lose money 90% of the time and that can be a very intimidating thing to face all the time. This applies not only to customers and the outside world, but even with my staff, who are trained to vocalize when they think I am wrong or not on the right track. Sometimes it is this process of defending what I believe that galvanizes my thought processes and solidifies my ideas, allowing us to move forward. It means more pain, effort and energy, but that is what is steeling my body, mind and soul to push forward. We cannot stay as we are and no one can in this environment. We either grow big or we begin to die and I am not interested in the latter option.

I am now at the point where I can tell, in many cases, what people will say as they are beginning to say it and they take my impatience at their comments as arrogance. In fact, it is a simple matter of trying to save time by saying I know what you are thinking and I have already considered it. I am making this decision, so let's move on. I can see how it can be frustrating dealing with me because one may think that I think I know everything, when in fact I am simply trying to move faster. I give my closest staff and advisers the ultimate compliment of believing they can think at warp speed and we are all traveling together. Again, it can be a very frustrating thing for them at the time, but it is the highest compliment I can pay them.

I remember my dad telling me the same thing when I started out. He said I had to process information and think faster. It is a skill like everything else and when pushed to the limit, this can increase your efficiency to an amazing degree. Of course, being around people who don't embrace the same skill can be frustrating. It can also be of extreme benefit because you can often think and plan ahead of them.

As I look out the window I can see the flags on a neighbor's flagpole waving on this cold, clear, blustery day. I think thermal underwear, a mask, goggles and heavy clothes are in order. I will meet Uncle Dave and hope for a pleasant journey. It has been a while since we biked together. It seems hard to believe I was in Malaysia last week, Boston this week and that I leave for Europe a week from Monday. I still don't know when I have to go back to Malaysia, but I am also due to go see Alex in St. Louis on May 1st. It amazes me that he is a junior already and graduating next spring. I should have gone to see him there before, but at least I am going now.

No Road Is Ever Straight

3/28/10
9:22 PM EST
Home, NJ

As is typical of a Sunday, I try to take it a little easier and, as often as not, I go crazy the whole day, like today. It was breakfast, tennis, snack, biking, snack, clothes to my office, check on some financial records, lunch, go to two supermarkets to prepare for the Jewish holiday of Passover, go home, snack, and then make Choruses, a wonderful holiday dish of various types of apples, spices, nuts and raisins. Then I had dinner, cleaned up, read some more about Malaysian British law, weighed myself (so far so good there), took my bath and am ready for sleep soon. I really like busy days and so far my body seems okay with it. Ben, Jeroen and I are traveling together for a few days. It should be good to get things in order for the future.

3/30/10
2:52 PM EST
My office, NJ

Yesterday and today were both spent in paperwork, getting our new patent application ready for searching and getting the latest rendering done for our new "non-lethal assault responder" anti-pirate system, which is already on its way to a potential joint venture partner in Malaysia. Last night was the first night of Passover celebrated at my sister Irene's house. It was quite a crowd and a lot of fun as we went through the service showing how the once enslaved ancient Jews won their freedom and set out on a 40 year journey through the desert. The food was really good as usual and I was quite full by the time I got home.

Tonight, the second day of Passover and another traditional feasting night, is at Barbara and Cliff's with another big crowd expected. Ben and Katie are coming in from Manhattan and Kayla will be able to stay for most of it before going back to Cornell. I will miss her a lot. Business has been better and I am calmer. I hope it continues to move back upward.

3/31/10
5:33 PM EST
My office, NJ

Kayla was driven back to school by her friend late last night. I was a little apprehensive because the weather was not great, but I got a text this morning that all was well, which meant I was going to have a fantastic day.

I went to the urologist today. It is always a frightening experience both because my father and grandfather had prostate cancer and because I had a scare some years ago. It went well and I won't have to go back for six months. I will try to forget about it for awhile. Meanwhile, things at the office are going well and we are working on our new anti-pirating project. My Monday and Thursday tennis partner tore his left rotator cuff. He is trying to fix it with physical therapy and I hope it works. He is still playing in the meantime.

APRIL

4/1/10
4:20 PM EST
My office, NJ

It is a beautiful spring day outside and I long to be out in it. I leave in about 75 minutes to rendezvous with Wendy for dinner. I have been working on the changeover of Ideal Jacobs Netherlands to a standalone Netherlands company and we have had our glitches along the way. I am going there next week and can do the final preparations in person. If it is not going to happen, I will know quickly and we can make other arrangements, like starting a new company in Belgium. Igor from IJUS wants to move to the area and his girlfriend is Belgian, so we are in good shape. Our radome samples are shipping out today for the composite company in Malaysian.

4/2/10
4:43 PM EST
My office, NJ

It is Good Friday and the day's pace has been laid back. Not a great deal has been happening, so I took advantage of the time by editing my new book. I am finding advantages to editing it twice myself in that I can make the changes immediately without having to wait to see them later. I am mentally preparing for my trip on Monday. It is gorgeous outside and my plants are in bloom. I am looking forward to dinner with Wendy.

4/3/10
10:03 AM EST
Home, NJ

It is a gorgeous spring day here in New Jersey and I am scheduled to meet Uncle Dave at our normal spot at 11:30. Wendy and I already had breakfast, which is a nice thing to be able to do since I no longer have the radio show and no children are home. In fact, today is Kayla's 19th birthday so they are all on their own. I write that mostly with joy, although it does mean we are moving on and getting older. We actually talk about having grandchildren and the thoughts are positive. I look in the mirror and see more grey hair, which is another sign of moving on, but nothing terrible. My life is where I want it to be, so I am contented. To have the chance to go after your dreams is an amazing blessing and I understand well how good I have it.

I have created a new goal that may never be achieved. I want to have created 10,000 jobs by the time my career ends. I may not even have a way to measure it, but it is something concrete and a legacy I would like to leave behind. To me, giving someone the chance to be self-sufficient and the ability to move toward their passion is one of the greatest achievements possible and I would like to help give that to as many people as possible.

In the meantime, things are progressing. I am in daily contact with my partner Ben and our plans for going public, while not always smooth, seem to be moving forward. I am waiting for the next date I am supposed to be in Malaysia and am hoping they give me a few weeks notice. The patent for our new composites technology will take a few months before it is ready to submit. We sent radome samples out to our potential customer in Malaysia along with a proposal to work on a joint venture for protecting ships from assaults. There has been no word back on the proposal yet. Having actual products to sell is much better than just data sheets. It puts us into the position of a partner rather than just a material supplier. My latest invention has to do with a portable levy loosely based on our barrier that would be able to stop floods from destroying lowland areas. It would be a breathing, living formation and would flex, so it would be able to give with the largest storm surges while remaining intact. A little water getting through is not a problem as long as the bulk still goes downstream. Brett is working on the insides for the anti-boat assault invention. Once this is done, it should be relatively easy to make drawings for and prototype the rest of the unit. Al is due back from Switzerland on Monday. It will be good to have her home, especially since I am leaving the same day for Europe.

4/5/10
4:33 PM EST
Newark Liberty Airport, NJ
Lufthansa Lounge

I have spent the last two days getting ready for this trip. This entailed a lot of paperwork, including editing my new book. Alice is back! It is a very good thing and I think she is happy to return, although leaving her grandson was tough. Our holiday of Passover is officially done for me at 5:00 PM, which is less than thirty minutes away. Although I am not very religious, I have not eaten bread, muffins or anything else that contains yeast since last Monday and I have a sandwich poised and ready for me to start munching on at the appointed time.

I hope I did not lose an opportunity before. A very nice gate person offered to get me on an earlier flight to Germany, but it would have meant rushing like crazy through the security lines and hoping I did not get stopped to make it in time. I would have gotten to Heathrow earlier, which is my final stop after a layover in Frankfurt. I decided I might risk not having any seat at all, so I declined. It was nice of him to ask, but I have been through the lines here before and for some reason I hesitated. I spoke to an old friend who works at EPA and he is on loan to the Department of Education to create an environmental management system. I have been itching to get back into some EPA related volunteer work, so I offered to audit the work he has done. He liked the idea and we will talk again in a few months so I can spend the day to tear apart his systems. Believe it or not, it sounds like fun to me. We all have our strange areas.

I have been emailing with my partner Ben, but there has still been no word on when we have to go back to Malaysia. I started talking about taking a vacation today. That is a sure sign I am tired and need a few days off. Unfortunately, I do not know when that will happen regarding my travel schedule. I want to go up to the Berkshires with Wendy in June so I can sleep outside on our porch and look for the fireflies at night. It is strange how exciting it is to see fireflies light up. I mean, it should not be a big deal, but it always fills me with sense of awe. It only happens for a short time during the summer and it brings me back to my youth.

I wonder if there are any newspapers in this lounge? I am out of ice water anyway; it is time to make a search.

4/6/10
3:32 AM German time, 9:32 PM EST
In flight - 622 miles per hour over the Atlantic Ocean, 3:48 to go

The great news is that we are approximately on time, which should give me lots of leeway to make my connecting flight. The not so great news is that I can't seem to sleep, but that is easy to understand since it is not my normal bedtime yet and I had a nap. As is normal, time has stopped and I seem to be in a time tunnel hurtling towards my next destination. Strangely, I thought I just heard thunder, which is highly improbable since I am listening to the group Clanad on my iPod. I have been downloading a lot of music from iTunes and transferring a bunch of my CDs to my portable device, so I could be as ready as possible for whatever music mood to hit me. My eyes are starting to burn. It is time to sleep again.

4/6/10
8:05 AM German time, 2:05 AM EST
Frankfurt Airport Lufthansa Business Lounge

I feel pretty good. So far so good to get to London on time. I have emailed my contact there that I should be okay for our noon meeting. I have never met this man before; he is a referral from Paul from Trelleborg. It looks like a beautiful day here, which I hope continues into Munich when I get back here later tonight. I am due to arrive at 8:00 PM to meet up with Jeroen and Ben for a two hour drive to the hotel. It promises to be a long day with a lot of naps.

4/6/10
9:07 AM German time, 3:08 AM EST
Frankfurt Airport, at the gate

I have traveled to a lot of different places and never once was the small capsule of glue that I carry ever questioned. That is, until I got to the gate security for my flight to Heathrow. The guard read the contents and declared it a harmful substance, bringing it over to his supervisor. By this time, I was starting to sweat and get really nervous. Transporting a hazardous substance could mean a lot of trouble. The person in charge brought me to a small room and told me she was sorry, but she had to confiscate the container. By that time, she could have had almost anything she wanted, so I signed the form and she let me leave. I was very happy to get to the gate.

4/6/10
3:29 PM London time, 10:29 AM EST
Heathrow Airport Lufthansa Lounge

I made it to the the Hilton Hotel, our rendezvous point for my meeting, at about 11:50. I rushed to get changed in the men's room (sorry to the German businessman who walked in on me, though happily, my pants were on). I was ready by about noon and got an email from Paul that the man I was seeing was delayed. I had some extra time, so it wasn't a problem. I found out later he had been involved in a minor car accident. After he arrived, we sat, talked and had lunch. He works for an aerospace firm and is after a piece of business that may have an application for our composites. We agreed he would send us an NDA so we could do some immediate evaluations and send test panels as soon as it is cleared by our export attorney. It was a great meeting with a lot of future potential. It made the whole trip worth it by itself. Well, that and meeting Wendy in Amsterdam, so I am quite happy.

Paul was nice enough to drop me off at Terminal 1, which was no easy task. This airport is one huge maze, especially with construction going on. Here I sit, waiting for my flight. I am very tired and have already entered the realm of sleep deprivation. I have been falling asleep immediately and having very strange dreams. I bought Kayla a flying pig toy. I hope it gets to her and is still functional since I took it out of its case to save space.

4/7/10
2:23 PM German time, 8:23 AM EST
Munich Airport

The flight to Munich was flawless and I met up with Jeroen and Ben at the car rental counter on schedule. From there, it was about two hours to get back to one of my favorite hotels located way back in the German woods. I get the feeling I am one of the few Americans who go there and I am pretty sure Ben, being from China, will be unique. It was dark by the time we arrived, but the combination of a few naps and jet lag made going to sleep a difficult prospect. I went out for a walk before starting that process. The stars were brilliantly shining, set against the background of a clear, black sky. It reminded me of the family trips to the Adirondack Mountains in upstate New York when I was a child. I loved those voyages and remember them often at times like these. I called the office while I was out there to find out that the big barrier project we had been working on for the last few months was definitely not going to happen. Their organization, although small, apparently did not communicate with each other and the person we were dealing with had neither the power nor authorization to embark on a product line upgrade, which meant our work with them was useless. It was not a complete waste of time for us. We got paid for some of it and the new information we got from the research and testing has enabled us to move forward in our new hurricane barrier and ballistic technology. It is rare that any effort is worthless and although I am disappointed, the project was never meant to be. I am glad we went as far as we did.

Everything else is moving along well there. Al is very capable, as is the rest of our team. Then it was back to the room. I got about five hours of sleep, which was definitely not enough considering the last traveling day. It was tough getting up this morning, but I did my bands (a workout using thick elastic) and then went walking again. It was just past dawn and it was going to be a crystal clear, wonderfully chilly, beautiful day, which was fine because I was dressed to combat the cold. I wonder if anyone was watching me as I was listening to my iPod. I was feeling good with bursts of adrenaline and, yes, I was actually singing and dancing a little. I walked to the nearby lake and through the resort. I met Ben and Jeroen for breakfast and we planned our strategy for our 10:00 AM meeting. They are easy traveling companions. As we were about to leave, I ran my hand over my face and realized to my horror that I had not shaved. I come from the old school of sales and you never go to a customer inappropriately dressed or groomed, unless you have been traveling all night, lost your baggage or both. This was a temporary disaster, so I halted our progress, literally ran back into the hotel from the parking lot and shaved. We were back on our way within fifteen minutes.

The people at Rosenberger, the company we were visiting, were very nice and even showed us a pair of nesting pelicans in one of their smokestacks, which was fascinating. The meeting went well with talks of future business and the expansion of our distribution center to act as a midway stop for the materials we produce in China and deliver to their facility in Hungary. Around 11:30, we were on our way to the Munich airport for our flight to Amsterdam. Both Ben and I napped while Jeroen drove; he is a wonderful navigator.

We found out that my plane ticket was not valid upon arriving, so Jeroen got me another one. Here we sit in the lounge, ready to go to the gate in a few minutes. We are on an earlier flight than we originally planned, which means I may get to take a walk once we get to the Netherlands.

4/7/10
3:50 PM Dutch time, 9:50 AM EST
In flight

As we were getting ready to board, we spoke about finishing the process of getting Ideal Jacobs Netherlands to become a standalone Dutch company, changing the name to Ideal Jacobs Europe. Jeroen and I can review it tomorrow, get the changes back to the attorney and be ready to close on Friday. I also suggested the four of us play badminton tomorrow evening. Since none of us play much badminton, I don't think much blood will be drawn. It would still be good if we could all get together, finish work and have some fun. We need to get the company changed by the end of the week and plan an expansion for new possible business coming in from Germany and the Netherlands. Igor, from our office, is due in Friday morning. He needs to meet everyone and we all need to be on the same page as to where the company is going, who is involved and what the plan of attack is. We should land, have our baggage and be in Jeroen's car to the hotel within an hour. I think they both just had a snack, so I have no idea when dinner will take place and if we are eating together. If I have the chance to walk in the gorgeous sunshine after we get to the hotel, I plan to do it.

4/8/10
Our Hotel
9:18 AM Dutch time, 3:18 AM EST
Driving along A12 highway, somewhere in the Netherlands

We got to the hotel on schedule, but we had more work to do so my walk never happened. We discussed the options during dinner and then I went back to the room. After speaking with the office and my wonderful wife, I went to sleep. I got up early again this morning and went to the gym at about 5:30. It was wonderful there. I was alone and was able to do my band workout and use the treadmill for an hour.

4/8/10
7:15 PM Dutch time, 1:15 PM EST
Our hotel

Tomorrow we will see a current customer who wants to put up a plant in Serbia as a joint venture. I plan to persuade them to use a holding facility here in the Netherlands instead. Time will tell.

4/9/10
2:07 AM Dutch time, 8:07 AM EST
En route to Amsterdam

Once I got downstairs last night, I had some time before Ben and Jeroen came down. I indulged in a glass of hot tea outside on the chilly terrace while I waited for them. It was a beautiful time out in the twilight. When I finished my tea, I called Al to tell her about the day. I had figured we would eat dinner at the hotel, as it was simple, fast and I was tired. Ben and Jeroen, however, wanted to go out, so we found a nearby restaurant after some searching. I was really tired by the time we sat down and as soon as I saw the menu, I realized that it would not only be an expensive but a time consuming dinner. The advantage was it gave us more time to talk about the changeover to IJ

Europe. The bad part was I lost an hour that I could have used for sleeping. Regardless, we were back at the hotel by 10:30 PM and after calling Al one more time, I went to sleep.

I was up at 5:30 AM, exercised and then walked outside. Realizing there could be some bumps in the changeover from Lencon Patents to IJ Europe, I tried to come up with some alternative plans in case our original ideas did not work out. It has been my experience that when you are dealing with people's livelihoods like their careers and businesses, you can never be sure who will react in what way. I am trying to cover all bases in case of turmoil.

I met Jeroen and Ben for breakfast and after checking out, we went to a nearby train station to pick up Igor from our office. His fortunate choice of a Belgian girlfriend meant that he had no trouble with the idea of permanently locating to the Netherlands and working for IJ Europe. First, he has to meet the people involved to make sure everyone gets along. We got him at the station and Jeroen and he seemed to get along right away. We all went to Lencon's office, where he stayed with Yolanda, one of the office managers, to go through the IJ Netherlands system. His girlfriend will pick him up this afternoon and Jeroen and he will meet up again next weekend to get better acquainted before he comes back to the U.S. He is currently scheduled to go to the Netherlands permanently in September, but that date could be moved up.

Then we were off to a customer who wanted to joint venture for a plant in Serbia. I am not a great fan of putting manufacturing facilities in countries where I have no good contacts on the ground and know nothing about the governmental system. The business will also take a while to get going, if at all. Once there, I offered the alternative of producing in China, having the products tested there and then having them tested again here in a new distribution center that we will create in the future. We would also finance a month's supply of full-scale units, so our customer's customer will always have stock on hand and can put their mind to rest about waiting for units from Asia. The customer liked the idea and he and Jeroen will go see his customer next week to get approval. Then we will get drawings so we can put together a formal proposal.

4/9/10
10:53 PM Dutch time, 4:53 PM EST
Grand Hotel Amrath Amsterdam

We got to the hotel by about 3:00 PM and as normal, Ben and I went our different ways. He went for a walk while I had some work to do, and then I went for a walk. The city of Amsterdam is a bustling wonder filled with people from all parts of the world. Since the country is below sea level, there are waterways everywhere to help move the water to safer areas. Amsterdam is filled with canals and boats of all types and the action there is unceasing. I walked for awhile and seemed to enter a time warp. I was in an old part of the city that contained the "Coffee Houses," places where you could smoke marijuana legally, as well as shops that catered to all possible tastes. It was like being in the 1960s.

It was a gorgeous spring day with mild temperatures, a blue sky and the journey was both amazing and interesting. On the way back to meet Wendy, I passed a Mexican restaurant and decided to stop inside. A short time later, I had a burrito, two salads and an order of rice. Once back at the hotel, I met up with Wendy, who had a good flight coming over, and we eventually got ready for tonight's dinner. I was a little apprehensive, but the first good thing was the restaurant had two dining areas and the main one was not being used, so I chose that in case it got loud. The second good thing was everyone was there to have a good time and that is what happened

Ben is leaving tomorrow morning, so I won't see him again until I go back to Malaysia, probably next month. I hope to get a good night's sleep tonight and to relax with Wendy for the rest of the weekend.

4/10/10
6:57 PM Dutch time, 12:57 PM EST
Grand Hotel, Amrath, Amsterdam

I slept until 8:00 AM this morning and probably would have slept a lot longer, but I set my alarm so as not to lose the day. I went downstairs to the hotel Wellness Center, a very nice gym area with New Age music, where I did my workout. Afterward, I changed and went back to the 1960s section of Amsterdam, where I got a little lost before buying some fruit and heading back to meet Wendy. We went to then Rijks Museum, which featured some of the works by one of my favorite painters, Rembrandt. Once we got to the museum, there was a group waiting to get in and nothing seemed to be happening. After trying to get information and receiving no reply, we went in front of a waiting group and got inside. Some of the people still waiting outside were good-naturedly yelling about us going ahead. Once we were past the security barrier, one of them playfully mentioned that I had scissors with me, for which I broke out laughing. They were a good-hearted bunch and had I been a drinking man, I am sure they would have been fun to have a round with. The Rembrandt paintings were magnificent and I also liked some of the other painters, not to mention a few pistols and rifles from Amsterdam's early history. Afterward, we had a quick lunch near our hotel and then it was off to a one-hour boat tour of the various waterways. I had been on such an expedition with our people from Ideal Jacobs Netherlands a few years ago, but was happy to see it again. It is amazing what people can do when they are forced to push back against the ocean and they have done an amazing job of reclaiming land from the sea. We also passed by numerous houseboats and beautiful buildings including Anne Frank's house. Seeing it reminds me of what the Dutch did for our people during World War II and I am filled with admiration for their decision to uniformly try to protect us.

After the boat ride, we went back to the old section of the city. Wendy wanted some french fried potatoes she had seen people with and we eventually found some. After getting some more euros, we went back to the hotel where we are taking it easy until dinner. It has been a fun, relaxing day. I heard from Jeroen, who was happy with the way the dinner went last night and is hopeful everything can be worked out for the new company next week. We also saw Ben as he was checking out this morning. He had asked me four years ago to help sponsor the schooling of some children from the Chinese countryside. The kids are graduating high school this year and have done fantastically well, so I agreed with Ben to continue the program for a new group of youngsters. He should be in the air by now on his way back to Hong Kong. I will probably see him at the end of next month for the next stages of going public.

4/11/10
5:44 PM Dutch time, 11:44 AM EST
Grand Hotel, Amrath, Amsterdam

We had a wonderful day today. Wendy and I got on a bus at about 9:00 AM this morning bound for the Keukenof Gardens located outside Amsterdam. After transferring to another bus at one of the local museums, we were at the facility around 10:00 AM.

As soon as you enter, you are met with an onslaught of flowers in bloom that are both dazzling and mesmerizing. The colors covered the spectrum and the various types of tulips, Narcissis (daffodils), irises and much more were amazing. We stayed there almost three hours and the whole time it was quite chilly and windy. It was fine since we were dressed for it and could duck into the greenhouses, which contained even more flowers. I had no idea of the number and species grown here in the Netherlands, but I have a much better appreciation for them now.

I also like the Dutch people. We had met a man on the way to the museum yesterday, who was almost 90 years old and looked like he came out of a Dutch renaissance painting. He was an architect who had been to South America for many years, but was now firmly planted back in his homeland. There is something about the people here. The men are often very tall, good-looking and pleasant; greatly represented by Jeroen. We got back about at 2:00 PM and went to the same lunch place as yesterday, where I had a smoked salmon sandwich again. I am a great lover of that dish and have been indulging a lot while here in Holland. Later, I worked out at the gym while switching between a good John Wayne movie and some iPod music. There was a heated pool in the area, so I changed and went back for some laps and even a few minutes in the jacuzzi. Wendy and I will have dinner tonight here in the hotel restaurant and tomorrow we leave for home.

During the trip today, Wendy mentioned that people here don't wear helmets when riding their bicycles and motorbikes. I emailed Jeroen and he said it was not part of the national custom. I thought about it and decided if we could make a helmet that was good looking, safe and included other great features, maybe we could create our own market. I emailed him to start doing research of how many head injuries there have been in the Netherlands and

Europe and we will compare them with countries like the U.S. and Germany who have laws requiring the use of helmets. That will be one way to help push the concept. I also emailed Ben so he would know what I am thinking because they could also be used in Asia. I know it is a long shot, but trends happen in strange ways and if our new design happens to take off, then it could be a whole new area for us.

4/12/10
3:05 PM EST
In flight - Approximately five hours to get to Newark/Liberty Airport

Dinner last night was laid back and peaceful, not to mention a nice ending to a wonderful weekend. I got good night of sleep and was up early to work out in the gym and go once more to the 1960s section of Amsterdam to walk along the highly interesting streets and canals. The weather was beautiful, crisp and clear and after my walk, I had breakfast with Wendy. She went off to find the painter Rembrandt's house and I went for a last swim. We then checked out and got to the airport with plenty of time. The only problem I foresaw today was getting to Zurich in time to catch our flight. The plane ride was exactly on time and we rushed forward when we landed with only had 45 minutes. We proceeded through passport control, to an underground train, to a security checkpoint, where I ran into a problem since my carrying case was brought back to recheck. By this point, we were really getting tight on time. We hurried through, only to have to go through another passport check. Finally, we raced onto the place. As it turned out, we were not the last ones to arrive. My travel people booked us both aisle seats, but not together. I had forgotten to check that. Right before we took off, Wendy persuaded another woman to change seats and we are now riding together. For the record, my wife is a wonderful traveling companion and we balance each other well. I do some of the tourist things with her that I would never do alone, like visiting the museum and the flower area, both of which I enjoyed. She is okay with getting to the airport earlier than normal and with the gamut of my various types of checking.

Meanwhile, emails have been going between Jeroen, Allan and Ben throughout the day regarding the new projects for Europe as well as working some on the bicycle helmet idea. I was working on what I would want to see in the perfect helmet and we can check it when I get back. At this point, I hope to nap an hour or two before we land, but no more since it will probably keep me from sleeping tonight.

4/12/10
7:04 PM EST
In flight

We seem to be getting in early!! Once we are through immigration, baggage claim and customs, we will find Mike, who is picking us up. The weather is supposed to be beautiful and I look forward to being home and seeing Bailey.

APRIL

4/13/10
7:19 PM EST
Home, NJ

We got home at about 9:00 last night. I was asleep by 11:00 and up at 3:45 AM. Between our ISO 9001 audit and various meetings, it was a great day.

4/14/10
7:35 PM EST
Home, NJ

I think I have a bit of jet lag from last week and except for some bursts of adrenaline, I am tired now. Our ISO quality system audit was completed today. The two day event went very well with only one suggestion for change. We decided that we needed to do some preliminary product testing for the hurricane panels. We are building an air launcher for a 2" by 4" by 8' plank to be launched 100 mph into our panels. If they are punctured, they fail. It will be a great way to pretest our ideas. All parts for the cannon, thanks to Brett and Vinnie, should be in by the weekend and Brett will build it next week. I am proud of our team. They can seemingly do almost anything. With every birth there are always problems, as we see in companies here and with IJ Netherlands. I know it is tough for Jeroen and I want this settled one way or the other. Igor is in Belgium and will go to the Netherlands in a few days both to meet his girlfriend's relatives and to have a meal with Jeroen and Tamara to get acquainted. There are a lot of changes happening.

4/15/10
9:45 AM EST
Home, NJ

I got some great news today. Katie emailed me to say she wanted to come back as my editor. Since she is competent and I totally trust her judgment, that is fantastic news and a great load off my mind. I already emailed her months four and five from last year and will send more soon. I sent a proposal to Vincent in Malaysia regarding joining forces for R&D, test development, marketing and potential buying and selling from each others' companies. I also sent him a customer list. The next step to move forward is his. If we do, it will help satisfy the desire to have R&D and development at IJM. I wrote a proposal for Wan at the government owned composite company in Malaysia. If they like our product, I want to build a plant in his area and have his company buy a small part of ours, both to protect our intellectual property and to market, produce and sell worldwide. I am waiting to hear back both from Ben on the proposal and Wan regarding the sample testing before I send the next email.

The air cannon construction moves forward. We should be ready for tests the week after next. If the samples pass, then John can start marketing immediately.

No Road Is Ever Straight

4/15/01
9:57 PM EST
Home, NJ

It is Friday night and I am in dire need of sleep. I hope to go until 8:00 AM tomorrow when Wendy and I are scheduled to go out for breakfast. Right now, Ben is in Kuala Lumpur. He will stay there off and on or the next two months guiding our public offering. We both agree he needs to be there in person to keep it on schedule and make it happen.

I have now contacted two California based companies regarding take-overs and both have ignored me. Strangely, I get the feeling they are talking to each other about merging and my timing is bad, but we will see. I have been inventing again with some help from our team. Kayla got her flying pig toy and loved it. It was wonderful to hear her smile over the phone.

4/16/10
9:56 AM EST
Home, NJ

I have been wrestling with a new invention. I was not even sure what it was until it came to form this morning. It involved making a new mixture of materials to protect fuel tanks. Of course, what is in my head may or may not work. That is what makes it interesting. We started sending out our latest idea, the acoustic buoy, yesterday. It is a matter of the odds. If you send out enough ideas, one will either work or invoke another idea in someone else. It is all in the percentages. It is often easier to be creative when the problems are shown and people don't tell us what to do.

I feel overweight and have been eating carbohydrates like waffles and muffins in addition to breakfast in preparation for my long bike ride. It is not a great combination, but I am also tired, so I am hoping the extra food will enable me to get through the ride and burn up the calories in the process. I did not sleep well last week and I don't have time for a nap now. I also wanted to go visit my parents before Wendy and I went out, but I am not sure that will happen.

There is a giant cloud of ash from a volcano in Iceland that is causing havoc with air travel throughout Europe. A lot of the planes are grounded and I am not sure when Igor will get back here. In the meantime, I may start him working at IJ Netherlands to get his feet wet. It is not the worst of things to happen, especially for him since his girlfriend is in nearby Belgium. My tulips and other flowers look beautiful. We are having our house exterior cleaned tomorrow. We also plan to recoat our outside wood porch against inclement weather and maybe work on the driveway and outside walkway. There is always stuff to do and I am incompetent at all of it, which means I go to the office and do what I am good at. I tried to do tasks around the house decades ago, but after ruining our front lawn and messing up one of our bathrooms, we all decided where I was most useful.

4/17/10
4:12 PM EST
Home, NJ
Sunday afternoon

After working out downstairs and playing tennis with my brother indoors, it was back home to get ready to go into Manhattan. I was scheduled to meet my son Ben at 11:45 and after parking at my office and dropping off my clothes for the week, I made it to the nearby train station on foot with a few minutes to spare. Ben was waiting for me at Penn Station and we took the subway to get to one of his favorite diners. For those of you who do not know what a diner is, I believe they originated as a sort of mobile restaurant known for good food, large portions, affordable prices and long hours. They are a favorite of my family and I always like to try a new one. This one was especially small, but we were able to get some space at the counter and had a very pleasant lunch. From there, we walked to a street fair that had all types of vendors selling clothes, jewelry and food. It was a pleasantly cool day in New York City and we talked as we walked, covering such diverse topics as dealing with his new boss, what is happening with my business and religion. We browsed through a very large book store on the way back to the train station and he left me at my train pickup spot while he returned to the subway. He is a fine man and I am extremely proud of him. He is also joy to be with and I am glad I made the trip. It was a quick train ride back to Maplewood, where I walked to my car. I plan to have dinner with Wendy soon.

4/19/10
3:30 PM EST
My office, NJ

I did not do it. I will keep saying it even though it may not be true. My email database self-destructed this morning and we all know how bad I am around electronic equipment. Mike set up the repair and it failed after six hours, so he has moved the repair operation to another desk. It is a smart move, since I will not be within wrecking distance. One of the problems with moving as quickly as I do is that I sometimes hit computer keys that I should not, often in combinations that were never meant to occur. I take full responsibility, but will not change. That is why I have Mike.

Elsewhere in life, there is progress on the Ideal Jacobs Netherlands front and I am hopeful for a completion of all contracts by Wednesday morning. Business for the month is good so far and I am pushing to get more. Kayla called on Sunday extremely upset that she dropped her computer. It is damaged and Apple will not cover it even though she has a warranty. I calmed her down and today we air shipped her older one up to Cornell as hers went in for repairs. I think she will be calmer once she gets a working computer back in her hands.

Despite the volcanic cloud, it looks like European Airlines is starting to run again. It is a very good thing for everyone except Igor, who probably hopes it stays that way indefinitely so he does not have to leave his girlfriend.

4/20/10
5:09 PM EST
My office, NJ

I awoke this morning to an email from Jeroen. A shipment to a customer in the Netherlands from Asia cost way more than it should have and it was causing big trouble. The customer was threatening to leave, so we had to work fast. I instructed Jeroen to pay for the shipping charges above what Jeroen had thought they would be. Once he did that, the customer was fine and working with us again. I feel confident it will be settled tomorrow. Unexpected charges can be a quick death for an account and you have to move quickly not only mitigate the problem but also use it to get more business by building trust that we will take care of problems that come up.

I got the contract to change Lencon patents to Ideal Jacobs Europe. I signed it and sent it back to Jeroen. We should have it tomorrow along with a copy of Jeroen's employment agreement with Lencon, which should finish out that part of the process. It will be good to be able to move on. Ben emailed that we are being forced to give a six-month financial report for IJX to the bank, which means we are may not go public until September. Ben is doing his best to move quickly, so I am not upset. He also said that 20% out of the 25% of the stock we are giving for the offering has already been spoken for by one large fund. It is a very good sign and also means that instead of a lot of little stock holders we are going to have a few large participants, which will make doing business in the future an interesting time. I have been doing a lot of selling for new material and specific products. We just have to break one to launch; I know it from experience and it is no problem to continue. We are starting the first in a group of patent searches for the new material. It will be expensive, but it is necessary to protect ourselves for the future.

4/21/10
4:37 PM EST
My office, NJ

I have come to the conclusion that I am addicted to iTunes. I have been writing down various songs, mostly from my younger years, and going to my office to download them onto my system to later move to my iPod. I really enjoy listening to a plethora of music and I can pick the songs I like without having to buy the whole albums. I find the whole experience enjoyable. I am not gambling, drinking or messing around so this is not a big deal in the big scheme of life, but it is still good to bare our chests occasionally.

I have spent a lot of the day sending emails about our new product line and showing examples of what we can do with our new composite plastics. My fascination for the whole process has not diminished and I know that we have to keep pushing until we get someone to buy it, hopefully starting an avalanche of sales. Business has been good enough that we have been rehiring and I hope to hire our first new person in the next few weeks. I have no idea what will happen, but we will proceed with the idea that things are improving here in North America. On that note, I am getting ready to go down to see our people in Mexico at IJ Mexico probably at the end of next month. I emailed the copyright attorney to begin proceedings for IJ Europe to register the Ideal Jacobs logo throughout the common market. Mr. Obama is attempting to force the big banks to put money into a fund to cover their brethren that fail. I am skeptical of participation and that it will function.

4/22/10
3:47 PM EST
My office, NJ

You have probably noticed that my latest entries have been in the afternoon and not at night from home. The reason is that I am trying to get to sleep a little earlier. My nightly rituals of letting out Bailey, locking the house for the night and checking to make sure things are turned off all take time and if I am to have a clear, peaceful mind to get to sleep, those things can't change. Being obsessive compulsive has some wonderful attributes; it forces you to finish something once you declare that you have to do it. It is wonderful for making you keep your word, hold your integrity in tact and adhere to ever increasing standards of behavior that you define. The negative parts are the continuous checking and other repetitive behaviors that can drive you nuts. There are drugs to treat that, but they also affect the creative parts of your brain and adrenaline output. I count on both for help in inventing and being able to propel myself forward in the areas I choose. It is a double-edged sword that I gladly wield.

I was texting with my son Alex earlier, telling him about a lot of the basic work I do like following up with customers and looking for new business. It is largely repetitive work and can drive you crazy, but it forces up the odds of success and is therefore necessary. I don't want him to think my job is always glamorous and fun, which it is not. Besides, you have to earn the great parts by doing the preparation to get out there. I don't just travel to exotic places, see clients, have a great time on an expense account and let the money roll in. Like everything else, there are fun parts and not so fun parts. I owe it to all my kids to give them a view of reality and the advantage of having a passion for what you do because it is that feeling of love for my job that easily gets me past the other parts.

My trip to Mexico is now set for May 3rd and Ben emailed me that I will probably need to be in Asia the first week of June. Going public is now set for the first week in September.

Our porch has been re-coated, our front walk re-grouted and our house's exterior has been cleaned. The only thing left to do this spring is plant flowers next month and maybe have a new driveway put in. Our house is not cheap, but I love living here.

4/23/10
10:31 PM EST
Home, NJ

The air cannon is now built and Brett is testing it. The auxiliary equipment will be ready for Tuesday and we are scheduled for full scale tests on Wednesday. In the meantime, we will run a patent search on the materials involved and set up formalized testing. Jack is making panels of new materials for testing and possible patent applications. We are into new science now and it is very exciting to be pushing the barrier of what is possible. I had left my portfolio at the IJ Netherlands office when I was there and Jeroen was supposed to give it to Igor to bring back to me. Both of them forgot and Igor got an email thrashing today. It will be the first of many as his tough training as a manager has already begun. His raw talents are great, we just have to get him structured to be able to handle the pressure of command. Jeroen will need him as his backup, confidant and ally for what will be coming. We continue to spend a fortune on the new composites area. I hope I am right regarding the amount of potential business.

4/24/10
9:52 AM EST
Home, NJ

It is a beautiful Saturday here in New Jersey and I am scheduled to ride within the hour. It looks to be about 60°F while I am out there and I look forward to a calm solo ride. Uncle Dave is busy today so I am on my own, which probably means I will be thinking about a lot of stuff. As I exert more physical energy, my mind will move into a different dimension where it can wander peaceably and focus on whatever is needed at that moment. I often come up with some of my most creative ideas and make big decisions in this state. It also gives me a time to dream about what can be and let my mind soar above what is possible. It is for all those reasons, not to mention breathing fresh air and getting great exercise, that I love the great outdoors.

The airways in Europe seem almost back to normal now, as the volcanic ash problem has subsided. Europe, however, still has another big problem, which is Greece. They will need a major bailout and judging by the rate of their borrowing and the inability to reduce their expenditures, they are on the way to default. Whether they officially default or it happens unofficially, the results will be a general weakening of the European Union and a decline in the euro. My guess is that, since Greece will not reform its monetary policies, it will eventually be asked to leave the union. Otherwise, it will force the decline of the entire union and I don't think the strong members like Germany will allow others like Spain to bring them to their knees economically. I think there are major changes coming. It is not easy to act as one unit when the parts don't do what is best for themselves or the group as a whole. Fiscal responsibility is a cornerstone of necessity for the common market and if its members don't participate, then they cannot continue to function. I do not see countries like Greece and Spain submitting to the discipline and order of countries like Germany. In good times, groups can get along much more easily than when times are tough and the different views of governments becomes much more apparent.

4/25/10
3:23 PM EST
Home, NJ

My ideas for inventions are often cumulative from various stimuli. For instance, after watching the movie "Twister," about the attempt to figure out how tornadoes are created and can be predicted, I started to think about big storms in general. Added to that was our current work on the hurricane and tornado panels. Those, along with the recent problems with huge hurricane devastation in the middle of the U.S., all coalesced to form an idea. If our new material passes the hurricane tests on Wednesday, then I can make the assumption that with additional reinforcement the same material will pass the tornado test. If we can stop the effects of a tornado in a defined space, then it creates a whole new group of potential inventions. We could build a fifteen foot wall that sloped down and outward from the top with riffled sides like a gun barrel, so that any air going up the sides would be spun in a specific direction. If we could change the direction of a tornado while it is going up our wall, then the energy could be dissipated. If we built a wall with an area at the bottom that had wind turbines and those turbines were powered by the oncoming tornado and reversed the direction of the wind rotation, then when the twister hit our wall it would effectively kill the tornado. In other words, we would use the force of the storm to kill itself. Continuing on that idea, what if you could attract tornadoes in the first place? Perhaps we could harness a huge amount of usable energy from them. How do you make a tornado move where you want it to go? How does a lightening rod work? If we set up a line of these walls, connected them by power lines and released something in the air that would attract a tornado then we might be able to create a virtual wall of attraction and capture its energy. I spoke to Brett about it and he found it intriguing, but said he would not test it in person. I understand his hesitation.

4/26/10
3:43 PM EST
My office, NJ

Great news! Ideal Jacobs Europe has been born! Now we can start acting as a proper standalone company. The first things are to get the website up, create new business cards and stationary and move forward with all of the new potential business. There are still some details to work out, but we are on our way.

The tornado killer idea did not work. I spoke to Don and apparently tornadoes' power emanates from the top and not where it touches the ground. So much for my great ideas. It is no matter; most don't work and just a few will. We move forward.

I spoke to Mark from WOR. I like to keep in touch both because it is my connection to radio and because I like him. His daughter is going to Cornell this fall so that I am hopeful his daughter and Kayla can meet.

4/27/10
4:32 PM EST
My office, NJ

It was a day of lots of paperwork including going public in Asia and making sure all of the necessary supplies for the hurricane tests are ready tomorrow. We now have two potential interns for the summer. I want them to work on the new composite areas and also check my theory of action and reaction regarding storms of all types from one part of the globe to the other. We had a customer in for a plant tour today and it went well. More business appears to be possible. We have to keep going after business everywhere to support our R&D efforts.

4/28/10
2:45 PM EST
My office, NJ

I got an affirmative reply from Jerry at WOR regarding using his name in my new book and also sent a message to Joe Bartlett, my mentor and partner for the Saturday show both asking his permission and opening the door to come back in the fall. Something inside me wants to be back on radio. The feeling of seeing the light go on and being live on the air is an adrenaline rush that never seemed to fade. I am having lunch with Elana tomorrow so we can go over the possibilities. I have once again been going through our database regarding finding customers not only for the new plastic thermoplastics, but also our blank circuit pack panels with our custom EMI shielding and latch design. Orders for them have risen considerably and we all feel there is more business out there so I am going after it. I have an eye doctor appointment this afternoon and then date night with Wendy at our favorite local Italian restaurant.

4/29/10
4:45 PM EST
My office, NJ

We had high hopes that we would have success with the hurricane panel testing today, but it was not meant to be. The panels are currently being held in by a picture frame-like device that only comes in about an inch from the end. The force of the 100 mph 2″ x 4″ x 10′ plastic nosed piece of lumber is so tough that it is pulling the test sample away from the compression holders. Brett is going home and will reduce the aperture, or size of the window, meaning we can have more area to grip the samples so they will not give when fired upon. We feel this will result in a true test tomorrow and then we can ensure that the wood spears will not go through our material. It was another day of paperwork, customer follow-up and sales mostly through email. It is grinding work, but it will prove out. I leave to see Alex this Saturday and then I go to Mexico on Monday morning. I am already worrying about the flights. The weather for Guadalajara looks hot and I have two airports, customs and immigration to get through so I will pack my suit and wear informal clothes until I arrive. Our first sales call is not until 2:00 PM so Paulina can get me to my hotel, I can check in and change there and then we can move forward. We have test panels at multiple sites and it is difficult waiting for the results. We have no choice of course, but it is still tough.

MAY

5/1/10
8:45 AM EST
Newark Liberty Airport, Newark, NJ

Great news yesterday: we passed our first hurricane test. Through the great efforts of both Jack and Brett, we were able to come up with a formulation that passed the rigorous test. The next stop is to refine the material for the best combinations of strength and shock absorption with reduction and price. It is a great start, but a lot more work is ahead of us. I also worked on two new problems yesterday that actually started the night before and cost me a good night's sleep. That is part of the job. By the end of the day, everything seemed to be worked out. It is amazing how problems can seem world changing, but as soon as you have a plan their power recedes until you can almost forget what was driving you crazy a few days later. Our business is based on many climactic events for our customers, which is the reason we get a lot of business. Tough, difficult rush jobs always have a price regarding the amount of both positive and negative energy they produce on all sides. When that effort becomes too high a price to pay, either you give up that type of business or retire.

I slept well last night and bade my wonderful wife and dog goodbye this morning. I am on my way to see Alex in St. Louis and except for losing my boarding pass since I printed it yesterday – which meant I guessed wrong and parked at the wrong terminal, which meant a walk to the right gate area – everything is fine. It is going to be a very warm day here, but I think it will be cloudy and mild when I see Alex. So far we are on time. I have a sandwich with me and plenty of work for the flight. It is a new month. April was good in sales and I am hopeful it will continue. It is fantastic not have to be worrying about the economy, business and laying people off. Every day is like a mini mental health vacation and will stay that way for a while. While I never take good times for granted, the last eighteen months have been a somber reminder of what can be and to always be grateful for what I have.

5/1/10
11:07 AM St. Louis time, 12:07 PM EST
In flight

As part of going public, there is a huge amount of paperwork. Although I am not involved in a lot of it, requirements occasionally come through and their request for detail is extreme. I am working on a director's document since I have that position for the new public company. They ask many questions, including everywhere I have lived my whole life. I finished the latest group and will submit it back to our coordinator Jossie in China for her to check some data and fill in some final information. When I go back to Malaysia next month, there is a good chance they will want to go over every question and answer on the latest form, so I will be prepared for a long meeting. It is part of the process and getting annoyed will accomplish nothing. It has to be done, so the best thing is to do it quickly and get it back for review so it can be finalized and off my "to do" list.

5/2/10
7:01 AM St. Louis time, 8:01 AM EST
St. Louis Airport
Sunday morning

We arrived on time yesterday. I had a great taxi ride from an Ethiopian immigrant and we discussed the difference between Ethiopian and American women. He was not prepared for the culture shock when he got here, but seems to be adapting. The Chase Park Hotel is beautiful, and Alex, who looks wonderful, came to get me after I checked in. We zoomed off to lunch. Alex seemed a little harried and stressed, because of the show last night and from facing four final exams. After lunch he gave a me a tour of the campus, which is old, well laid out and beautiful. Obviously, there have been a lot of large donors involved and the school reflects a great deal of alumni support. Alex had to prepare for the night so I took his car back to the hotel and went down to the gym to do my band workout. I went for a walk later through the park, which is filled with bike and jogging paths, a waterway, golf course, art museum and lots of other stuff. I walked past a small pond and noticed a turtle on one of the logs jumping into the water. I stopped for a few minutes and what seemed like a ballet erupted in front of me with various turtles coming up to the surface and then diving underwater again. Combined with the ducks, other birds, roses and flowers it was a beautiful, serene moment. Then it was back to the hotel where I ate dinner. I had been well prepared for last night and had a suit ready to go. I made my way back to the designated parking area, very pleased that I found it and up to the fashion show entrance. Actually, it was relatively easy to find. All I had to do was follow the pretty girls who were stylishly dressed in very high-heeled shoes. I had a great seat to see the various fashions, especially Alex's, and all were very interesting. I am not a connoisseur of clothing, but I did enjoy the event. Afterward, Alex invited some friends and we all went to a nearby cupcake store and had a fun time. I actually met Alex's first year roommate and his sister who also goes to school here. It was electric being around intelligent and highly motivated college students, ready to go out into the world and seek their fortune. Alex dropped me off at the hotel and went back to his room to study.

I got up early, did not work out since I was planning to bike when I got home and had another great taxi ride to the airport. This time I was driven by a former captain from the local fire department and we had a good chat about work, kids and keeping our wives happy. There is a tornado watch for part of this state, but so far we are on time to get out so I am hopeful we can get into the air. The plane is at the gate, which is usually a good sign.

There was a terrorist attempt in Times Square in Manhattan, apparently involving a vehicle with some type of bomb inside. The oil spill near Louisiana is getting worse and they have still not been able to stop the problem. The environmental impact could be huge and will do nothing to help the offshore drilling program the president had hoped would happen.

5/3/10
4:25 AM EST
Newark Liberty Airport

The flight home yesterday was great and I was back at the house by 1:00 PM. After a quick lunch, it was off biking in very hot weather, which was fantastic. I drank all of the water I was carrying and was happily exhausted by the time I got home. It was wonderful to get a hard workout after traveling. Later I started to repack for today, went to the office and got dinner, cash and supplies for this week. It was great seeing Wendy and Bailey. I got up at 2:45 AM this morning, Mike picked me up and it seemed that the stormy weather we were supposed to get last night was not delaying our flight. I am already running on little sleep, which means that my obsessive compulsive systems of constant checking and germ phobia will get worse. I can usually control it pretty well when traveling. We will see how it goes.

5/3/10
11:19 AM Texas time, 12:19 PM EST
In flight

Although we landed a little late, I was able to get to the right terminal and to the Continental Lounge. I was even able to get a copy of my favorite paper, the Financial Times, before getting onto this flight. We are on schedule to arrive at 11:40 and I can meet Paulina after I get through immigration and baggage claim. Since I just ate my second sandwich and some pretzels, I probably won't need lunch, but some ice tea would be nice. I look forward to being back in Mexico. Guadalajara is a nice city and we have done well here. I am prepared to show off our new composite materials in addition to the video I have with me. I have been emailing with Brett and Jack and tests will continue this week. I want to finalize the formula for the patent application by the end of the week. I am making progress on editing my book from last year. I should be done in another month and then it is up to Katie. It is supposed to be very hot so I will bring my suit jacket but I may not wear it. Paulina has scheduled twenty people to see over the next three days, so we should be very busy.

MAY

5/3/10
8:08 PM Guadalajara time, 9:08 PM EST
Intercontinental Hotel

We arrived in Guadalajara on time and Paulina was there to meet me. She is happily married and it shows; she looks well and at peace. As we sped off to the hotel for me to check in, we caught up on recent events. We had lost a big piece of business here, but she has successfully replaced a lot of it and I am very proud of her and her team. Once I got changed, it was on the road to Flextronics. It was very hot today in the 90°F range, but there was no humidity so it wasn't that bad being outside. As we got to the customer facility, there was a fire along one of the nearby hills. Paulina told me it had been burning since yesterday and you could see the flames not that far away. It would have had to jump a large highway to get to us so I was not very concerned. Once inside the complex, we visited three buyers who were happy with our company, which is always great news to hear. We showed them the video for the thermoplastic drop test and I am hopeful we made a big enough impression to stay on their minds for future business, at least for a while. I was pretty tired by the time we finished and Paulina drove me back here. After a quick snack, I did the band workout and was on the treadmill. I wasn't sure I was going to make it the whole way, but I managed to before getting changed back in the room and going to dinner. Hotel rooms can be lonely at night, so I stayed downstairs after eating for a while to answer my emails. It wasn't crowded in the dining room. The staff was very nice and they left me alone, so I gave them a good tip. I will get ready to go to sleep soon and tomorrow we have a big day seeing customers and having dinner with our former employee, Marisol. I called home and spoke to Wendy. She misses me, as I do her.

5/4/10
6:24 PM Guadalajara time, 7:24 PM EST
Intercontinental Hotel

I slept about 8 ½ hours, which I definitely needed, got up at 6:30 and went down to the gym. There was another man down there trying to get one of the treadmills working and I helped him. He tripped on it a little later, which concerned me greatly. I helped him back up and he was fine from then on. It is always nice to help someone both for them and myself. After my workout, I was running a little behind schedule so I raced to my room, changed and went to the breakfast area. I asked the person seating me for a bottle of water and the check. I got some fruit and went over to the egg station. There was a little problem with my Spanish instructions, but a waiter came over and translated to the cook. Soon, my seven scrambled eggs and mushrooms with cooking spray were on their way. As I finished my fruit, the eggs appeared and I think I was out within ten minutes. I raced back to the room, got ready and was right on time to be picked up by Paulina. We went to Flextronics again and met four people with different positions and levels and all seemed happy with us. On the way out, Paulina noticed that the security had put a boot on her front tire. She had mistakenly parked in a reserved spot, which cost us about 45 minutes while they came and removed it. It was not a big problem, it simply meant we would not go out for an iced tea between appointments. We had two more calls, then met our former manager Marisol for an early dinner at a fantastic restaurant. Since neither Paulina nor I had eaten lunch, we had a great deal of food and a really fun time. As the day progressed, it became apparent that there was more business to be had down here but, as per a year ago when we were thinking of putting in a plant, maybe partnering with someone already here was the best way to go. It is much easier to join than begin from scratch, but it would have to be the right kind of company with the right focus, product lines and quality and environmental systems. I will think about it more along with creating a world based plan to better coordinate how we are doing business from IJ Company to IJ Company. We are stepping on each others' toes now since we share the same customers and it is starting to become a problem. I will think about it more over the next few days. I also spoke to Brett regarding a new type of panel that will be hurricane resistant, fire resistant and insulating. He is checking on the possible price ranges; something else for us to sell. It is relatively early here and I have already eaten, which gives me time to work out again and have dessert when I return. There I go, living on the edge again. To me, it is a nice treat to be able to work out twice in one day and since I had a very unusual three glasses of iced tea at dinner, I have plenty of caffeine in me to work off. I will call Wendy later. It has been a good day.

5/5/10
8:31 PM EST
In flight to NJ

I was asleep by 10:00 PM. I have to revamp how IJX and IJUS work the business with IJ Mexico. I will need to think about it.

I was up at 4:40 this morning and was alone in the gym, at least for a while. There were a lot of machines out of order, however, and I ended up on a Stairmaster. I had never used that machine before, but I found it enjoyable until I vacated to give it to someone else as the room had filled up. I went to the outside pool and walked there for thirty minutes. The sun was coming up over the city of Guadalajara and it was gorgeous. I met Paulina and we were off to Sanmina-SCI and saw a total of eight people of various positions. We were hoping to get approval next month to be on their daily delivery system which, although expensive, will put us in the pathway for more business. It enables the customer to cut their lead times because they can get daily deliveries. There was a lot of talk about us getting chances at other label and gasket business.

During the morning, I got an email from Hing regarding the composite company in Malaysia that is testing our radome materials. He had lunch with the head man and they are interested in doing a potential joint venture. It would seem that the renderings and offers I sent to build product together achieved their desired effect. I made the decision a while ago to be myself everywhere in the world. I used to try to be different in Europe and Asia regarding their various cultures. What I found out was that being my aggressive, polite, straightforward self is what people expect and can relate to. We have people on the ground to smooth over any missteps I make, which works out well since they can be the good guy if my actions cause disturbances. They want a full proposal on how we can work together and I started writing it as soon as Paulina dropped me off at the airport, right after I finished the second draft of the May newsletter. We had a very good three days together. I am proud of her for the great job she is doing and I told her so, which made her feel good. I always like to tell people when they are doing a good job. Money is nice, but being told you are doing well is also very important. On the way to Houston, I sat next to a counselor for a community college in California. She was very pleasant, but had a tough route trying to help a lot of people who were unemployed and going back to school to try to increase their chances for a good job.

The plane to Texas was on time. I got through immigration and customs and went to the Continental Airlines lounge. So far, this flight seems is on schedule and I am getting tired and grouchy. This was evident to both Al and I when I spoke to her and got overly upset at a potential problem. She is having a medical test tomorrow and won't be in until the afternoon, which is probably a good thing because I will not get much sleep tonight and will probably be even more irritable by then. I will work as long as I can. They just told us what they were serving for dinner and I am glad I had a sandwich and a banana before since I am not eating it. Maybe they have some pretzels. I am not going to drink any more diet soda because it might keep me up tonight, but I may risk a cup of tea. I am glad I went to Mexico. It is important to see the customers and support Paulina in person. I told her, the fact that I leave her alone is a compliment and a testament to her good work. She wants to learn from my experience and I must make sure to give her the chance so she can grow with the company.

Sleep deprivation is beginning to take its toll. I am listening to music from the American President and it is making me emotional. I look forward to being home, seeing Wendy and my dog, my parents, Ben and Katie this weekend and of course my brother for tennis. What a fortunate man I am.

5/9/10
8:17 PM EST
Home, NJ

We landed on schedule and Mike the Driver was already there and to get me home by midnight. After having some dinner and seeing Wendy and Bailey, I got to sleep at about 2:00 AM and was up again at 5:00 AM. As predicted, I got slaughtered by my Wednesday tennis partner. I played better than expected, but he was virtually flawless and I stood no chance. Undaunted,

No Road Is Ever Straight

I spent a fantastic day catching up back at the office, working on our new projects and generally happy to be home. I had lunch with Gary, who was supportive in our new efforts for expansion as always and I ended the day talking with John our export attorney about the joint ventures we were attempting in Malaysia.

The British elections were today, but there has been no word yet of which party won and who will be the new prime minister. The terrorist who planted the car bomb in New York City was apparently incompetent and his mission failed. The stock market dropped 1000 points today because of one trading mistake and Proctor and Gamble's stock was cut in half. The day ended with the DOW being down over 300 points. I am glad we are spread out across the world in various economies. People are very skittish about Greece, Portugal and Spain; who knows if the Common Market will survive. Ireland and Scotland's airspace is still closed due to the volcanic ash cloud from Iceland. The oil slick in the Gulf of Mexico continues to grow, but they are trying to cap off the leaks now. I hope they are successful. The only advantage is that in times of extreme stress, people will listen to those with potential answers who would have had no voice before. It is like us with our customers, who now look to us for potential solutions. I got documentation from one of our customers in Mexico regarding signing us up to do daily deliveries, which usually means the potential for a lot more business. We have our chance at getting more and growing and we are going for it.

5/7/10
5:25 PM EST
My office, NJ

I spent a good part of the day preparing a joint venture proposal with the state owned composite manufacturer in Malaysia CTRM and a memorandum of understanding with the Malaysian Defense University NPUM. My plan is to set up partnerships with both so we can do research and joint manufacturing throughout Asia. All in all, it has been a very productive day and even some inventing, which I cannot write about. It is amazing to me that the ideas we are coming up with here may have merit not only in the commercial world, but also military and defense areas. It is a humbling thought to think we can increase the safety of our soldiers and maybe even save lives.

5/8/10
5:31 PM EST
Home, NJ

There was a threat of rain today, so Uncle Dave did not ride with the fast group and came early with me. Unfortunately, although it was a very enjoyable ride, we did pass through an intense rain storm and we got wet but it did not dampen our spirits. After changing, I picked up my mom for her Mother's Day lunch a day early and we had a great time catching up on family and business. She is always interested in what is going on and it is wonderful having the unconditional love that she pours onto me. I dropped her off and then went to the plant store. I went through the prospects for the public offering for IJM and realized that the numbers I had been seeing were in Malaysian and not U.S. dollars, which meant that we would not be raising as much as I thought. It sounds ridiculous to make that kind of mistake, but there is so much paperwork going back and forth and so many facts and figures that it is difficult keeping everything straight. No matter; we are still going ahead. After the flowers arrived, we brought them to our porch because of the high winds. My very smart wife thought they might get destroyed if we left them outside. We are due to have dinner tonight with Dan and Elana at a Mexican restaurant. My, how life has changed for me. Judging by the shadows coming over my laptop, the beautiful sky is turning somewhat cloudy. The winds should be calm tomorrow, so I hope to get all of the plants in the ground.

5/9/10
8:56 PM EST
Home, NJ

I have been telling people we can solve a great many of the world's problems, those involving mechanical solutions like the oil spill in Louisiana, new types of protective armor and new hurricane shutters. We had better score soon or I will lose my credibility. It was Mother's Day and after tennis, I began planting the mountain of plants I bought yesterday. Around 11:45, I left to pick up Ben and Katie at the train station. That began a wonderful three hour adventure, which included lunch and a visit from Barbara. I went back to planting as Wendy took the kids to the station and it became apparent I had not bought enough topsoil. At about 5:00, I ran out of dirt, cleaned up, watered the flowers and surveyed my work. I think they will turn out beautifully and Wendy agreed. I will order more dirt this week and plan on finishing the balance of the planting on the weekend.

5/10/10
3:32 PM EST
My office, NJ

It is a beautiful spring day here in New Jersey with a bright sun and a blue sky. I am going to try to leave a little early so I can stop by the plant store and buy more dirt. I may get some Black-Eyed Susans and daises if they have any. Who knows what else will catch my eye. It has been a day of a lot of paperwork and email sales. The stock market is up over 300 points with the trillion-dollar bailout of Europe. The euro has been dropping, which has been affecting our business there since we are buying more expensive products in China and importing them into the Netherlands. We may be forced to raise prices there. I am in the midst of rechecking how our companies worldwide are doing business, and as a whole it seems to be working well. The volcano in Iceland is spewing again and there have been plane disruptions in parts of Great Britain. The oil leak in Louisiana is still happening and turning into one of the worst environmental disasters in a long time. Al has booked her flight to England to see the new grandchild that is supposed to be born within a month.

5/11/10
4:53 PM EST
My office, NJ

I got home last night to dinner with my in-laws, Barbara and Cliff. It was a beautiful evening and I truthfully only wanted to be outside, water my new plants and wash the dirt off my car. This morning's emails relayed bad news of problems that new hurricane regulations in the U.S. were apparently made lighter so now our process might be too good and expensive for widespread use. Couple that with a problem with an expensive prototype that we will probably have to replace and it was a lousy day up until 3:00 PM when someone turned a switch and things got better. Don Argintar's soap dispenser monitor that shows how many people are using it every day seems to be working and tomorrow's meeting should finalize the first prototype order. I also spent the day sending out loads of emails with our hurricane panel information and tests. I am tired and am going home soon.

5/12/10
7:15 PM EST
Home, NJ

My day was good, which is a quantum leap above yesterday. A lot of what went wrong seemed to be getting worked out. The job gone wrong from yesterday, which will probably cost us $6000 to redo, was to be discussed today. However, the customer had some technical problems so we are delayed until tomorrow. I think our team is on a clear path, which, as usual in cases of trouble, is to make the customer happy. I anticipate a swift, positive meeting tomorrow so we can move forward and take care of the various issues involved. The stock questions about IJM were discussed with Gary and we sent information over to Ben to check with our consultants. Being able to give stock to our people is extremely important and I want it done. It is simply a matter of finding the best way to do it. There has been no word yet from our contact from Anderson Window, but that seems to be moving forward. We heard from one group testing our material in Malaysia and hope they are finished by the end of May. We are working on more projects and business at IJUS is good for the month so I am reasonably calm, which is a major change of events from the beginning of the week. Sometimes you have to have a few bad days to appreciate the balance. I don't usually need the reminder since I try to count my blessings continually, but it does heighten the appreciation. Elana stopped in and brought me some of her amazing chocolate muffins. I did not eat bread for dinner in preparation and they were delicious. She is a very nice person and I am very fortunate to have her as my friend. Wendy and I had date night tonight and it was extremely pleasant. She is always a very fun date and companion.

MAY

5/13/10
5:25 PM EST
My office, NJ

I spent the afternoon in a meeting with the people from the 3 Tex Corporation. They were knowledgeable, pleasant and wanted to do business both to supply us with composite cloth and to partner for new projects. It is always exciting to be around people with a totally different set of knowledge because you can learn so much in a short period of time. The face to face meeting, three of them and three of us, was fun and it was good to size each other up to see if we can deal in the future. They will get us a price on Monday and information for some potential work together. Let's see what happens.

5/14/10
4:15 PM EST
My office, NJ

One of my obsessions came back to bite me. I have been downloading a lot of songs and movies from iTunes and today my computer rebelled and refused to keep going until we drained some of the music and movies. I spent part of the morning reviewing patents from people regarding similar types of hurricane material we are producing. I think we have a clear road and I sent out a summary. They are still trying to plug the oil leak in the gulf and maybe by the next decade they will call us to help. The euro has been dropping and my brother thinks the European common market will breakup. Countries like Germany will not prop up those like Greece forever. We are working on a new type of acoustic buoy that can monitor all types of river, lake and ocean traffic, be it fish or boats. It is fascinating to work in new areas. I have emailed my main contacts at WOR, both to get permission to use their names in my newest book and to open the door for going back to radio in the fall. I miss being on the air.

5/15/10
5:30 PM EST
Home, NJ

I got up in time to cook Wendy breakfast and read before going to my office to meet Elana. Working out with her is an experience because she is so focused, disciplined and unbending regarding form and structure. Anyone better be ready before stepping out on the floor with her. I was not disappointed and I think she was happy with the effort I put out. It is always wonderful seeing her and I hope she has a good time at the wedding she has been planning all week. It is for one of her cousins and is taking place in Long Island, New York so I hope all the effort turns into a fantastic blast. After I left her, I went home, ate again and went for a bike ride, which was amazing. The weather was a perfect 70°F. I had plenty of water and had a great time. Unfortunately, Uncle Dave could not join me. After biking, I still had planting to do and amazingly enough, I ran out of dirt again and will have to buy more tomorrow. Still, the flowers I did get in look great so I am motivated to finish the job. That will probably be it for the summer, unless of course I get too close to a plant store, get pulled in by the gravitational force and buy more. I am delightfully tired and it feels great. I am mentally running on full and ready to start working on new ideas.

5/16/10
7:07 PM EST
Home, NJ

The news from Thailand continues to get worse and I am now worrying for the safety of our people and the operation itself. There are new deadlines imposed by the government and the few thousand Red Shirt protesters will soon lose their chance for free passage out of the barricaded quarters in Bangkok. I hope it ends soon with the least amount of violence possible. The ash cloud from the Iceland volcano is back and threatening parts of Europe. More airspace, especially around southern England, may be closed. The Chinese World's fair in Shanghai has begun and the officials there are hoping for more than 70 million visitors over the next six months. Since I do not like crowds, I doubt I will be one of them.

There is a big 4-state primary election on Tuesday. The incumbent politicians are worried they will lose their seats due to the anti-government and anti-politician sentiment in the country. I think they are right to be concerned.

It was another beautiful day here in NJ. I played tennis, went biking and also finished planting. Now we wait to see which plants don't make it and I can decide if I want to replace them then.

5/17/10
5:27 PM EST
My office, NJ

I spent the morning working on sales and setting up how we were going to handle the dropping euro in Europe. At this point, if the euro goes to parity with the U.S. dollar, then the goods we buy from IJX will cost 40% more than they do now. Therefore, some of the business we have there will become unprofitable. Like many other companies, we will have to either raise prices or give up the business. There will be lots of changes there, as I expect the economies of Europe to worsen in the coming months. We will have to be careful, but when there are radical changes, there are often chances for new business and product lines. The afternoon was spent in grinding out more emails advertising our new hurricane materials. I know on a percentage basis they will produce inquires and sales, but it is tough to go through thousands. No matter; it needs to be done and I will do it.

MAY

5/18/10
5:32 PM EST
My office, NJ

I went to play tennis this morning and my Tuesday partner told me his brother died last night. He had been sick, but this was unexpected. I asked myself what I could do and the only thing I could think of was tell him I will try to beat the hell out of him. So ensued a battle for the next hour. I tried my best and I lost, but it was close and he was smiling by the time we finished. Later, I texted him and my brother, who also plays tennis with him, that I sent three trees to would be planted in memory of his brother. He liked that and I was glad we could do something positive. I now have a definite trip for Asia and spent part of the day trying to schedule the plane rides. I hope to finalize them in the morning. Titan requested that I write a letter from the chairman for the new IJ Malaysia website. I hope they liked what I sent. I also wrote my version for the working joint venture between us and the composite company in Malaysia. That is looking positive, so I wanted to get my thoughts down before forgetting them. I am incredibly fortunate that I can write well enough to be able to get our ventures off the ground. I am no Hemmingway, but the talent I have is enough to get done what is needed and not enough to have spent my life trying to be a successful author and starving along the way. As I said, I am I know when I am well off. I am off to go get Stella's back bicycle tire that was punctured last Sunday. It is raining so I hope I get a close parking spot.

5/19/10
4:41 PM EST
My office, NJ

I booked my flights today for Asia and found out a few minutes ago that I got aisle seats for most. I have one left to check. Having an inside seat makes me feel trapped, so I will do a lot to try to stay on the outside seat. I am leaving on June 5th, a Saturday night, almost at midnight and will be back late Thursday night of that week. In the meantime, while the main leaders of the Thai Red Shirts gave up today, their followers decided to start burning and robbing Bangkok. It is a very bad situation and I am staying away. I feel very badly for the people there, especially our own team. There were some midterm primaries yesterday and a long time senator who had switched parties to become a Democrat to try to stay in office was beaten. It looks bad for incumbents of all types and as far as I am concerned, the more new faces the better for the next year. My quest to have a two-handed left side backhand is going well, so eventually I will have backhand and forehands for both sides. When or if I get hurt, I just switch sides with little loss of power and accuracy. That is the goal, though I am not sure if it will ever happen. Business is good here, which is a pleasure.

No Road Is Ever Straight

5/20/10
5:20 PM EST
My office, NJ

It continually amazes me how much paperwork can be involved with everything. More came in last night regarding the public offering, not to mention the joint ventures with the two groups in Malaysia as well as trying to set up the hurricane panel and home building panel systems here. I had a staff meeting with our VPs for all of the current projects and the various testing going on worldwide. There is a lot to keep track of. The other part of my job, which is taking care of trouble, came into play today with a Canadian customer who, being pushed by their customer, needed a part we were making in China in an impossible delivery. After going back and forth with various suggestions and alternatives, I have to follow up with IJX tonight and try to get an expedited delivery from them. Just because we are all part of the same global team does not mean I can snap my fingers and everything I want magically happens. All of our groups have their own schedules and I have to work within them. We still have no orders on the new composites or the heat extractors and the R&D dollars are continually mounting up. We are bringing on more lawyers and finance people to try to make sure we are covered in all of our new areas. It is expensive and grueling trying to keep up, but there is no choice. I find the vast majority of it a lot of fun. I sometimes even find it hard to go to sleep because I am so excited about what is happening. It has been a beautiful day here in NJ; about 80°F with low humidity and a gorgeous blue sky. It is supposed to be a little warmer tomorrow and I got to pick up Miss Rose from school. We should get home at about 10:00 PM and I can't wait to see her. The stock market dropped 376 points today, more than 10%, and we are in an official "correction." The euro shows no sign of recovering soon, which means we are in for another interesting ride. I am hoping the U.S., Mexico, Canada and non-Chinese Asian countries went through the bad times and are on the way up. I hope.

5/23/10
4:55 PM EST
Home, NJ

Tennis with my brother this morning was an unusually rollicking match with lots of effort and the use of my left handed forehand and new two handed left side backhand. I tried to go biking afterward, but found I had pulled a muscle in my right leg, which made it uncomfortable and a worry to continue because I could affect myself for my tennis game tomorrow. I went back to the house after cutting off my ride and worked out with my bands in the cellar and used the treadmill for a short time. Then it was off to New York City with my wife and Kayla. Thankfully, Wendy drove and we had a wonderful meal with Ben to celebrate his 24th birthday. Katie and Alex, who had stayed in the city last night, also joined us. Our children are getting older and they continually to become more fantastic as they mature. They are wonderful people and it would be an honor to know them even if we are not related. As it is, I am very proud of them and talk about them and my wonderful wife incessantly with people all over the world.

Obsessive compulsiveness takes many forms. Unfortunately (or fortunately), our children all seem to have it to some degree. Its forms can be anything from the inability to handle the repetition of non-structural tones to specific behaviors of conduct like having five alarm clocks that all have to be checked every night for the correct time. One of my son Alex's became apparent today on the way home from Manhattan. Alex plugged in his iPhone into Wendy's car system and it became apparent that he had an incredible need to keep changing songs before they were finished. Not only that, but he sang along with them and rarely knew the words. Until this point, I thought I was the only one who did that in the family, but it seems I have once again passed down a unique behavior to one of my children. I am not sure he is thanking me for this one, but as I always say, we are whole packages so I hope the goods far outweigh the negatives.

After we got back, I took a short walk. Then I pulled out a special spray nozzle for our hose and blasted the moss, grass and weeds from between the tiles in our front walk. It was actually fun, but now I need to get some sand to fill in the cracks I created with the water jet. I am responsible for dinner tonight. It will only be Alex, Wendy and I. Kayla went over to see Max, her former boyfriend, and his parents. They are friends now and it will be good for them to see each other.

I found out yesterday that Abul, our agent in Malaysia who is helping with the deal with the Defense University, is seeing the head person at 10:00 AM their time tomorrow, which is 10:00 PM our time tonight. He hopes that they will sign both the NDA and MOU so we can get started. It will be a very big deal if they do and I hope I can sleep tonight knowing what may be happening. I will try.

Wendy tells me that sometimes I look like I leave mentally for a while and go into a cocoon when things at work are incredibly stressful. We have a lot of big things working right now, including a huge potential meeting in the morning and the effects are taking their toll on me. This is why I am working out so much. I am incredibly thankful I do not smoke, drink, take illegal drugs and almost never gamble so that my obsessions are usually channeled to good areas, which only turn to fortify my energy and mental well being. A lot is riding on the agreements with both Malaysian groups. I mentioned to Wendy that I may want to go back on the radio. She thought I was done with it and that I should think about it some more before making a decision. I agreed. It seems that the oil well in the gulf is mostly stopped, but the devastation will be increasingly horrific for a long time.

5/24/10
8:46 PM EST
Home, NJ

I found out early this morning that the Malaysian Defense University signed our NDA but not the MOA. They plan to sign it when we meet in person next month. That gives us time to get ready for the third area they wanted us to research, which is setting up offshore living modules for their population. They want to be able to move some of their people to live in the water and we want to be part of the project. I sketched out some ideas last night, including an underwater rail system, a mixture of composite materials to set up freight cars and a general submersible living complex. It was fun to work on and I even got some of the ideas past Al and Mike, who can both be very tough on my inventions.

I spent the balance of the day doing more paperwork for IJM and getting ready for my upcoming trip. The details are multiplying and I am trying to stay ahead of things the best I can. It can get very complicated. I also got my car washed this morning which I find relaxing for some reason, not to mention to enjoyment I get from having a sparkling clean car. After dinner, I toured my flowers and most are looking well. This is another five minute relaxing journey that I try to make daily. There has been no word yet from the composites manufacturer in Malaysia, which is the last big deal we are trying to close now. If it happens or at least moves ahead, I hope we can close that next month. There is a lot of potentially giant stuff and a very fun time.

5/25/10
5:23 PM EST
My office, NJ

Alice is extremely nervous as her new granddaughter was due to be born today in London, but has not yet made an appearance. We have already dubbed her the "English Muffin" and we all look forward to her healthy, happy debut.

We redesigned the new floating house idea for the Malaysian Defense University and Eric is rendering it. That, along with a bunch of other renderings, will come with me when I go to Malaysia. More paperwork is needed for the people taking us public in Malaysia; Ben's patience is amazing. We are working on reducing the panel thickness for the hurricane panels and getting pricing together. The world markets are down again. It figures; there may be a war with North and South Korea and the euro is still heading downward. What a time to go public! I think the timing is good and I am happy we are doing it.

5/26/10
4:50 PM EST
My office, NJ

There are long term goals and short term triumphs and today I went for a quick shot. We already have an NDA with the Defense University in Malaysia. We have an NDA with the Composite Technology Research Malaysia group (CTRM) and we are hoping for a joint partnership agreement. I saw the initial documents for it written by Hing and although it was well written, I spent part of the morning adding more information. By the time I finished, I realized there was no way the people from CTRM were going to sign that within a week. Looking for a quick success, I suggested to Ben that we write an MOU, which is only one to two pages. We can see if we get that approved so we have a basis for working together right away. He agreed and I sent my version to our able export attorney John for review. This will give me something to sell and I can push hard to get it signed.

5/26/10
5:31 PM EST
My office, NJ

My son Alex is coming to realize that when he graduates from college next year and is theoretically on his own, his standard of living will significantly drop. He is understandably worried and I offered some advice as to how to get an extremely high paying position when he finished school. He has an internship at Tommy Hilfiger for the summer. He had created a new design concept that they loved and he begins work there next week. In my opinion, the best way to forge ahead of everyone is to have a complete marketing and sales plan ready when he walks in. He knows the president of the division and I think she would be happy to look at it. She may appreciate the effort and may put it into work. My son is a perfectionist, does not think he can do everything needed in a week and will probably decline my advice. In order to achieve perfection, a lot of time is needed. I have often found that 95% of an idea and preparation is enough to sell it and I have beat the competition because they were waiting to be perfect. It should be interesting to see which of us is correct.

I sent an MOU to the head of the composite company in Malaysia this morning and am waiting to hear back. If he signs, then we can work on a formal partnership later. I want something in writing now. I have been putting together the costs of the new composites plant with Jack. I like doing this kind of thing and hope the final results show we can make a good profit on the hurricane/tornado panels. I am spending part of my time going after old customers and contacts and it is achieving results. It is also good to be in touch with people I haven't connected to in years. Besides, as the saying goes, it is much easier to activate an old customer than find a new one.

5/28/10
5:47 PM EST
The Berkshires

Yesterday was a good day. We worked a lot on the new land/ship project I plan to submit to people in Malaysia and a few even said they would want to buy one. If we can make it eco-friendly and cool enough, then perhaps we have a shot at building something truly great. Whether the effects of global warming are from people or not is irrelevant if you figure it is coming anyway and have to deal with it. Receding land means a great amount of land will be changing from dry to marshy to under water, and housing has to be adaptable. I hope our new design can meet that challenge. Eric is working on it this weekend and we hope to have the final ready for Tuesday. The deadline for getting my new book to press is approaching. August 1st is not far away, so I spent the balance of yesterday afternoon editing and I am up to about the middle of last September.

Last night Wendy and Kayla went to Manhattan to see the cast from the television show Glee. All in all, they had a great time. Meanwhile, I was using the bag of leveling sand Vinnie had nicely gotten for me to fill in the cracks created when I water jetted the area between the stones on our front walk. It was a nice night and Bailey kept me company. This morning I was up early to get ready to come up here to our house in the Berkshires of Massachusetts. We are renting it out for the month of July since we are not here much and we spent part of the afternoon cleaning and throwing stuff out. My wonderful mother-in-law helped us and we are going to have dinner with her and Jeff in a little while. After cleaning and doing laundry, I went mountain biking for the first time up here since last September and it was a fantastic ride. It is peaceful up here and Wendy and I agreed to come up more.

There is a scent in the air, a combination of flowers and wood smoke, that suddenly brought me back to the summers my family spent a two week vacation in the Adirondack Mountains in upstate New York. We were really far back into the woods, so there was no distortion from city lights or pollution when trying to see the stars at night, which were numerous and dazzling. That was a long time ago, but the fond memories remain.

5/29/10
3:04 PM EST
Home, NJ

I checked multiple times last night and I even found a firefly in the house, but they weren't sending their glowing tail signals last night. Perhaps they will next time we are up there later this month. Dinner with Bunny and Jeff was very pleasant. I was up by 6:00 AM and rode my new bike. You find out a lot about a bicycle on the first long ride and this was no exception. She is a wonderful street bike, sleek and fast. However, she does not have the mass and stability I need for off-road biking in the woods. The weather was about 65°F, clear with no humidity and I had a wonderful time. Afterward, Wendy and I packed up our house to ready it for our July renters and had a great breakfast with Bunny and Jeff. Bunny is planning a big party for Jeff in September and all our children can come. Both Wendy and my parents are getting older and their health is not great, excluding Bunny. The horrible time is coming where they will be too sick to live where they currently do or will pass on and leave the other behind. I do not look forward to the prospect. As far and Bunny and Jeff are concerned, it has been a wonderful relationship over time and I feel lucky and honored to be their son-in-law. As for my parents, there will always be things I would have done differently as I am sure the same for them. The process of getting older, wiser and learning to see from other points of view has made us all better people. We are all human with our pluses and minuses and when they are gone, I hope I can remember the majority of the good and let the balance fade into oblivion. It is impossible not to have regrets and alternative preferences as opposed to what actually happened. That is life.

5/30/10
2:46 PM EST
Home, NJ
Memorial Day

I had a beautiful ride this morning and the weather was 75°F and clear. As I hoped, I was able to get to Maplewood before the start of the Memorial Day parade and watched almost the whole thing. There were police and rescue people, various scout troops and groups of all kinds. It made me feel proud to be a part of it, if only from the sidelines. I finished the ride from there and afterward, Wendy, Kayla, Alex and I had lunch. I bought some flowers to replace some of the ones I put in that did not do well. As it turns out, Dan and Elana are coming for dinner so I will begin cooking in about 30 minutes after some great help from Wendy and the kids.

JUNE

6/1/10
4:47 PM EST
My office, NJ

It was good to be back in the office. I know it has only been since Friday, but I miss the action. It was mostly a day of paperwork and updates. The semi-final design for the global warming floating house community is done and out for review before we finalize them for my trip on Sunday. I spoke to the head of the CTRM in Malaysia this morning and they are reviewing our MOU.

6/2/10
5:35 PM EST
My office, NJ

I spent a lot of the day working on the new patent application for our ballistic material, information for going public and cleaning up loose ends so I can leave on Saturday night with a clean mind. I got approvals from our export attorney for the last of the information I want to take with me to Malaysia. I just sent a job offer to a young man who is the son of a woman who cuts my hair. She is an immigrant from Poland. I like immigrants, as they are usually very hard working and have an incredible desire to succeed. I hope that translates to her son, so we will see.

6/3/10
4:49 PM EST
My office, NJ

The young man I offered the job to last night had until 11:00 AM to answer back if he wanted the job. Last night, my daughter told me that one of her friends, a young man I have known from our Synagogue named Zack, also needed a job. Since I knew him and his family already, I worked it out that he would have at least a part time job helping Jack make samples and do research for the composite panels. The 11:00 AM deadline passed with no word from the first young man, so Zack now has a full time job until he goes back to college. It is amazing how things work out.

Kayla lost her cell phone last night and it still did not turn up after a lot of searching. Since I am in charge of the family telephone plan, I needed to be at the Verizon store to get her a replacement. Of course, this gave me a fantastic opportunity to also have lunch with her and we spent a wonderful two hours together. She is so much fun to be around and I will miss her greatly when she goes to camp in two weeks. She is ready to be there, so it will be best for everyone when she goes.

Speaking of leaving, Alex is moving into Manhattan tomorrow in preparation for his internship. I have not heard of any problems, so I guess things went well. He too will be much happier on his own in the city.

6/4/10
Approximately 5:00 PM EST
My office, NJ

The main stock market here in the U.S. dropped 323 points, below 10,000. So far, the recovery is continuing here in the U.S., but with few jobs being produced. Hungary sounded an alert as to their financial situation today, which was another bad sign for Europe. The BP disaster in the Gulf continues. Their latest fix may be working, but no one knows for sure right now.

Another humanitarian boat is on its way to try to get through the Israeli naval blockade of the Gaza Strip. The last flotilla was boarded by the Israeli Army and people died. It is not a good situation. Turkey has shut down relations with Israel.

6/6/10
9:33 PM EST
Newark/Liberty Airport
Eva Airways Lounge

I had a fantastic day so far. I got up early and went biking. There was a threat of thunder storms for the day and I wanted to beat the potential rain and be back with plenty of time for lunch with my mom. Uncle Dave could not ride, so it was good to think by myself and let my mind roam. I got home in plenty of time and finished most of my food preparation for the trip. I was trying to pack everything in a carryon, but ended up needing an extra cloth bag that I hoped I could get through security. Lunch with mom was great. We talked about where we were going in the business, my trip to Malaysia, what I hope to accomplish and, of course, family. Their 60th wedding anniversary party next month has an added bonus as her brother, my Uncle Allan, is coming in from Texas. I saw him a few years ago and it will be great to see him again.

It is always nice to hear that your mom is proud of you and I am glad we were able to have lunch alone together. I hope to do it more. I went back to the plant store again and then home to plant and prune. I can't seem to stop myself from buying more, but it is probably a harmless addiction. The rest of the day was spent resting. Kayla was home for dinner, which is an extra bonus and as always it was very tough leaving both of them for the airport. Kayla is due to go see her best friend Alexa, who works for a whale watching company in Massachusetts, and she will be back next Friday. I am due back next Thursday night. I am excited and nervous about this trip. There are some things that need to get done quickly and the next few days will be our best chance. One unfortunate thing the airlines did made me check my main bag so now we are separated. It is a little disconcerting, but EVA Airlines has always been a great company so I am hopeful it will meet me in Kuala Lumpur when I land. In the meantime, it is easier traveling with only two pieces, so I will focus on that.

6/7/10
2:53 AM Alaska time, 6:53 AM EST
Anchorage Airport, Alaska

Coming in for landing, I noticed that the sun had not set even though it was the middle of the night. It is up almost all day this time of year. The flight here was on time and extremely pleasant. I supplemented the airline meal with the chicken I brought, but I must say their fruit and two cookies were excellent.

One of the advantages of being the boss and the rainmaker, which means I am responsible overall for new sales, R&D product lines and customer relations, is that I know how hard it is to get customers, but I also have the power to tell them to leave. It is an option I rarely use, but these are extreme circumstances. I got a few hours of sleep on the plane, which was enough to be functional. The next nine hour flight should give me the chance for another three to four, and then I will be good enough for the meetings I have when I arrive. Given a choice, I would have preferred to get to the hotel, work out for an hour, get a shower and change before seeing people. That is not happening, so I will go with the flow. The extra advantage of this is that since I will be very tired, my temper will be shorter and I will be more difficult to deal with. I never want to be too consistent in any one direction and a little bit of unusual behavior keeps people on their toes and not too complacent.

All of our IJ people worldwide are counting on me to do the best for us and I do not plan on letting them down. I will go back to my final edit for last year's book.

6/6/10
8:48 AM EST
In flight to Taiwan

595 mph, 32000 feet, -65°F, about to go over the Pacific Ocean

We are on schedule. Additionally, I wrote to Jeroen that growing pains are just that. Change and growth means stress and problems along the way. We will get through it. I also offered to go to Europe to help him sell. Igor is due to move to the Netherlands so Jeroen will get a lot more direct support.

I will keep editing until I pass out, get hungry or can't do anymore; whichever comes first. The only slightly negative thing is the airline is not serving a full meal for another seven hours and the snack they have is so calorically intense that I dare not eat it. I have plenty of my own provisions, although they are carbohydrate based, which means my plan to stick to protein and fruit is not going to happen. It is a very mild problem and I will not be hungry, which is the main thing because that will make it very hard to work. In the meantime, I decided to go into a caffeine high, though I am not sure why. I am double drinking green tea and diet soda, which probably means I will not be sleeping anytime soon.

I am listening to a collection from the Carpenters, a singing duo. They were very popular when I was in my teens and I have always liked them a lot. Their music brings back memories of my first girlfriend Karen, some of which were good and others best left in the past. As I mentioned to my mom during lunch, I have no urge to be any other age than I am now. I hear people who would like to be back in college or in their 20s again and that is not for me. I am very happy where I am. I have the job I always wanted, a fantastic family, my health and our worldwide teams, positioned for major expansion. I have always dreamed that the inventions and ideas that come out of my brain will one day be used to not only help people and make us more successful, but legitimize us on a worldwide basis, earn us the respect I think we deserve and the chance to be brought in when a crisis occurs. I know our team can do amazing things and it has taken us decades to get into position.

That is why this week is so important. If we have two formal MOUs in place and both groups agree to our proposals for innovation, R&D, prototyping and production then we will be launched onto the world stage. I know there are risks besides the financial, including being an American company and working on commercial inventions that could have military and defense applications. We will have to be extremely careful to follow the correct path to cover ourselves and still be able to launch forward. We will not get another chance like the ones we have now for the foreseeable future. We have to go for it, everywhere at the same time. I am happy to be the point man and let the results, good or bad, fall on my shoulders. We are following my dream and the bigger it gets, the more companies and partners involved, the higher the responsibility, the higher the chances for success and failure and the greater our ability to make a difference in our world.

I can feel the caffeine surging through my veins. Again, I am not sure why I did this, but it feels good for a little while. I will capitalize on the rush and go back to editing. I cut myself off from any more, at least on the short term.

6/7/10
2:06 AM Taiwan time, 2:06 PM EST
In flight, approximately 2:56 to landing in Taipai/Taiwan

I did not get a lot of sleep, but it will be enough to keep me going, so all is well. We are scheduled to eat in about an hour. I hope to be at the first meeting by 3:00 PM Malaysian time, which will be thirty hours from door to door.

No Road Is Ever Straight

6/7/10
6:02 AM Taiwan time, 6:02 PM EST
Taiwan Airport Eva Air Lounge

Things are good; I have my boarding pass for Kuala Lumpur and about 2 ½ hours before going to the gate. I may go for a walk and stretch my legs. It is a definite advantage not having my main suitcase for that endeavor. If I can get one or two hours of sleep on my next flight, which is about 4 ½ hours long, then I should be okay for the meeting with Ben, the meeting with the stock people and dinner with the two head men from CTRM. I am hoping for a break before we go out to eat so I can at least get a shower, change and maybe workout a little. A nap would be an added bonus. Regardless, I know what I have to do and will focus on getting it done.

6/7/10
10:11 AM Malaysia time, 10:11 PM EST
In flight to Kuala Lumpur

I did get some walking in while waiting for this flight, but did not get to sleep. As it turned out, I am sitting next to a pilot. He is on his way to Malaysia for a seminar. I always feel better having an extra driver in case of trouble. He is very pleasant and spent a lot of his flight school training in the U.S.

We have about four hours to go. After lunch, I will try to sleep again.

6/8/10
11:12 AM Malaysian time, 11:12 PM EST
En route from Kuala Lumpur to Melaka

The plane arrived on time yesterday and we got to Kuala Lumpur at 2:15 PM. I was having trouble finding my bag that I had checked in because the electronic board was not showing my flight. Figuring either it was late or just not listed, I started walking down the many carousels in the luggage area and fortunately found my suitcase quickly. Ben was there to meet me in the outside reception area and as we walked outside I was hit with a wave of very hot, humid air. Figuring the temperature would be in the mid nineties, I did not bother to change my clothes before going to the meeting with the consultants helping us to go public. I was told this was to be a short thirty-minute meeting to go over some financial matters and to instruct me on the duties of being board member for IJ Malaysia. Ben handed me some notes before I went in and what ensued was a quick discussion of how to handle buying and selling the stock shares IJUS would receive for going public. Then in came two of the main people in charge of our offering and as it turned out the rest of the meeting was not about my duties as a board member, which I had already studied in New Jersey, but rather about our prospects. They wanted to be convinced, to be sure that potential stock buyers would be, whether I thought the plans and goals set out for the corporation were suitable, doable and whether they followed my vision for Ideal Jacobs worldwide.

I had left my house in New Jersey about 30 hours earlier with not a lot of sleep. A heavy dose of adrenaline kicked in and I not only met their questions head on, but attacked back. We spoke about cash flow, banks, where assets would be used, who decided how things would go, our partnerships and even what happened if I died or retired. The last was not an option as long as health was not an issue. By the time we finished, I believe they were convinced of our sincerity and abilities, and agreed with our goals and paths to potential great success. I believe they were convinced in the end and they both agreed we were a solid company well worth anyone's investment.

Once done, I went to the Crowne Plaza, our regular hotel here and realized that I barely had time to exercise before I needed to get ready for dinner. After 15 minutes of my band workout, I got really tired and went back to the room, showered and changed. I cannot describe the incredible feeling of getting out my of clothes that I have had on for quite awhile and have hot water hit my body. It was great. After I changed, I made the mistake of turning on the television for a few minutes and actually passed out twice before I forced myself to go downstairs to meet Ben. Hing was also there and it was wonderful to see him. I had been a bit worried about an 8:00 dinner after I had been traveling so long, but once our hosts and the two head people from CTRM, Rosti and Wan, came another round of adrenaline kicked in and I was fine until dinner ended. We spoke about the MOU that they planned to sign today, went into our various backgrounds and discussed how fate had brought us all together. It was very pleasant and good to be out for a social evening. I got back to the hotel at about 10:30 and since I had prepped everything before I left, I had little to do before getting to sleep by 11:10 PM.

A great event had occurred while I was traveling. Alice's new granddaughter was born! Both mother and daughter are fine and the excitement level is off the charts. I got up at 6:30, which was definitely not enough sleep but adequate to get by. I exercised and walked around the outside tennis court. It was hot and humid, but very nice to be outdoors. While there I called Wendy, who is doing well and misses me, as I do her. Kayla was out babysitting, which meant I did not get a chance to speak to her. As always, the emails between me and all my crew are going back and forth. Ben, Hing and I now we are on our way to CTRM. As I have mentioned, this MOU along with the one for the Defense University are critical to an increase in sales, not to mention for heightening our credibility, visibility and the chance to put us into other new areas. We are in a beautiful, large van and I chose the way back seat both to be near my laptop case in the trunk area, but also so I can sleep. Ben and Hing are speaking Mandarin, so I can do as I want until we get there.

6/8/10
5:24 PM Malaysian time, 5:24 AM EST
En Route to Kuala Lumpur

We got to CTRM with time to spare so we went to an open-air café for lunch. Hing had very nicely packed sandwiches for me and I enjoyed myself with some iced tea, especially since it was not uncomfortably warm yet. Our meeting began after an overview of their system from their head of operations, Wan, who we had dinner with last night, at about 2:00 with various members of the composite company. I spoke about how we could work together, some of the new product ideas we had been working on for them and the Defense University. As it turned out, they had been working on an idea of their own for composite housing and it looked very possible to marry it with ours to create a hybrid system. There were other areas where we could work together and everyone seemed happy and excited. We signed the MOU and took some pictures, one of which we will use for the next edition of the Ideal Almanac. After a plant tour, we looked at two pieces of land on their site that might work for a composites plant and spoke about partnering there with one of their divisions specializing in new products. I have a sample of their material to bring back to the U.S. to see how we can bond our product to theirs. I will write a schedule for various products, testing and other areas to send next week. Then we can all agree of what needs to be done and the necessary timing.

We got what we wanted. They are very nice people and the potential for both companies is huge. We are on our way back and just passed through a speed trap, which we were thankfully not caught in.

6/9/10
6:08 PM Malaysian time, 6:08 AM EST
Taxi in Kuala Lumpur

After we got back to the hotel last night I worked more, bought some food, walked a little and ate. I got up early and exercised with my bands, almost creating a commotion when the serving table I had anchored my bands to fell over. Luckily, there was no damage and I went outside to the pool area to walk. I called Wendy, who is good, checked in with Alice with an update and called Brett for his progress regarding the hurricane window and door sales launch.

After breakfast I met Ben and Hing to sign some papers and work on the strategy for the day. They were going to the IPO meeting and I went with Abul. I would meet them about noon. Abul was with the same two men who had gone with us on the last trip to the University. We got there in good time and were ushered through all security points easily. It helps when your compatriots are former high-ranking members of the military themselves. We met with one of the representatives from the Defense University from last time. He was exceptionally pleasant and was very excited about the renderings for the new projects, our new relationship with CTRM and that we would all be working together. He also offered their test facilities to help with the new products we would be joint developing. We got him an updated version of the MOU, which would be from IJ Malaysia, and he said he would have his legal department work on it right way to get it back to us by early next week. On the way out, we met the new man in charge, another major general. The last head of the Defense University had moved up to an extremely important job in the army, so we were dealing with very senior people. Then it was over to the IPO meeting and the progress was slow but steady. Before lunch, I gave a short speech on the importance of getting IPO out for later in June and how it is imperative that there are no stopping points. At about 2:30, the lack of sleep got to me and I laid down in the next room. Ben saw me and sent me back to the hotel via Hing to rest for awhile and after a good two hour nap, I am on my way back there now. Traffic in Kuala Lumpur during rush hour is intense, more so than even New York City. In fact, I could have walked it faster, but did not want to due to the rain and extreme heat. I will be there in about fifteen minutes and then I have no idea how long the balance of the meeting will last.

6/9/10
10:21 PM Malaysian time, 10:21 AM EST
Crowne Plaza Hotel Kuala Lumpur

I got to the meeting in time to sign the needed documents and we were all out of there by 7:45 PM. PK, Ben, Ku, Hing, Jossie, Titan and I went to dinner at the pleasant open-air restaurant we had been to before. It was a calm, productive dinner where we spoke about what had happened, plans for the future, getting the final pieces of information for the public offering and my next trip here, probably in about eight weeks. Then it was back here, where I will pack and go to sleep. I will check the office once more before doing so.

6/10/10
7:48 AM Malaysia time, 7:48 PM EST
Kuala Lumpur Airport

I got up before my 3:30 AM alarm, exercised, walked along the outside pool in view of one of the Twin Towers, rushed back upstairs, showered, finished packing, had a quick breakfast downstairs and now I am here at the airport. There was no traffic and I was almost through to immigration when the guard looked at my two carryon bags and decided one was too large. A primary rule of traveling is never to argue with a security guard, so I turned around and checked one bag. It will make travel until Newark easier but will delay me at the other end. I got through to the lounge without any further problem. I even remembered to buy chocolate for my crew, so all is well. My first attempt at calling Wendy was unsuccessful, but I did leave a message on the answering machine as I have done many times before, announcing where I am in the world and a short message. She likes to listen to them when I am away. It makes her smile and she can hear my voice anytime. Meanwhile, the airport window is showing a rainstorm that may or may not make it to the airfield. I was not able to buy any food for the long trip from Taiwan to Newark, but I hope I can do it on the next leg of the trip. I have a lot of work to do and will keep going until I feel like stopping. There is World Cup fever here; they talk about it a lot on television and in the local newspaper.

6/10/10
12:15 PM Taipei time, 12:15 AM EST
En route to Taipei

We have less than two hours to go and I am already starting to have trouble sitting. I have a five hour layover and then about 15 hours to Newark. I will relax once I am on the next plane. I got the template done for the new triad partnership between IJ worldwide, CTRM and University Defense. I will probably flesh it out later. I don't think anyone will have a problem with the structure. Once that is defined, it will make it much easier for everyone to deal with each other, create trust and exchange information.

6/10/10
4:12 PM Taiwan time, 4:12 AM EST
EVA Airlines Lounge

We landed a little late, which made no difference since I have a long layover. When we boarded, I helped a woman to store her violin above my seat. As we were walking off, we got to talking and it turns out she is a dentist from the U.S. whose husband got a job in Asia so she went with him. She was also fortunate to find a job here and they have been relocated for a few years. She is going back for a month visit and her husband will follow soon. She is a pleasant woman who went to Princeton and Harvard but with no attitude. I wish her well on her journey to Los Angeles.

When I first got to this lounge, I figured I would boost my power supply and to my major concern, I realized I had put my laptop charger in my other piece of luggage. I did not have enough power for the ride home. Since I hoped to put in a lot of work, I set off on an adventure to find some food and a charger for the trip back. The first store I went to did not have the right brand, so I kept walking and found a place where I bought two small salads. Then it was off further away to the last computer store that I had been told about. If this one did not have it, I was out of luck, they did and I am charging my battery as I write. I am hopeful they also have an outlet on the plane, although I will probably have about four or five hours of capacity by the time this one is fully back on line. On the way back, I bought eight lotus leaf bundles filled with chicken and sticky rice. I have no idea what they taste like, but I have been on long flights without enough food and it is not fun, so I am hoping to be okay with the provisions I have left. Currently, there is a thunderstorm going on outside. I have to remember not to eat the lotus leaves!

6/10/10
10:43 PM EST
In flight towards home

Less than 11:00 hours to land. 604 mph 32002 ft.

We are somewhere over the Pacific Ocean just moving past Japan. The plane seems to be running a bit late and we are scheduled to get in before 9:30. As per my wife's great advice, I am not getting up at 4:00 AM, but probably an hour or more later. Then I will go straight to tennis and meet my brother.

I have more work to do on the project proposals for our new partners. The people around me are asleep or watching their video screens. Time has stopped, so I will take advantage of it, be calm and work until I pass out again. Now that I have unlimited power, I can even watch some of the movies I brought; a nice treat.

6/11/10
12:06 PM EST
In flight

I finished the initial project write-up for the first five projects. YES! I will send it to the VPs for review when I get back in the office tomorrow. Time for some sleep.

6/11/10
6:32 PM EST
In flight

We have 2:51 to go; our estimated time of arrival is 9:24 PM. If that holds and my luggage is on time, I should be home by 10:30, which means I can be asleep before midnight. I am going a little stir crazy and want to be home. This log is ready for review by my VPs tomorrow. I want them to pay particular attention to the project information for our people in Asia. If they approve, I will send it to Ben for review and get it to CTRM and the DU on Monday. I will go back to editing last year's book for awhile. Food should be coming in about an hour, which is good since I did not like my main food supply of sticky rice with chicken. The flight attendants did, however, so thankfully it did not go to waste. My emergency oatmeal package is in my suitcase under the plane; not good planning on my part, but a very minor issue.

6/12/10
4:31 PM EST
Home, NJ

I got home around 11:00 PM on Thursday. It was wonderful to see Wendy and Bailey and I got to sleep by about 12:30 AM. Yesterday, I slept in until 5:15 but still had to drag myself out of bed. Tennis with my brother was very pleasant but it was tough to keep my motivation and energy up, as anticipated. Then it was to the office and a day of catching up on paperwork and meetings. Things went well here while I was gone and our VPs reviewed my project proposals for our new partners in Malaysia with a few small additions. I sent it to Ben and will check with him on Monday morning so I can send it out to our people in Malaysia. Al is in England with her new grandchild and her duties were ably covered by Eileen and Mike. Business for the month has been good and our projects are on schedule except for making a sample of the acoustic buoy. The replacement labels for the oil company that I wrote about should be ready by the middle of June.

I got more than ten, very welcomed hours of sleep last night and then went biking. I got a nice surprise part of the way through; Uncle Dave had finished his long ride early and met me. We had a very nice, peaceful time together. I puttered around my flowers for awhile and then had lunch with Kayla. We were speaking about her major, environmental biology, when I got an idea. After we got back, I wrote it in my lab notebook. It is a new type of support area for the land boats. Just in from the ocean, we will have staggered layers of storm surge protectors. The gaps between the barriers plus the flexible cabling keeping them together will enable some of the water from a storm surge to get through, thereby not breaching the wall permanently. Behind the wall will be a new ecosystem making a salt water lagoon with trees, a fish hatchery and some salt water crops. This area will help provide not only protection for the houses behind them but also a food supply that can generate money. Behind that is another row of barriers and then the land houses. This intermediate area will create a great buffer zone for the houses and add a valuable food source. I will check with our VPs to see what they think on Monday. For tonight, we are going over to Cliff and Barb's.

6/13/10
4:35 PM EST
Home, NJ

We had a great, relaxing time at Barb and Cliff's last night. Jess is pregnant and due sometime in December. It is the first of the next generation for us, which also moves Wendy and me one higher on the line. When our parents pass, we will be the oldest generation. We may have grandchildren within the next ten years, which is a sobering but mostly good thought. I do not mind getting older. I will work harder to stay in shape in all ways.

I played tennis outdoors today with my brother. It was beautiful and my jet lag appears to be mostly gone after another good night's sleep. I biked and came back to look at the building I want to buy. It occurred to me I did not have to have all of the cash necessary and could simply get a mortgage, the old fashioned way. We will see; I don't have to make a decision for another eighteen months. Afterward, it was home for lunch and then to the office to bring my clothes for the week and complete some paperwork. I sent the project proposal for the new Malaysian partners to our export attorney for review. He needs to stay on board to keep us out of potential trouble, especially since our Asian group wants to go into military and defense applications. I also sent more suggestions to Jack and Brett regarding our patent application. Some of them are pretty far out, but there are no limits when reaching for the stars. I am trying to figure the furthest edges of where we can go with our new composites. By then, it had begun raining, which was great for my plants, I picked up dinner and am now home. Wendy had lunch with all of our kids and everyone had a very pleasant time. I look forward to a peaceful evening and a crazy day tomorrow, packed with meetings that could all mean great advances.

JUNE

6/14/10
7:05 PM EST
Home, NJ

Jack and Zack are making samples to give to all potential sales people involved. I got a call from Jerry from AL. A small group from a company that does technical and repairs for AL is ready to break off and form their own company. Jerry thought they might benefit from our support and give us a chance to get into the business. I agreed and am waiting for their call. Our export attorney says we need a formal agreement with the U.S. government regarding sending technical information to Malaysia. It will cost about $7500, but I feel we have no choice and will go ahead.

Paul, my tennis instructor, goes in for a hernia operation this Thursday. He is out for about three weeks. This Wednesday I will bike and I have replacements already the next two games. I hope he has an easy time of it. Mr. Obama is trying to pressure BP to put money into a trust fund to pay people currently living with the Gulf oil spill. BP has already lost a fortune in stock value and to their corporate brand by the way they have handled this disaster. We continue to work on the global warming floating house program and have developed a new ecosystem idea to build between the initial barriers and housing to act as buffer. It will also feature a salt water lagoon with a fish farm and various trees. A lot is happening. Mostly, I just have to let our people move forward on their own, though sometimes that is hard.

6/16/10
5:33 PM EST
My office, NJ

We got the actual prices for the composite presses and tooling today and they are in line with our own estimates, which is great. We heard from Al and her new English baby granddaughter is precious. She returns this weekend and it will be good to have her back. Business has been good for the month so far. I am hoping the U.S. recovery continues so we can build on it. I hope to get a signed MOU from the Defense University tomorrow. My trip back to Malaysia is now set for the first full week of August. I hope to go on actual sales call with our partners with high ranking government officials and their customers.

Tennis outside was beautiful this morning. I had three heavy workouts in a row. Wendy and I had breakfast with Kayla before she drove to her camp for the summer. I miss her already, but she will be back to visit a couple of times. My son Ben called me last night. He is liking his job much better and successfully completed a major in-house electrical reinstallation. They also like his composing abilities and may use him for actual commercial production. It is wonderful to hear him happy. There has not been much word from Alex, only that his internship is going well and his course is boring.

No Road Is Ever Straight

6/18/10
5:05 PM EST
My office, NJ

The ISO audit has been moved to July, my trip is set for next Friday and Wendy is okay with leaving Thursday night. I am nearing the end of the final edit for last year's book and look forward to a break afterward. BP is setting up a 20 billion dollar trust fund to pay people for the problems from the oil leak, which is still going on. Brett has been testing more hurricane panels and our research there is almost done.

6/19/10
2:52 PM EST
Home, NJ

Elana emailed me last night with an offer to train this morning at my office and I rarely pass up the chance to work out with her. She is a tough taskmaster and lets nothing pass regarding form, motion or intensity. In other words, I had a very tough, but invigorating workout. I like being around her. She is a positive force and our time together was very pleasant. She even made me a new type of muffin. I love her baking and ate a bunch of them in preparation for my solo bike ride back at home. It was about 80°F, but I had plenty of water and an apple, so I had little trouble finishing the route. After lunch, I thought I would plant some new Honeysuckle seeds I bought, but after reading the directions I had to wait. They have to soak for a day first, so maybe I can get them in tomorrow.

I decided it was time to write about something that has been bothering me. Being an American and traveling the world means that I often hear what people think about us. Sometimes I am called on to verbally defend what our government is doing, but more often people want to know about the U.S. and our people. They love America. It seems like two separate subjects: our leaders versus the country with our people. I understand the way we seem to others and often cannot defend some of our policies. Sometimes I simply say that if I was in power, I might do things differently and mention they probably don't agree with everything their leaders do. They usually agree and the subject changes.

But religion is different; it is a much more personal matter and one that cannot be as simply explained as where you live. Maybe it is because it is such a personal thing that crosses over world boundaries that makes it such a volatile issue. I, for one, do not normally bring up the subject, but will not shrink from it if discussed. The problem is that being Jewish often gives people in many parts of the world an immediate link to Israel and the combination of the two do not often get a great reaction. You might say that I should be strong enough to want to fight for both my religion and the origin of my people and normally you would be right. However, getting into a fight with anyone regarding such an amorphous and emotionally based subject is a no win situation.

JUNE

Being an American Jew traveling the world makes it an even more difficult issue. When going through parts of Asia with high Muslim populations, I have been cautioned by my people there, while not to keep it a secret, not to broadcast my religion. As I said, I do not advertise that I am Jewish when I leave the U.S. In fact, I leave my religious necklace at home and am generally extremely quiet when traveling, being courteous, polite, and not looking for confrontation or trouble. However here is where the problem lies. I will not tell people I am not Jewish or an American and I will not stand and listen to either of them being berated. Israel is a slightly different matter, since I am not Israeli, a fine point many non-Jews do not understand. I have not been there and do not agree with a lot of the things they do. I have friends in Asia and want to do business there. I do not have to be Jewish to them, as they don't have to be Muslim to me. It does not have to be an issue where we all agree to get along, do business and help each other. I have often said that the one true path to peace is when everyone is dealing with each other because you will never kill someone you trade with, as long as the relationship is positive to you both.

I have been reading the Koran, the Muslim holy book, and like the Old Testament and the Dead Sea Scrolls, it is very violent and preaches a specific point of view as to what is correct, what is acceptable and who you can deal with. I am still reading it and am hoping to find information that will enable me to counter claims, if they come up, that all Jews are bad (and since I am one, I am also bad). The Koran does talk about righteous non-Muslims and how they are okay and I am hoping I can someday reach that category. In the meantime, I will keep reading and hope to garner enough information to counter any claims if they come up. So far, everyone has treated me with the same high level of respect and good will that I have extended to them. I feel that, given time, our religions will not matter. For now, I need to be ready if that higher state of trust cannot be reached before a breach occurs. It will be a wonderful world when we can all treat each other as individuals and we are all judged upon our individual actions. I will continue to tread carefully and hope to build relationships so they will have some chance of lasting before outside forces can tear them apart.

6/20/10
9:48 PM EST
Home, NJ

It was Father's Day here in the U.S. It is a role I take very seriously and to be thought of as a good dad is extremely important to me. I got a call from Kayla on the way to play tennis this morning. She could not come home because she was undergoing training to be re-certified as a swimming instructor. She wished me a happy holiday and was very sorry she could not come home. I miss her a lot.

After tennis, biking and gardening (yes, I did go and buy more plants and dirt and put them in), Wendy, Ben, Katie, Alex and I went over to Irene and

No Road Is Ever Straight

David's house to celebrate Father's day. My parents, my brother, Eve, Rachel, Jeff, Rebecca and her new boyfriend were all there and it was a lot of fun. My nephew Jeremy and Ira's daughter Lisa were away, but maybe we will see them at my parents' 60th wedding anniversary party the end of next month. My dad is going to be 86 years old on his next birthday. He has defied all odds and is not only walking around and alive, but still enjoying life. He says he can't walk as much as he could before, and may cut out one of his medications. He has gone his own way with treatment since his first cancer was diagnosed more than twenty years ago and at this point his doctors leave him alone to do as he sees best. I feel extremely fortunate, viewing my life and the wonderful people around me. I owe a lot back and hope I am spreading some positive energy in return.

6/21/10
4:55 PM EST
My office, NJ

Al is back! Two men came in who work for a spinoff group from Alcatel-Lucent. They want to start their own business to work on legacy products supporting them in software and new updates. They may want/need some help from us to get started and I offered them the extra space we have in Millburn. It could be a new hardware area for us; they take their end, we would do ours and who knows, it could be another chance at something new. There have been more growing pains with our companies getting along worldwide. Part of my job is to keep the wheels of communications greased. It rained after I planted yesterday, which was a very good thing.

6/22/10
5:18 PM EST
My office, NJ

I finished editing my latest book!!!! It is big news for me and now it goes to Katie for the final edit. Our MAC guys will probably read through it one more time to make sure I did not say anything that could cause trouble and then we go to artwork and the press. We are scheduled for release in August. It is a very sweet moment to have this completed and I am very happy. The new Ideal Jacobs Malaysia website is almost ready to go online and it looks good. As time allows, I am emailing information about the new composite to people in our database. I hope to get through almost everyone. It will probably be about 4000 people by the time I finish.

6/23/10
4:43 PM EST
Home, NJ

It is very hot here in New Jersey at 91°F. I am glad I played tennis early this morning. We had a meeting with Dan regarding day lighting for the new global warming floating houses and it looks like a natural fit. Brett will make some drawings for the interior of the first projected house so Dan can figure out how much to daylight, meaning bringing sunlight into the houses with solar tubes. We feel that people in Malaysia probably don't need air-conditioning, but we still have to power evening lights, a refrigerator and other electronics. We can probably use bottled propane for the stove. It is a very interesting project and everyone is excited to be involved. I sketched out an idea last night to make kit houses like Sears and Roebuck did during the last century. We would save on not having to put in foundations for the pilings or labor to assemble and could then sell the kits much more cheaply; another idea to give to John for review. We are also going to create a version for New Hampshire, which will be different to fit that very different geographic region. There continue to be growing pains with IJM. We are trying to increase our systems to take care of the potential problems and it is tough to stay ahead.

6/24/10
8:10 PM EST
The Berkshires

After a hot workout this morning on the tennis court, it was back to the office with more work on the global warming housing project and a potential breakthrough in the manufacture of our panels with a new idea I hope will not only extend the life of our panels, especially in wet conditions, but also create an additional patentable area. The background on our patent searches continues and I am hopeful our attorney will be ready with a full report within two weeks and then we can finish the application. It was then home to pack, pick up Wendy and up here to Massachusetts. The ride was longer than usual with a lot of traffic. It is strange how the car flow goes. It is slow for some miles and suddenly opens up with no cause showing for the delay. Regardless, we made it and were off to see Bunny and Jeff and pick up one of their spare cars since I am on the road for business in the morning.

We were going to go to a Chinese restaurant for dinner, but both Wendy's parents said it had gone down in quality. When we passed a new Tex Mex restaurant, I suggested we go there. The uniqueness of my suggestion because I only recently began to explore Mexican food, was such that Wendy immediately agreed. Once seated, two things became immediately apparent. The waiter we had, Daniel, was a little "slow" mentally, which only created admiration for him for trying as tough a job as being a server and the restaurant itself for not only hiring him but giving him a helper. The second fact was there was obvious trouble in their kitchen and the service was going to take a lot of time. We had no more plans for the evening and I was determined to react to the waiter pleasantly. We started speaking with the couple next to us who were also waiting and it was a nice way to pass the time. About 45 minutes later, however, the wait had gotten to us and others, including the couple next to us who had walked out, and my wife was on her feet going to look for the manager. You may not know Wendy well, but trust me, when she goes after someone they will know they have been spoken to. We finally got our food at that moment, ate quickly and gave Daniel a good tip; the problems in the kitchen were not his fault. He mentioned we should come back for lunch. Coming back there was the last thing we planned, but I asked him if the kitchen was better during the midday and he smiled and said no. It struck me as very funny, both for his honesty and the smile when he said it.

It is my belief that leadership has to start from the top. There was plenty of help in the restaurant and there was no reason why the entire operation was running so badly, except for bad people in command. I modestly believe that given one day, I could radically change the corporate culture and make it immensely more profitable. Regardless, it is the way of most businesses. People put their life savings into operations when they have no clue about customer service, efficiency, effective systems and making money. This place can only have first time customers because probably no one will go back. I do not give it much hope for survival, which is too bad. They have the basics, but their management team is lacking.

Afterward, we went to a nearby shop, bought some chocolate and came back here. I have two phone calls to make tonight; the first to our Malaysian partners at the Defense University and the second with the composite company. I am hoping I can jump start our projects with both. The weather has turned beautiful and I plan to sleep outside on the porch. I will search for lightning bugs and sleep to the sounds of nature and occasional cars going nearby.

President Obama fired the general in charge of Afghanistan and is putting in General Petreus. The overall consensus is that it is a good choice.

6/25/10
5:40 PM EST
The Berkshires

I generally love sleeping on the porch here and get a great night's sleep. Some of the lightening bugs were out, but I did not sleep well. I got up at 6:00 AM and was out before 7:00 to meet Brett. We went over the plans for the composites and agreed that the global warming house was the fast track project everyone seemed to want to get started right away. If we can get the groups in Malaysia to officially sign on a partner, then that should be enough to get either loans or grants to begin immediate construction of a plant.

6/26/10
1:58 PM EST
The Berkshires

Dinner was very pleasant last night except for the phone call from Kayla. The people running the organization at her summer job are incompetent and everything is in hysteria. My daughter thrives on order and intelligent structure and she is getting none of that. I told her if it gets too bad and they were not doing as they promised for her employment, then she could come home and work for me. It was very upsetting to hear her crying and unhappy, but she called back later, spoke to Wendy and was much better. I am very protective of my children and want to enforce ruthless retribution when any of them are wronged.

I got a better night's sleep, but it was still not great on the porch. The weather was cool and beautiful and I maybe saw one firefly. After a wonderful breakfast of oatmeal, banana, cinnamon and blueberries it was off biking. It was a spectacular ride and it gave me additional time to think. I emailed both Ben and Hing regarding the legality of starting a joint venture with CTRM and because of our public offering, it is not possible right now. On the way, I also saw some wild turkeys, which are fascinating to watch. After a shower, Wendy and I took Jeff out for an extended Father's Day lunch. It was fun and he looked like he had a great time. Then I dropped off Wendy and she and Bunny were going to hang out together for the afternoon while I gassed up the car for tomorrow's ride home and got dinner for tonight's Prairie Home Companion show at Tanglewood.

6/27/10
9:13 PM EST
Home, NJ

Tanglewood was a little rainy last night but still beautiful and the show Prairie Home Companion was as good as usual. It was a very fun night. We dropped off the parking pass back to Bunny, who gets to stay in a special member's lot. Then it was home to a reasonable night of sleep. I woke up an hour early and since Wendy was up also, we closed the house, ate a quick breakfast and were back home before noon. Our house in the Berkshires will now be rented for a month to friends of Bunny's and I hope they enjoy it. This is the first time we ever rented it out and I am not sure if I like the idea, but we shall see. I went biking this afternoon alone because Uncle Dave could not go and stopped at our friends' on the way home. Their eldest son Alex is interning for us in July and his father Doug asked me to wait while he changed his clothes, as he decided to ride back to my house with me. There were two minor problems with this. One was he was not tired from the ride I had already done and he was on a thin tired road bike as opposed to my thick tired mountain bike. Suffice it to say, I saw a lot of his back but it was still pleasant. After getting home and watering my plants, it was off to the office with my clothes for the week and catching up on emails.

6/29/10
4:43 PM EST
My office, NJ

We have our first telecom cabinet to redesign from scratch. We will get the customer's current cost this week and will need to be at least 40% lower including testing, which is an interesting challenge. It was a day of a lot of paperwork. Things are moving forward.

No Road Is Ever Straight

6/30/10
5:00 PM EST
My office, NJ

We are almost done with the first design of the global warming floating house project. Eric has to tweak the last rendering which shows the area adjacent to the ocean or river that has the potential to overflow, flood or have a storm surge. The double storm wall should slow the water's surge and help with soil erosion and the tree buffer should help stop the flow inland. The salt-tolerant vegetation we plant in the inland flooding area will help to purify the water and the fish farm will help to feed the people living in the houses, which are protected by an additional storm surge wall. Brett will test our new anti-pirate cannon. One of our reps thinks the U.S. Coast Guard might have an interest, which is a very cool thing to help stop bad people and without killing them. I heard from Kayla last night. Camp is now going well and she is due in on Thursday night. Alex is getting in on Friday and dinner is a good possibility with both.

JULY

7/1/10
5:27 PM EST
My office, NJ

Today was our 4th of July office picnic. I know it was a little early, but it was the best day schedule wise. Wendy was able to come as well as two of our interns. It was a great time and I think everyone enjoyed it. Our interns will now be moving into a marketing survey for hurricane and tornado panels made of our composite materials. It is good timing they are here since we will have a lot of research to do. We have been back and forth with the export attorney. It seems that we are responsible for our military/defense inventions outside the U.S. even if they go past who we sell them to. In other words, if we help create a product with our Malaysian partners and they sell it into China and we know about it, then we are responsible for the security breach with the U.S. government.

7/2/10
5:10 PM EST
My office, NJ

Today marks the beginning of the Independence Day weekend here in the U.S., which is a fantastic time of celebration, parades, sport events, firework displays and remembering how good we have it here. I had lunch with Kayla, Wendy and Barbara before Kayla goes back to camp tonight. She looks great and I will miss her. An additional treat: Alex is home for the night, so we are all having dinner. I am leaving a little early to go see them.

7/3/10
5:07 PM EST
Home, NJ

It has been a momentous 24 hours. I got home last night to a wonderful dinner with Wendy, Alex and Kayla and then Wendy and Kayla went to the movies. Wendy and I had a talk, which prompted some major reevaluation on my part.

I am 54 years old and it is time to make some changes. My ability to continue at the current pace is beginning to ebb. The current and ever increasing stress and demands on my time worldwide are increasing and I decided on the following changes. This morning I ordered a duplicate piece of exercise equipment that I have in my office so when it arrives I will no longer need to go into the office before going to play tennis. I will start sleeping between 30 minutes to an hour longer. I will also begin leaving the office at 5:00 PM each night instead of my normal 5:45. This means I will start watching my email sometime around 5:00 AM instead of 4:15 AM each workday, which probably won't cause major trouble. It means I will get home early enough and in better shape mentally so Wendy and I can take Bailey for a short walk or take it a little easier. It doesn't mean I won't answer my email and it doesn't mean everything won't get done. It simply means I will sleep a little later and get home a little earlier. I also hope that the extra energy I should get will help me to think clearer and better for the time I am working. I will also be more creative when I am not in the office. Experience has shown that a lot of my best ideas happen in off peak hours and, since we need those ideas on an ever increasing basis, this should be a good situation for everyone. I am curious to see if the company does better with me in the office a little less. My guess is it will since I am no longer in day to day operations anyway.

I emailed with Ben this morning in China. I got an idea with CTRM to utilize their original ultra small plane product for newly rich Asian millionaires. Ben will run a quick market survey and then we can talk to CTRM and NDUM. My main jobs now are finding and bringing in new customers, creating new product lines, fixing problems and overall management worldide.

I went riding with Uncle Dave today and he will check on the costs if we buy the building I wanted in April 2012. That will be one year before our lease is up and I think we will not be spending much more to rent as opposed to buying. I feel reasonably confident that the banks will give us a mortgage for the building, but I have no idea what other collateral they might want. Wendy and Alex are in the Berkshires and should be at the James Taylor & Carol King concert in Tanglewood by now. There will be many thousands of people there, which is way too crowded for my taste, so I hope they have a good time together. I went to see my parents today and they seem well. Bailey is looking contented since I just fed him. Kayla went back to camp last night. I still have no idea if our inventions will sell. It is like my writing; it was never taken seriously until its importance with our branding and marketing became evident. I will have to prove myself here as well.

7/4/10
10:18 PM EST
Home, NJ

The fourth of July!

In my quest to change my life to the new goals I spoke about yesterday, I have been informing people about my change of hours to make sure I force myself to do it. Both of my sons were surprised and happy at the change and thought it would be good. I played tennis with my wonderful brother and then went biking. I stalked my usual building and even heard from Uncle Dave how much it would cost for a mortgage although we still have 2 ½ years before our current lease is up. Wendy and Alex got back from the Berkshires.

The concert was great and they had a wonderful time together. After a lot of sleep, last night's bad headache is mostly gone. I am hoping for some more good rest tonight to get rid of the balance.

It is hard to believe it is already July and more than half of the year is gone. The days are already getting shorter again. I will make plans for my usual Florida visit to my in-laws in January. I was watching a program on television about what is right about the U.S. and there are certainly many good things. It is an extraordinary place to live, work and thrive. The chances for success are abundant and allow the optimum in following your own dreams. The level of self expression and personal rights is amazingly high and most of the time people let everyone else have their space and get along. It is truly a paradise for those who want to rely on their own wits, will-power, innovation, competitiveness and need to go for it. It is one of the blessings we have and this should always be remembered. A lot of people have died, been injured and have made great sacrifices, so we have and keep it. Although I consider myself an internationalist, I am an American in determination, spirit and will to fight for what we believe in. As always, I try to count my blessings continually and living here is definitely one of them.

7/5/10
2:37 PM EST
Home, NJ

It is a holiday and except for some emails from IJ Europe and IJM and a note from Mike that his iPhone was destroyed yesterday in a wet sprinkler accident and he needed a replacement, things are calm. The general buzz is that people like the idea of reproducing the two-seat airplane from CTRM and there is also interest here in the U.S. and possibly Europe. There are tons of regulations to get through, but the initial interest is heartening. Now I need to think of more non-military and defense ideas worldwide so we can produce and distribute them anywhere. I played tennis this morning with one of my tougher opponents. It was very warm and it should be about 100°F by late this afternoon. I was prepared with lots of sunscreen and water to stay out there for awhile. It was a very good match, although I was losing. The courts were crowded and we were kicked off about an hour and a quarter later. I exercised at home before and after and by then I had enough for the day.

I have been watching my computer carrying bag for a week since we came back from the Berkshires waiting to be repacked for traveling. I accomplished that today along with making enough pancakes for my weekend breakfasts for the next few months, so it has been very productive. As I mentioned, it is very hot outside and the sprinkler system only works for the front lawn and not the flowers in the backyard, so I will change my clothes in a little while to go water the back. It has been very dry in New Jersey for the past few weeks and water restrictions are beginning to appear. I hope it rains a lot soon. We are scheduled to go to Barbara and Cliff's for a cookout in about 90 minutes, so I had better get moving on the watering. I need to think about new ideas and I am hoping the change in my schedule will help.

7/6/10
4:10 PM EST
My office, NJ

Last time I checked, it was 104°F and the humidity was starting to climb. I played tennis early but it was still close to 80°. Brett, Al, Mike and I had a meeting with our three interns Alex, Jack and Zack. They now have their jobs defined regarding the marketing information necessary for the composite materials and should be finished before the summer is done. I am going through one final edit for the book, cutting out duplicate, unnecessary and sensitive information and also wrote the foreword, acknowledgments and dedication. I started sending out the global warming floating house community idea to people and the response has been good. It would be nice to get enough so we can actually build it, but it will be a massive and expensive effort and I am not sure if we will get the necessary support. As per my resolution, I plan to be leaving at 5:00 PM for home today, which will be strange. I will probably water the plants in the backyard as they will be thirsty from the heat.

7/7/10
6:58 PM EST
Home, NJ

I have left early the last two days and except for getting delayed in the parking lot for a phone call at work, I am usually home by 5:20. So far so good, so I will endeavor to keep it up. My Total Gym is due in by Monday so I will then engage phase two of my plan, which is to sleep a little later, workout in the basement and go directly to tennis. It reached about 97°F today and is supposed to get progressively cooler as the week continues. I went to a funeral of a member of my temple today. I had not had contact with Eva Lou for probably five years, but we had been friends in the previous decade. She was remembered today as tough, fiercely loyal and a good friend. Her husband passed her about a decade ago; I hope they are together and happy once again. Funerals are often very sad, but she had lived a long, fruitful and happy life so it was as pleasant as it could have been. Alex, the head of our interns, is having a lot of good experience not only working on the market research for the composite plastics, but also leading his peers. All three of our interns are fine young men and it would be great to have them back as potential full time executives in the future. I am always looking for good talent.

7/8/10
4:35 PM EST
My office, NJ

The heat wave is starting to break but high humidity has now become a part of our weather. Playing tennis outside is a little crazy, but at least we do it early in the morning. I felt an injury this morning in my left foot and I am hoping that rest will take care of it by tomorrow. If not, it could be a painful journey. We have to set up video conferencing on my MAC laptop for a conference with our people in Malaysia helping us to go public. My plane and hotel are now set for my trip to Ottawa in two weeks. I just need to secure a car and driver. My timing is too close to get a car and find my locations for calls and besides, the stress and potential liability of driving in another country is not worth the effort. I will get there on a Tuesday and leave Wednesday afternoon. I will bring extra clothes in case weather stops the flight home. I have emails out to customers for potential calls there.

7/9/10
4:43 PM EST
My office, NJ

My new "Total Gym" an all-in-one work-out machine, just arrived here at the office, though it was supposed to go to my house. Regardless, I will set it up and should be able to start sleeping a little later starting Monday. The first stage of marketing research for the composite materials will be done Monday. They are putting a new cap on the well in the Gulf and British Petroleum says it will be leaking more oil over the weekend until the pump is working. They also said their new well to divert oil from this broken one should be done by the end of the month. The disaster continues.

My trip to Ottawa is now rescheduled for late August. Kayla comes home tonight for one day from camp! The new rendering for our air cannon-anti-pirate boat is ready and I sent it out for evaluation. One of these days, one of these inventions will take off. The more we do, the better our chances.

7/10/10
4:03 PM EST
Home, NJ

David and I had a new compatriot on our bicycle ride today, Howard. I have known him for many years. We all went to the same high school, although he was in David's grade and one year older than me. Interestingly, he too is in the printing business. What are the odds of having three people in the same field all riding together at one time? He is an exceptionally pleasant man and even though three is often a bad number for communication in any group, it was a pleasant journey. The printing industry of two or three decades ago, where we all prospered, has changed in radical ways. Much of what was printed is now done via computer or online and never reaches paper. The balance like annual reports and standard printing is under continual price attack and many have left the bushiness. David has moved to real estate and ad specialties, we moved into labels and other niche areas long ago, but Howard has mostly stayed in printing. We are all under enormous continual price pressure and competition from all sectors. We are forced, encouraged or, in our case, obsessed to reinvent ourselves and utilize our brains to find new exciting places to be. Niche markets with good profits are sometimes already available, but often they have to be created. That is our space.

After lunch with Wendy, Kayla and her friend Mira, the girls left to go see Kayla's friend from high school. Soon after, I received one of those phone calls that all parents dread. They had been in a car accident. Someone had hit them from behind and she had tapped the car in front of her. I raced to get there with Kay on my cell extremely upset and wanting me to be there instantly. I moved as quickly as I could and her phone call was heartbreaking. When I finally arrived, her car was in bad shape, but fortunately the girls were only shaken up. After the police report was done, Wendy had gotten there with Alex, who took Wendy's car while we dropped off Kayla's car at a local collision shop. I know the owner from previous accidents and, even though it was Saturday, he was there. We took everyone home and after filing the report with the insurance company, everyone seems reasonably calm now. Wendy will take the girls back to camp tomorrow. We want to make sure they have no bad affects after a good night's sleep, which also means both Kayla and Mira get the royal treatment tonight and anything they want. At the moment, they are calm, relaxing and watching television. They were extremely fortunate to get through this with only damage to the car. As I told Kay, it is a car, a piece of machinery and can be replaced. She and Mira are what I care about. She was very happy I did not hold her responsible, as it was not her fault. It is just as well that our trip to the Jersey Shore was postponed. If I had already gone, I would have felt terrible for not being there. I am a dad first and foremost and that responsibility and honor will never be taken for granted.

7/12/10
4:49 PM EST
My office, NJ

The non-lethal air cannon idea seems to garnering some interest and we will run more tests tomorrow. It is a product we can design and build. Tomorrow I start my new hours for coming in after tennis instead of first thing in the morning. It will be very strange. We passed our ISO 14001 environmental audit with no problems. It is a wonderful thing to have a great team and system in place.

7/13/10
4:45 PM EST
My office, NJ

As it turns out, we will need a scale model for the global warming house for a National Guard convention we plan to attend in August. We are also planning on doing a scale model of the new air cannon attack boat. Mike and Vinnie make the house and Alex and Jack will work on the boat. Brett is currently testing the air cannon for length and if all coordinates well, we should be ready with some incredible presentations by next month. I also put out a feeler for our local state senator to maybe buy a building in Millburn for a new facility. There is no word on Kayla's car with the insurance company. I will start following up on Thursday.

7/14/10
3:00 PM EST
My office, NJ

We will probably change our patent work to our export attorney's firm because I like the way they operate. The patent for the composite and other areas need a lot of attention. We continue to spend a fortune in R&D. I hope we are right that it will bear fruit.

7/15/10
4:40 PM EST
My office, NJ

I have developed a certain uneasiness by our not having a capability to make large composite panels of various types, so today we took action. We will have two suppliers to outsource orders by the end of August. That will give us the breathing room necessary until, or if, we build our own facility. I spoke with the chief of staff of our local state senator and she will try to help us regarding economic development aid if we choose to set up a plant in Millburn.

7/16/10
4:55 PM EST

We now have a base price list for our composite materials and it is being reviewed by our VPs. Once done, it will be ready to share with everyone. We are trying to work out a marketing collaboration with Trelleborg Offshore. We have invited him to share our booth in Texas next month at the National Guard show and we can discount each others' price lists when we are out in the field. We almost had a fire in the plant last night; one of our motors overheated in our jigsaw and was causing sawdust to smolder. Luckily, our amazing staff saw the problem, called in the landlord and dealt with it. Gary was in today as expected and we are doing well. Most of our profits are going back into the company for R&D. If we are right, we should make a great deal of money and if not, we are learning a lot. It is stimulating and we are having an amazing time. Jumping off the cliff is always exciting.

7/17/10
5:41 PM EST
Home, NJ

Kayla came home last night from camp to stay the night. What a joy she is. This morning I biked alone and worked on the marketing plan for the CTRM aircraft in Malaysia along with some other areas. Although I like having Uncle Dave along, I also don't mind some time to myself to think and let my mind wander. It was about 80°F and not too bad riding. As the day grew on, it increased to the 90°s. Once back from riding, I met Kay and Wendy for lunch at a local Mexican restaurant. After that, Kay and I went on some errands; any time with her is fun. I went to see my parents this afternoon and they are both mostly fine despite feeling some effects of getting older. They are looking forward to their 60th anniversary party in two weeks. My dad still likes to talk about business, philosophy and the world and we don't agree on some areas, but that is normal. Tonight it is out to dinner with friends and Kayla goes back to camp. We got word yesterday that her car can be repaired, so I am hoping she can get it when she comes back for their party in less than two weeks.

7/18/10
6:51 PM EST
Home, NJ

It was another hot day here. Tennis outside with my brother was great, as was my bike ride afterward. Wendy had gone into Manhattan early with our friend Carla to go to a museum and to meet Alex. The rest of the afternoon was spent in going to the office, preparing the marketing plane for the Eagle aircraft and setting up our next trip with CTRM and the Defense University. We need to get concrete programs stated and I am hoping for the plane and global warming floating house project. Then I went to the supermarket for provisions for our road trip tomorrow and back home to start calling my ushers for the High Holy Day services. As usual, it was tough to get started, but once I got a few people on the phone, they were pleasant, making it more of a fun chore. Then Wendy and I had dinner. It is Sunday night; I hope I sleep.

7/19/10
12:44 PM EST
In transit

Mike, Jack, Alex the intern and I are on our way back from visiting a plastic extruder and laminator. Our plan was to have them extrude material for our various types of composite materials and then cook them according to our specific recipes. We need at least two suppliers for sub-contracting until we can get up and running on our own and I think this company has good potential to be one of them. I brought Alex, both to give him the experience of being in a real business situation as opposed to college theory, and to see how he handled himself in case we wanted to utilize him more in the future. The meeting went well with four of the suppliers' top level engineers and sales people. We discussed what was possible and all signs look good for doing business. We will get a statement of work to them tomorrow and they will supply samples in September. We will then make up samples of our cloth, additives and plastic for them to process and it should be done by the end of September. Our ETA for being back at my house is about an hour and 45 minutes. I have been getting emails from Ben in China. They are doing last minute preparations for the big meetings about going public tonight. I will print out more information when we get back and further prepare. It will start at about 10:00 PM, which is late for me, but I am hoping an adrenaline shot of energy will happen when the phone rings.

7/19/10
9:49 PM EST
Home, NJ

The meeting in Malaysia with the securities commission is on, but I have been pushed back to 10:30 PM. This means I will have been up since 4:20 AM and I am still hoping for an adrenaline surge when the phone rings. I have been going through lots of additional data from IJM and at this point, I have put everything down and plan to try and relax until it is my time. It is strange how these moments become temporarily frozen in time and things slow down. Normally, time passes very quickly for me and is usually filled with a high degree of energy that makes me move from project to project. Now I am glancing at the clock on our oven and wondering if the new 10:30 time is accurate. I have never been in a situation like this, where a foreign government body will determine whether something I am highly involved in can move forward. Of course, the alternative is that they will simply turn down our application and we will continue as a private firm with a lot more control. On the other hand, being public will give us a new road to moving on to the next level exchange in Malaysia and increased worth and power. It is one of those big moments in time; a crossroads as to where we will go. My stomach is doing some loops. Regardless, when the phone rings, I will go down to the basement so I can speak as loudly as I want without disturbing my wonderful wife and dog. As far we have come in so short a time, the team we have assembled in Asia has made it possible. Often, I simply get out of the way and let them do their jobs. I am under no illusion that we would not have this chance without them. Assuming the plans go through, I hope to reward our staff come September with pay raises and bonuses. They deserve it. It is now 9:57 PM and normally I am in bed ready to be asleep soon. My schedule is now off, so I hope it is to my benefit. I feel alive.

7/19/10
11:52 PM EST
Home, NJ

I got an email from Allan telling me my participation would be delayed so I went down to our basement so as not disturb Wendy. I am currently watching a show on the Food Network and an old Gregory Peck movie. It was a little surreal sitting there with one hand on the remote for the television and the other on the telephone to try to cut off the ring to keep from waking my wife. The call came in at about 11:15 and I lost them once, but the second time we had a good connection and the questions came quickly. I was well prepared by the questions and information sent by Ben and Jossie. The security and exchange people were mostly concerned about how our companies would work and support each other worldwide and how we planned to expand in the future. I think it went well and by 11:45 we were done. The meeting will probably keep going for a few more hours, but my part is finished unless they have more questions. Now I will try to wind down to go to sleep. If I can't, I will work out in the basement. What an exciting time. I loved it.

7/20/10
4:46 PM EST
My office, NJ

Surprisingly, I did get sleep by about 12:30 last night, as the adrenaline high wore off pretty quickly. It was not easy to get up this morning at 4:40, however. My exercises and tennis did not come easily, but I am glad I did it and it was good to be back in the office for a normal day of getting a lot done. From the email, it sounds like our meeting in Malaysia went well on all fronts and now we wait for any additional information needed and a date as to when we go public. Alex, Jake and Zack, our interns, did a great job on the marketing survey of the composite materials for the hurricane and tornado window and door market for the U.S. and Asia. I plan to use it in our presentations to get loans and/or grants.

7/21/10
4:57 PM EST
My office, NJ

It was a day of a lot of preparation for the calls for Malaysia, Thailand and the Road Show. We had someone in from the state of NJ regarding benefits if we put a new composites plant here as opposed to building in New Hampshire. In essence, if they helped us get a loan then we would have to use union labor to renovate our new facility. I don't like being told what suppliers to use, so we won't be participating in the program.

7/22/10
9:02 PM EST
My office, NJ

The leaking well in the gulf was capped last week. So far so good!

7/22/10
3:55 PM EST
My office, NJ

It always amazes me that people don't do what is in their best interest and usually have no idea as to their true intentions. We had a man come in and spend a day testing for a job as pressman. He has no experience and it will take us at least six months to train him. He wanted to start at a salary of a trained pressman because that was what he was making at his last job in a different area. Why should my company pay him a higher wage and also have the cost of training him? He will not be working for us.

Keeping your promises and looking from the perspective of others seems so basic, but almost no one in the world does it. Most people can't see past themselves. Perhaps that is good because our philosophy of helping the other guy first put us into a good position everywhere.

7/23/10
4:30 PM EST
My office, NJ

There was more preparation for the National Guard show in Texas. We decided to send a mailing to a bunch of the military people involved, which included a copy of my latest book and meant signing all of them. We are also working on the global warming floating house prototype for my trip to Asia as well as a proposal to the Malaysian government to buy some. It is summer, a slower time of year and a good time to go after new prospects and contact people in general. The people renting our house in the Berkshires are so happy, they jokingly said they would pay to build a garage there so they could live over it. I am looking forward to a few days off before Asia, which happens the first week of August. Sales for the month are good enough so I am not worried too much, though the concern rarely leaves entirely.

7/24/10
8:42 PM EST
Home, NJ

After biking early this morning, we were picked up by our friends Carla and Mitch for our second annual 'Tour de Jersey' shore adventure. I really like them for multiple reasons. Besides being good friends and really upright, fine people, Mitch also likes to drive which I don't, so that automatically puts him higher in my estimation. They picked Wendy and me up at 10:45 AM this morning and it was down the New Jersey Parkway. During this time of year and especially the mid-morning, it is often very crowded, but maybe it wasn't too bad because of the extreme heat and humidity. The temperatures were expected to be in the high 90°F.

We ended up going to the same fish restaurant for lunch as last year and it was equally as good. From there it was onto a tour of various New Jersey shore towns where we eventually parked in Point Pleasant and went to walk along the boardwalk, a pathway that paralleled the ocean. On this journey, we experienced a multitude of New Jersey inhabitants in various stages of swimwear, many of whom had tattoos, which was extremely interesting and one of the reasons we went there. We all like watching people and we were not disappointed. There were members of probably every religious sect, nationality and racial type in the world. The incredible melting pot was a small microcosm of our country as a whole and everyone was out for a good time.

Two of our traditions from last year were again enjoyed. The first was playing the various boardwalk games of chance, which included using water guns to fill targets and launching plastic frogs at a targeted lily pad to win prizes. I must faithfully report that I lost all games to Mitch and when Wendy and Carla joined in, I also lost to my wonderful wife. So much for my skill, or lack thereof, in the various games of chance. My wife reminded me I am talented in other ways, so I did not let it dampen my spirit. The second thing we did was stop to drink and eat. The various establishments had fantastic lemon and orange aid beverages as well as specially flavored ices. I got the hugest soft pretzel I have ever seen. It was so hot that we did not want to stay outside any longer by 4:00 PM so we went back into the car. We did a tour of other New Jersey shore towns until we got to Long Branch, both the scene of many summers of my youth and our chosen place for dinner. Passing the swim club/residence, which is being torn down for condominiums, brought back some very old memories, all of which were drafted by the first time I spoke to a girl when I was about 11 years old. I was scared to death of women but determined to break out of my shy shell. That was the first step. People who know me know it is probably inconceivable that I would be afraid to speak to anyone, but the truth is that it was a long and painful road of learning to be outgoing that continues still today. I relish the fact that I can force myself to talk to people in most situations, but the little voice inside of me that says I should not because I am afraid of making a fool of myself never completely goes away.

Regardless, we kept driving and then stopped at a newly built area of hotels, condominiums, stores and restaurants. We walked around and went in for drinks and dinner. As always, I did not drink alcohol as I don't like the taste, calories and especially the effects. I stopped the limited amount I used to drink about thirty years ago and except for an occasional mandatory sip of wine at a religious function or when it has been added to food, I have stayed clear. Dinner was excellent and we were home by 8:30. It was another great time with Carla and Mitch and we will schedule more time together in the near future. Alex called and we found out he had come home from Manhattan to go to a party and to stay here to he could work in comfort tomorrow since his apartment was not air conditioned. It was a wonderful day.

7/25/10
4:01 PM EST
Home, NJ

Yesterday morning before going to the Jersey Shore, I went bicycle riding by myself. I was under a time constraint since we were being picked up at about 10:30. I was moving pretty quickly and making good time. I was getting near the top area of one of the last set of hills when I noticed an old man slowly shuffling down the street. He did not seem steady and it was very hot, so I asked him if he needed a hand. Surprisingly, he said yes and for a moment I panicked, realizing I was being thrown off schedule. Then I got a hold of myself, got my priorities in line and helped the man down the hill. His name was Lionel, a World War II veteran and a citizen of Florida, which was why, he said, the heat was not bothering him. As we walked slowly, him holding on to my arm, he spoke about his past. He was based in the Aleutians during the war and they had been strafed by the Japanese once. A lot of his friends were killed, but he saved himself by ducking under his bed. We got down to the next block and crossed the busy intersection and I left him on the corner. He was going a little further to stop to see his friend but he was okay from there. I then raced back up to get my bike and proceeded home. As it turned out, I got home in plenty of time and was very happy that I had the chance to do a good deed as Lionel had done for me when he served during the war. It is amazing how you suddenly have time to do something when it is the right thing to do.

7/26/10
7:07 PM EST
Home, NJ

Sometimes things don't go according to plan. We got word back from one of our patent attorneys that the base application we were planning to submit to cover our composite material both commercial and ballistic, was not going to fly due to some new patents issued recently. In other words, the work over the last year and the million dollars worth of time, investment and salaries is now in jeopardy because we may not be able to move forward if we can't safeguard ourselves with a patent. With that chilling thought in mind, I came up with a new patentable area. Jack and I created another and I had one from a few weeks ago that we were already testing. These three new ideas might be the ticket necessary both for more efficient and better products and also ensure that we have our own coverable intellectual property. There is nothing like the potential for a mild disaster to make you think creatively. I am not done and we as a team are not done. By the end of the week we will set up new patent searches of previous information to see if we do indeed have new areas. If not, I doubt we would build a plant unless we could be sure we would not be stopped by someone saying we are infringing on their patent. It is very tricky stuff and we have to be very careful. I have no plans to go into debt and then be told we can't produce. Let's just say it was not a boring day and it was wonderful to come home to Wendy and our dog.

7/27/10
4:43 PM EST
My office, NJ

I spoke with Jack this morning. I decided to take over this area and I wrote a list of claims that were patentable, some of which I felt really good about. We will need to do some patent searches on three of the claims first and since we are switching patent attorneys to the same company as our export attorney, they will run the searches as a test for their speed, accuracy and cost. Today there was also more work by Mike and Vinnie on the global warming floating house model. Vinnie and Dave were working on setting up to make the 4' x 8' sample plaques and I worked on a brochure for the Texas show. We are making more plaque samples and attacking on all fronts, a barrage of selling worldwide in an environment which is not sure if the economy is going forward, backwards or staying still. British Petroleum has a new leader, an American, and I hope it goes well. Democrats seem to be running scared regarding the midterm elections in November. I think all incumbents should be concerned; people in the U.S. are very angry.

7/29/10
5:30 PM EST
Home, NJ

I went up to Picatinny Arsenal today to show our global warming model, some composite samples and our group of new inventions. The two people I saw both said that they were in the midst of quoting for new government contracts and having a partner like us, a small business, ITAR registered and not defense contractor, was an aid for their chances. I am hopeful we can work together. It is always an adventure going into a facility like that. The security is very tight and it is easy to get lost because not much is marked. It was originally built in the Civil War period so it has an amazing array of architecture spanning about 150 years. It would be nice to do business there. Vinnie and I had lunch with a potential supplier who can make the composite presses I hope we will need. It is a family business and this guy knows his machinery, so I would feel comfortable dealing with him.

I found this while searching through a drawer for something else:

My Son Alex, 12/5/95

For those of you who know me or my family, you have probably heard "Alex stories." Alex is my middle child and my second son, who was six years old (now 21) and is known as a "terror," whose life is constantly saved by his bubbling personality and incredible sweetness. If there is any mischief to be done, dares to be taken or girls to be chased, then Alex will be there and always leading the pack.

Watching him constantly get into trouble used to drive me crazy and my wife or I would yell at him and/or send him to his room. We would always worry when he was in school or at friends because we felt he would get into some sort of trouble.

What I did not mention is that Alex has a passion. From the time he was old enough to pick-up a pen or crayon, Alex has been drawing, painting or doing some sort of art project. I never understood why he never minded being sent to his room until last week. There was no television, CD player or video games, only his art materials. Then it suddenly hit me: his room was not an area of punishment, but his private world of creation.

He would rather draw or paint than eat, sleep or be outside. He has no use for most people. Friends are not important and he could not care less what anyone thinks of him. His reality is centered on himself and everyone around him must be under his power.

JULY

My son is a genius and, like most geniuses, he walks to a different drummer. I, however, am not and that is a good thing for us both. As much as I am attuned to discipline, schedule and order, he is attuned to emotion, creativity and wildness. He views the world differently than me or my wife. In fact, he looks at life from different perspective than almost anyone else.

I no longer look at him as a pain in the neck who messes things up just to bother me. I realize now that his actions are the result of an inner passion that he cannot yet control and may never be able to harness. My job is to make sure he can function in society while still being able to realize his potential. Alex's job is to understand he has to learn to cope with the world and its people, at least to a limited degree, in order to be able to live a normal life.

While I have disdain for anyone who upsets order for the sake of trouble, I have the ultimate respect for anyone with a talent they are trying their best to harness. I look at my son differently now. His label has changed from troublemaker to genius and my label from troubled dad to proud parent. We both have a long road ahead of us, but at least we can travel it together. Alex and I are now working on my first book about patents. I am doing the writing and he is drawing the artwork.

Father's note: It has been almost 15 years since I wrote the above article and a lot has happened. I am extremely proud to report that not only has Alex continued with his passion for art, but he is on schedule to graduate from Washington University in St. Louis next year with a double undergraduate degree in fashion design and marketing. He has worked hard to harness his incredible energy, potential and intelligence to become a fantastic human being, a great son and a good friend. It is a continuing honor to be his father and watch him soar.

7/30/10
4:47 PM EST
My office, NJ

My brother, sister and I had lunch with my Uncle Allan today. He is 86 years old and in good shape. Since he lives in Texas, we may not see each other again so we all wanted to go. It was a wonderful lunch catching up on old times, talking about family we rarely saw and being together. We will see him again tonight at my parents 60th wedding anniversary party.

The news is now talking about a possible double dip recession, which is not a good thing. Our country needs to come back and this will be a major drag if it occurs. Regardless, we will keep spending our available funds on upkeep, new machinery and new projects. It is the only way to move forward.

I wrote a White paper for a new project that we are teaming with a customer. It involved being able to track soldiers, good and bad, through various wartime environments. Our customer, a chemical specialist, has contacts in the military for a possible grant. One of our inventions or projects will be accepted somewhere and will launch us forward.

7/31/10
1:30 PM EST
My office, NJ

Last night was my parent's 60th wedding anniversary party. It was not easy, but we managed to get Kayla home from camp and Ben and Alex from Manhattan in time to only be about 25 minutes late. That being said and our apologies given (we had given previous), it was a wonderful evening with my parents surrounded by their family and friends. It was one of the few times when all of their grandchildren where together. They all looked wonderful. My brother gave a fine opening speech and others gave remarks, including me. I talked about the great time we had as a family going on vacation to the Adirondack Mountains when we were kids.

I got up this morning and went riding. The previous weeks of high temperature and humidity had burned off and it was a glorious ride under a cobalt blue sky. It gave me time to think but I did not come up with much, probably a sign of impending mind shutdown for the vacation that starts tomorrow in the Berkshires. I got back from riding to find out I was going to lunch with Kayla and Wendy, which was very nice. Then it was back here to leave a big piece of cake from last night for the guys when they come in on Monday. I will go home and get my clothes ready for the Berkshires and for Asia next week. We are due home on Thursday and I leave Saturday midday, so there won't be a lot of time when I get back to get ready. I am definitely excited about a few days off to ride my bike in the New England woods and sleep on our porch.

There is more talk in the media about a double dip recession; I hope it can be avoided.

AUGUST

8/1/10
4:38 PM EST
The Berkshires, MA

Mike the driver picked us up at 5:15 PM and we were in Manhattan by 6:20. We dropped off Alex at his and his cousin Barry's apartment, where he has been staying this summer. His instructions were to change and be at the restaurant down the street within ten minutes and Kayla went with him. Mike dropped us off. Katie was already waiting for us and we were all united at our table by 6:32. It was a wonderful meal, although it took two and half hours. It is always a pleasure to be with our family and Wendy had a super time for her birthday celebration. On the way back, Mike almost got a ticket for blocking an intersection, but happily the police officer let him go. Once through the Holland Tunnel, we were home in good time. Kayla was packed and left for camp at about 11:00 PM. It was sad to see her leave, but she will be back within two weeks so it won't be too bad.

This morning's tennis with my brother was cut short a little by torrential rain and a thunder storm. I then went home, changed, packed the car and Wendy and I zoomed up here to our small summer house. It is beautiful and I had a great ride in the woods. Our first tenants left our house in great shape. They are friends of Bunny's and we can talk if they want to come back next year. It is very calm and quiet here. Wendy is taking a nap and I plan on trying to do some serious relaxing before we leave on Thursday. I know it sounds crazy to have to try to take it easy, but it is not my normal nature, so I will give it a good try. Mike's birthday was yesterday and he was scheduled to have a giant birthday party from midnight to 4:00 AM at a club in Manhattan with a few hundred of his closest friends. I can only imagine what a wild time that was.

8/2/10
1:44 PM EST
The Berkshires

Wendy and I met Jerry and Laurie Levy for dinner last night. I have known Laurie since grammar school and Jerry since we played soccer together in high school. They are wonderful, warm people and the dinner was punctuated by periodic bursts of joyous laughter. We spoke about our kids (their son just entered Jerry's family business) and our parents. There are lots of similarities since we both come from family businesses. I slept until 7:30

AM this morning. The porch was wonderful, cool and very pleasant last night. I was warm with my sleeping bags. It is fun sleeping outside, my version of camping, while still having the screened windows and doors between me and the bugs, as well as the structure of the house between me and the various outdoor animals.

Wendy and I had breakfast at a local spot, which for me consisted of six scrambled eggs, some bread, three blueberry pancakes and water. Since I was going to be riding, I knew I needed a lot of food for energy. After going back to the house, I got dressed and in between checking emails with the office I was off on the road. I did the long route today, which included a path through the local woods to the paved road onto the Tanglewood Music Center and back home. I also picked up some tomatoes and apples from a local produce stand. Wendy got back shortly after I did and we had lunch. I am out on our porch. It is glorious and the pull of a nap may be too hard to resist.

8/4/10
4:22 PM EST
The Berkshires

Our teams are getting everything ready for the meetings next week, the trade show in Texas and the prototyping for the hurricane/tornado panels with two sub-contractors. I biked this morning and will again one more time tomorrow before we head back home. Kayla's car is repaired and will be ready for us to pick up and Friday should be a normal day. It will be good to be back on my regular schedule.

8/5/20
9:09 PM EST
Home, NJ

I awoke this morning to a slight rain, but decided to go for it anyway and I am glad I did. The rain held off, as did the thunder and lightening, and the mountain biking was phenomenal. I finished in about two hours and, having picked up lunch, raced back to the house. When I was in the basement putting away my bike, I remembered that there had been mouse traps set. I went back to check and one of them was out of place. Fearing the worst, I found it with a live mouse stuck on an adhesive pad trap. My choices were to try to save the mouse outside or kill it to put it out of its misery. I went for trying to save him and I gently took his feet from the pad outside and let him go on our lawn. He was shaken up, but I hope he will be okay. I have nothing against mice outside, but a lot against them inside our house. It is a quandary, but I left a message for the man who watches our house that if he uses the traps, to make sure to check them frequently so the mice don't suffer. I would rather have the spring kind of trap that kills instantly, but I am not sure how well they work either.

Wendy and I were out before 10:30 and on our way home. It was great to get back here and before getting to the house, we picked up Kayla's car, which happily cost a little less than expected. However, someone hit my car over the last few days and I got an estimate from the body shop that ended up costing the amount we had saved. In the end, it will probably be about even. I was really annoyed when I saw the damage yesterday, but I eventually calmed down. Once home, Wendy and I unloaded the car and it was off to the office. I was able to catch up on the balance of my email and get ready for Saturday's trip. I had a momentary panic attack when I could not find my flight information, but realized later I was going via Expedia and everything was where it was supposed to be. I picked up dinner on the way home and after eating, checking my flowers, which a deer or ground hog has mostly destroyed, I finished packing. It is really great to be home.

8/6/10
10:29 AM EST
Newark Liberty Airport

Yesterday was a blur regarding getting caught up in the office and final preparation for today's trip. It was wonderful seeing my brother again and playing tennis outside. Afterward, it was home to a great dinner and calm night with Wendy and Bailey.

As is normal for the night before traveling, my dreams were strange but not horrible. I got up my usual 4:35 time to go biking. I was a little worried it would be too dark to see, but by the time I actually got out on the road it was dawn. The humidity had cleared and it was a gorgeous sunrise with cool temperatures. Unlike normal, I did little constructive thinking while on the road and just let my mind wander. Once home, I had breakfast and said goodbye to Wendy, which is always hard. I will miss Bailey also. We did hear from Kayla this morning. She called to wish me a good voyage and she is very excited since she is a captain of one of the sports teams at the big competition at her camp. It is a joy to hear her happy. I got the last segment of my book from Katie, so all I have to do is go through the last two sections and hand them off to Rich. I will now work on the August newsletter.

8/6/10
2:18 PM EST

In flight over Canada on our way over the South Pole. 11:18 hours to go. We have 6324 miles to go traveling at aprox. 33,000 feet going 580 miles per hour. There was no problem in take off and we are on schedule. I was able to finish the newsletter I had started yesterday and already emailed it to Rich and Al. I have been giving him more responsibility lately and he has risen to task well. I continue to move through the "to do" list since lunch is finished, as is the final editing on my new book. I am hoping to have it all completed by the time I get back next Saturday. We are traveling on a new Continental Airlines airplane equipped with power plug-ins and flat seats. I look forward to some napping later.

No Road Is Ever Straight

Good news: these flat seats are wonderful and I slept about three hours. I happily have one of the greatest sleeping pills and that is putting on old Jean Shepherd radio shows from the 1960s and 70s. He was and is a hero of mine, a mentor whose two word answer of "keep writing" after I sent him one of my short stories propelled me forward. I will never forget what those two words did for me and I have tried to help others in return.

I am now going to indulge myself in an exercise, which is "what happens if it works?" We are trying to sell multiple programs worldwide at the same time with the idea that only one of out ten at best will work. What happens if they do?

Proposal 1: Forced Air Launcher

We build a modified version of our forced air launcher so that it can launch our projectiles at least 500 yards. The contents of the projectiles can be anything from food, water, medicine and other humanitarian related items to agricultural fillers likes plants and trees, seeds, fertilizer and insecticide. It can also be used for defense for stopping water or land based pirates or creating chemical based virtual fences to keep animals out of certain areas. As you can see, the uses are quite varied and the best part is that the training of the team to assemble, repair, move and utilize the forced air launcher is the same everywhere. So you can actually utilize troops for military, humanitarian and commercial purposes to their full potential instead of waiting around for an attack. The idea is part of a much broader based initiative to have weapons and troops no longer be solely sourced for the military, but have them productive all the time. When countries see that they can make money and help their people with the same troops, then perhaps they will be less likely to waste them in warfare and use them more in trading and doing business with each other to make money. The military threat will always be there since the troops and weapons are in constant use, but they will be utilized in a more productive way. I may be a little naïve, but when countries don't have to disarm, it is a baby step towards peace. Maybe best of all, is that this is an extremely inexpensive weapon and can be broadly utilized. We will have proposals to two countries for this program out by then end of September. The initial prototype phase costs $875,000, which includes me bringing a team of our people, a forced air launcher and projectiles filled will multiple formulas so that we can train a team of soldiers to handle military, humanitarian and commercial projects all at the same time. If someone actually buys the idea, we can be ready with a modified forced air launcher design within a month. The projectiles are already designed, so we would just have to work out the contents for the various uses and make sure they function correctly. For instance, if you want to plant seeds in ecologically fragile areas where you can't walk, then you want the projectiles to bury into the ground and decompose quickly. If you want to stop pirates, then you want the rockets to burst on contact as they hit a ship to spread various substances on the deck to stop the boat and people from functioning without killing them. Another great part about this project is the forced air launcher works on compressed air, so it is totally green. There is no gunpowder or explosive involved with launching the rockets. This project would be reasonably easy to have off the ground and ready to go within three months.

Proposal 2: Hurricane and Tornado Panels

We have already done a great deal of research and testing on materials that will be hurricane and tornado resistant for window and door coverings and even to make panels to build entire homes. This is a chicken and egg dilemma. We do not yet have any capacity to build the panels. Vinnie and Jack are going to two manufactures within the next two weeks to set them up as sub-contractors when and if we get orders. However, the capacity necessary to set up large scale and be able to sell at good prices will take at least 6-9 months. We would have to rely on subcontractors until we could build the capacity ourselves. The plant necessary to handle this type of mass run will cost at least $5,000,000. I am not going ahead unless we have a large piece of business to support it. The good news is that we can utilize sub-contractors indefinitely, so I am not that concerned. I am also just not sure if there is a market yet.

Proposal 3: The Global Warming Floating House

This project is so big it is mind-boggling. A single house, for which we have no actual plans yet, made with our composite materials and state of the art sustainable technology, would be a massive project that would tax every resource and asset we have. We will have a proposal out next week to sell either the first house or the next ten houses and can also include the tidal resistant floodwalls and salt water resistant planted habitat. I have a prototype of the house with me and it is amazing. We would need substantial help from either the Malaysian, U.S. governments or both to set up production. However, with the hottest summer on record in the world and the highest rate of storms, global flooding is quickly going to become more of a reality and we are the only ones, from what I can see, working with a solution on a global scale.

Proposal 4: Commercial & Military Composite Materials

Commercial and military based composite materials that can withstand storms, small arms fire and the effects of blast. We can manufacture almost anything now and the questions are finding partners to create the needed products. One of the reasons we are going to the Texas show is to find out what people need so we can build prototypes to work. Again, we can utilize sub-contractors to build our products on a low quantity scale and when the numbers are there, we can go into manufacturing.

Proposal 5:

We have our first real shot at not only cost reducing an electronic product, but the customer wants a proposal for us to build, stock, ship, warranty and repair their entire line. In other words, we would become a specialized contract manufacturer, which is just what we have been working on for the past 18 months and finally have a chance. If it works, we will need to hire more people and probably create an assembly area in Massachusetts near Brett.

As for all of our standard product lines like printed labels, metal and plastic parts, cable assemblies, gaskets and telecom products, business ranges from okay to great worldwide and we will continue to push there also.

Since I have never had a bunch of these types of proposals hit at the same time, I am not that concerned, but it is fun to think about. As always, we will keep pushing everywhere and deal with it as it comes. It sure beats being slow and waiting for the phone to ring.

Back to editing.

8/7/10
3:41 PM China time, 3:41 AM EST
Beijing Airport

We arrived a few minutes early and it was an excellent flight. My hope was that I could get a boarding pass without having to change buildings, but that was not the case. After finally finding the international transfer desk, I was told I had to go to a different terminal. They actually told me Terminal 2, but I only saw signs to Terminal 3 and hoped I could get a pass there. After taking the airport train, I made my way through to the Continental gate on the top floor. By the way, it is very hot in Beijing, like seemingly everywhere else I go. I was told I had to take a shuttle to Terminal 2. I still had about two hours, so I figured I was okay but moved quickly and got on the correct transport. Unfortunately, unlike other airports, Terminals 1 and 2 are far away from where I was and as I watched the clock move quickly and our bus move slowly, it became evident that I could run out of time if I had to come back to the original terminal. After sweating out the ride and making my way to the Malaysian Airlines area, I was relieved to find the flight was leaving from the terminal I was in and I was okay. It was a short move from check-in through multiple security points and passport control and I was in their lounge with plenty of time. I decided to leave there early and wait here for the flight. You never know with airports; things that seemingly should not take long end up seeming to take forever. While that slow moving bus probably really took less than fifteen minutes, it seemed like an eternity. I look forward to boarding soon, having a good meal and an on-time arrival.

AUGUST

8/7/10
7:35 PM Malaysia time, 7:35 AM EST
In flight

We have about three hours to get to Kuala Lumpur and I hope to be in my hotel room by about midnight. I have been reading the Koran and have about a third left. It is interesting, as is the Old Testament. Both are violent and, of course, proprietary to their points of view. I see no reason why we all can't get along and will go from that viewpoint, as I have in the past, with everyone we deal with. If it could only be so easy with the rest of the world. I was reading one of the Malaysian national newspapers and found two articles that may come in handy with our meetings with CTRM and NDUM. The first carried comments from the Malaysian Prime Minister saying that government money should be spent with wisdom and efficiency. In other words, he wanted to make sure the money is well spent and what better than our multi-purpose compressed air system that can be used in war, peace, humanitarian aid and commercially profitable ventures. The other talked about Malaysian joint military maneuvers with other countries and how soldiers are being cross-trained for humanitarian aid when needed. What better time to add a profit-based segment to that group to help fund the military? I will keep reading. A long, hot shower is going to feel really good.

8/8/10
9:22 AM Malaysian time, 9:22 PM EST
Crowne Plaza Hotel Kuala Lumpur

The good news was that we arrived early and it was a very nice flight. The bad news was that my luggage did not make it from Beijing. It is a very sinking feeling to see the last of the luggage come off the carousel and realize yours is not with it. The very efficient staff there traced my bag and knew where it was immediately. After going to fill out paperwork, I found I would not get it back until tonight in the best case scenario. Feeling a combination of extreme tiredness, annoyance and happiness that I had my samples and a spare set of undergarments with me, I made my way out to the airport lobby and got a cab.

On the way to the hotel, I spoke with my wife, who agreed that, while a pain in the neck, it was not a disaster. However, by the time I got to the hotel there were no stores open to buy a bathing suit or spandex shorts, so I might as well sleep later since I could not work out. I got to sleep sometime before 2:00 AM and got up at 8:00. By then, Ben was already tracing my suitcase with the information I had already emailed him and it should be here by 9:00 PM tonight. With that good news, I went to breakfast and realized that a lot of my sales materials were in my suitcase, so I was going to have to wing it for part of my presentation. Such is the life of being on the road and I will try to make the best of it. Meanwhile, since I did not get my usual workout this morning, I am off my schedule, which also does not sit well. I will go to meet Ben and Hing in a little while and we will travel down to CTRM. I like selling in a suit; I look my best and the power emanates from me. I will have to make up for it by moving energy from my inside out. It is a nice challenge, but I hope I get a nap on the way down, as I have not had much sleep in the last two days. As I like to say, if you can't take the challenges of the road, then it is time to retire. I am fine.

8/8/10
6:35 PM Malaysian time, 6:35 AM EST
Crowne Plaza Hotel Kuala Lumpur

Going on sales calls improperly dressed is a very risky thing. To go in casual clothes can be seen as an insult to your hosts who might think they do not rate in your estimation. The best procedure, in my experience, is an immediate attack, which is what I did. Our meeting with CTRM began on schedule and within the first five minutes not only did our hosts know that my luggage was still in Beijing, but it became a running joke that each time I did not have the correct materials, they were in the missing suitcase. Our reason for going there was to show our new products and to enlist their aid in joint venturing for one or more projects. As it turned out, the airplane project we had set up the advertising plan for could not work because the engine supplier they utilized was no longer making the same model, which meant new certification would be needed if they went back into production. Testing for a new engine meant at least 12 months and probably a million dollars plus six additional months to get the assembly line started again. No customers were going to wait that long, therefore the project was dead. Later we found out they might want to sell the whole design and technology to another company if we could find a buyer, so that is something we will look into. They were very interested in the global warming floating house project and I will send them a schedule of what needs to be done. They can help set up a meeting with the Environmental Minister and other government officials so we can try to get a commitment and funding. I had prices ready for the radome job they were interested in, but it is in my suitcase, which by the way should now be delivered here by 8:30 PM tonight. They also liked the air compression projectile project but I am not sure if they want to pursue it. It looks like radomes and the global warming house are our best shots right now and we will proceed.

8/9/10
10:24 AM Malaysian time, 10:24 AM EST
Crowne Plaza Hotel Kuala Lumpur

I needed to find some adhesive to repair the global warming floating house sample, but I was low on clothes and was afraid to get too sweaty in the hot and humid weather conditions. Hearing from Titan that I was confirmed to get my suitcase back tonight, I took the chance and made it to a nearby mall in good shape and bought some socks, a bathing suit, goggles and some toiletries. Happily, I found a convenience store and they had adhesive, so then I had everything I needed.

Once back in the room, I made the needed repairs and went to the gym to exercise, which I badly needed since the last time was Saturday morning in New Jersey. It felt wonderful and then it was back to the room to get ready for dinner. I met Ben downstairs and we had a great meeting about what was happening with IJ Malaysia and virtually all of the news was good. His team was doing a great job. We will be expanding in China again with a new plant, or joint venture or partner with another supplier sometime later this year after we go public.

I have been having internet access problems, which seems to be the way things are going for this trip. Things are getting done, but it is not going smoothly. I am hoping for a change back to high efficiency tomorrow. I got my suitcase!

8/9/10
4:18 PM Malaysian time, 4:18 AM EST Kuala Lumpur Airport

After a great night's sleep of eight hours, I was charged and ready to go. My workout went well and after a regular traveling breakfast of seven hard-boiled eggs and fruit, I changed and met Ben in the lobby. We met two of our sales representatives and were off on our way to the National Defense University of Malaysia to sign an MOU and have a meeting regarding our new products. Once we got there, something seemed up since there were people with cameras and lots of others waiting to go in. It then dawned on me that they were here for the MOU signing and I started to get a little nervous. That feeling only increased when we were ushered into a big room and were introduced to group of high-ranking officials. I was motioned to sit at the head of a long conference table next to the head of the university, a 3-star general. The meeting was started by a formal greeting by a master of ceremonies who asked the general to speak and then said I would be saying a few words. Realizing I was about to speak, I quickly got my thoughts together. After some very nice words from the general, I thanked him and the group and hoped our joint endeavors would produce many positive results for both military and commercial ventures. We then had the formal signing and we went into a reception area for lunch.

I had mentioned to Ben that it would be a day we would never forget. Lunch was amazing. I sat next to the 3-star general and we spoke about his journeys in the U.S. and how he came to become a general. It was great fun and gave us a chance to get to know each other. You could easily tell he was in charge since the moment he finished lunch and stood up, so did everyone else, including me.

Afterward, it was back up to a meeting with our contacts Jesbil and Ghanni, both heads of research and development. We got down to speaking about the two main areas, which were the global warming floating house and the air compression launched projectiles. They were very enthusiastic about the house and we decided to meet again this Thursday to begin writing a grant application to prototype a house with a storm surge wall. It was incredible to hear them enthusiastic about the potential, for Malaysia and other areas. It was great to be validated on the concept. It was then on to the compressed air projectile system, which they also really liked. In fact, they came up with another use themselves and we will begin writing a grant for that on Thursday too.

It was then back to the airport where we were met by our third representative Abul and we had some talks about how we would handle the potential sales and their participation. Ben and I will discuss it more later and they and I can talk when we meet again on Thursday. Once here we found out we were delayed 90 minutes because they had to switch planes. The first one had a crack, so we should get to our hotel about 9:00 PM. If so, I may get a chance for a swim. Since I have time I will probably do some editing. Good news: my internet access is now working.

8/10/10
7:13 PM Thailand time, 6:13 AM EST
Bangkok Airport

We got to the Intercontinental Hotel at about 9:15 PM and I immediately tried to go swimming, but it was an outdoor pool and a lightening storm was in progress. While beautiful, it was too dangerous to get into the water. I changed my plans and went to the gym instead. Then it was back to the room to a meal of oatmeal, fruit and pretzels. I got to sleep by about 1:00 AM and got up at 4:00 AM. I exercised and met Ben and Paul Jordan for breakfast. Ben and I had discussed moving Paul to the position of Asian VP of composite development to take advantage of his background and experience as an engineer. Happily, he liked the idea and will send me his schedule to set up coming to the U.S. right away to train with Jack. Meanwhile, Ben will hire a new Asian head of sales to coordinate everything except China. We met Suwaleerat after breakfast and then took a long ride out into the country to see new potential customers. They primarily were involved with reinforcing light trucks for military and humanitarian uses throughout the world. There is a chance that our plastic material might be of help and we agreed to exchange NDAs and then information and samples as to what is possible. We also showed them the global warming floating house and they had a referral for someone involved with building disaster structures for the United Nations.

From there, it was back toward Bangkok and a meeting with a potential composite sheet supplier. Their company primarily makes surfboards and seemed interested in branching out into the global warming floating house production. Again, we will exchange NDAs, data sheets and samples. Afterward, we made our way through very heavy traffic thanks to the great driving by Suwaleerat to IJT our plant. Vinnie did an excellent job laying it out and it is orderly and running well. That was it for business and Paul, Suwaleerat and Ben dropped me off at the airport. It was a very good quick stay. I am now in the Thai Air lounge and about ready to go the gate on my way back to Kuala Lumpur.

AUGUST

We landed near 11:00 PM last night. I retrieved my suitcase and took a cab to Kuala Lumpur. Sometimes you have cab drivers that are silent and others want to talk. This one was a very pleasant talker and after discussing politics, I told him about our GWFH program. He offered to take me around to see various types of housing next time I was here and we exchanged business cards. I always like to know a driver in the various cities I often travel to and he will be good to have around. I got to the hotel around midnight and to sleep by 1:30.

Getting up at 6:00 again was not easy, especially since my stomach went crazy yesterday in Thailand, but I was okay to exercise. I checked in with Al, Wendy and Uncle Dave while doing my laps around the tennis court and the exercise group that was working out there.

After breakfast, PK picked me up and long with one of the senior staff from CTRM we went over to the MIGHT Group, which are high-tech advocates set up by the Malaysian government to spur new inventions and business. They match inventors and entrepreneurs with other companies and financing. After I gave some background about us, they mentioned they have a new type of nano product that will reduce the heat of a surrounding area by more than 60%. Since the telecom industry is always trying to miniaturize parts with more capacity, resulting in them run hotter, this could be a very big deal. I then brought up the GWFH and they liked the idea, especially since they thought we could paint it with their new invention submerged in the paint. I did not like the idea of an uneven flow of material from paint, so I suggested instead we create an ink with it and print thin plastic sheeting that could be used as inserts on top of our panels. Not only could the inhabitants get the benefit of the heat deflection, but also as the houses got bent and dented from various types of storms, they could replace the inserts cheaply and even change the color of the houses any time they wanted. The MIGHT people liked that idea and said they would go back to their people for approval.

Abul picked me up at about 1:30 and we were at the NDUM by 2:00. We met Jesbil, Ghani, and Abul's team Mamu and the general. We spoke about the GWFH idea, which Ghani wants to be part of a larger project and the forced air launcher shooting projectiles. This is being converted into a compressed air device that shoots fire containers into fires, specifically for large buildings like in the giant Twin Trade Towers. We then spoke about the potential for a new type of armor that will have to be approved for export through our attorney and the U.S. government before we can produce it.

Abul dropped in at the hotel where I modified our proposals for the fire suppressant system and sent that file and the house file to Ghani. I was very tired and was going to go down the street to buy some glue to repair the global warming floating house model, but it was raining. I decided to go out to the pool area and sit under the plastic awning with a diet cola, which I probably should not have been drinking because of my upset stomach. I sat in awe at the power of the universe as a lightening storm passed by the Twin Towers, throwing bolts in all directions. It was an awesome display and I was enthralled.

I decided it was time for dinner, but found out the hotel dining room did not open for awhile. In the meantime, I got my laptop, came back down to the pool, happy to find out no one was killed while swimming during the storm and sat there with the sun setting above me.

Ramadan started this week, which means most Muslims are fasting from early in the morning to 7:30 at night. Abul told me the hotels here put out big spreads because people are so hungry and too tired to cook. I have never been in a place celebrating this holiday before and it is fascinating. The food is like nothing I have ever seen with salads, hot dishes, raw seafood, amazing desserts and food of all types. People are singing, playing instruments and praying. It is quite an event.

The storm passed and dusk was falling quickly. I could see the Twin Towers lit up in white and grey, looking magnificent against the blue-black sky. It was hard to leave.

The people in Malaysia as well as throughout the rest of Asia where I have traveled have been extremely pleasant and I look forward to coming here again. It is strange to think that you can make a change in the world. I believe our new projects can. I know it sounds idealistic and perhaps naïve to think that if I can get one army to modify its thinking regarding the use of its people and its weapons and turn them into a force for humanitarian good and making honest profits. I am thoroughly convinced, however, that given the chance, people will generally rather work together, build their lives positively and have good times rather than fight and kill each other. If we level the playing field for opportunity to grow and prosper, then fewer people will want to cause problems.

Yes, I am an idealist, but I am also a ferocious planner and believe in following my instinct. If nothing else, when I leave this world I would like to have left a positive mark on as many people as possible. Preaching the benefits of doing business over war will be something I hope I do until I am gone.

8/13/10
12:33 PM Malaysian time, 12:33 AM EST
Crowne Plaza Hotel

I got a decent night of sleep last night and after working out and having breakfast, I spoke to both Al and Wendy and they were well. Abul picked me up and we went to another government group who is in charge of certifying new materials. It is sort of like our underwriters laboratories. If our materials are going to be used here, we will most probably have to become certified. Both men we saw liked our products, including the GWFH, and they are ready to help in the future. They also showed us a new material, which was a combination of rice stalks and plastic, that might be of use when building the houses. Abul dropped me off, I picked up some lunch and here I stay until 2:00 when I go to the airport. I am looking forward to Hong Kong.

8/14/10
8:40 AM Hong Kong time, 8:40 PM EST
Hong Kong Airport

It is amazing that less than six years ago, I first met Ben downstairs here at this airport and started this amazing adventure. There has been a question regarding tax credits for IJT and it looks like we may have missed out on some because of missed deadlines. I suggested to Ben that if the fire suppression airborne projectile system works, then we can utilize IJX to make the plastic containers, ship them to IJT for mixing the solution, filling them, final assembly and then re-designate IJT a contract manufacturer. Perhaps then we would then be eligible again for some of the tax benefits. I am waiting to hear back.

The flight from Hong Kong was on time. I got through immigration and customs without a problem. The hotel shuttle was not going to run for 30 minutes and impatient, I hopped on the train, which I like to take better than a cab. I was in my room by about 11:00 PM. I had a snack and walked along the harbor. The lights and the skylines are almost indescribable in their dazzling beauty, but suffice it to say, whenever I come to Asia I try to come here for a night before I leave.

I got a few hours sleep, got up, exercised in my room and then walked along the harbor, which is also very beautiful as the sun is starting to rise. While walking, I spoke to Wendy. We both can't wait to see each other, which is very nice considering we have been married for twenty-five years. Even better, all of the kids and Katie may be coming Saturday night for dinner at the house, which should be great fun.

I got a cab to the airport and after buying provisions for the flight and chocolate for my crew at IJUS, I found a place to sit in the G16 Lounge, ready to go. Two major international events overshadowed everything else here. The first is the major fear of a second international economic slowdown and people are very concerned the U.S. is double dipping. The second is the incredibly hot temperatures around the world, especially here in Asia. Global Warming is happening and our timing with the global warming floating house communities is perfect. People are coming to the realization that something has to be done. If we can get the Malaysian government to adopt our system, then we will have a big jump in the rest of the world market. I am tired, happy and contented, at least for now. My plans for the flight are to finish editing the book. A lot has happened over the past few days and we are in excellent position to benefit from the changing times.

8/14/10
5:36 AM EST
In flight, 4295 miles and 7:46 to go, -36°F outside

We are just heading over the East Siberian Sea on our way over the North Pole. We are currently on schedule to arrive on time and I have already eaten twice. I finished editing my book! Now it can go to Rich, get the final permissions from a few people to use their names and we can finish typesetting and go to press.

Katie says she is ready for more editing, so I will start soon on my first round of edits for this year's book, which is now almost three quarters done. I am aiming to be finished by next August.

8/15/10
3:51 PM EST
Home, NJ

Wendy picked me up at the airport yesterday and we got home at about 2:30 PM. Kayla was home from camp and Ben, Katie and Alex were all in by early evening. We had a really nice family dinner with lots of laughter that extended into the night. I played tennis with Ira this morning and it was, as always, a pleasure to see him. After biking, I still had enough energy to get to the office and get a lot of prep work done for tomorrow. I am losing my energy rapidly, so it is time to stop and take it easy. Wendy and Kayla are in the Berkshires and due back tomorrow. It is good to be home.

8/16/10
4:55 PM EST
My office, NJ

We learned a few very important things from the failure of the prototype tests at the composite manufacturer last week. The first was that the ballistic material we wanted to make may be too expensive for the marketplace. The second is we have already modified the formulas and construction to decrease the price to make it more competitive and easier to manufacture. The third is that Vinnie and Jack need to travel together to make sure both their expertise can be utilized in this undertaking. I was very fortunate to be able to get to sleep last night considering the potential for jet lag. We heard from Ghani, who said he would start work on the grant proposal for the waterless fire projectile project next week. I am waiting to hear from Eric to get started on the renderings for the global warming water based project. It is wonderful to be back in the office and on my normal routine.

8/17/10
4:47 PM EST
My office, NJ

I had lunch with two former Lucent guys who want us to help set them up to handle legacy equipment for Alcatel-Lucent and other companies.

Their business plan is a little thin regarding sales flows, but they may have a chance. It is always impossible to know who will succeed and who won't. There are three things going in their favor. One is they have a well placed friend who can help steer business towards them; second, they have a big hunger to succeed; and third, they have us. Another plus is we may have a big piece of business we can use them for, which by itself may be enough to get them going.

Eric is working on revised rendering for the global warming floating house and the fire suppression system and should be ready this week. I ordered a basket of various American breakfast treats for the 3-star general I met in Malaysia. He gave us a gift and we did not know we were supposed to do the same, so I wanted something uniquely American. I hope he likes it. We have been trying to get a major defense manufacturer to test some of our ballistic panels and they tested the wrong firearms after months of waiting, so we failed. It is very frustrating since we were so careful as to what the tests should entail and they ignored us, failed us instead. Now we are probably shut out from any potential business.

8/18/10
4:25 PM EST
My office, NJ

We are not ready to make our next set of commercial/military composite panels so I called our potential supplier and put off the testing until next month. It is not easy to call a company that is already set up for testing and then put them off. They feel both disappointment that you will never come and annoyance that their schedule has been interrupted. Happily, my father trained me for telephone calls like this and I was able to head off any problem.

Sometimes customers seem to be snake-bit. We keep sending them jobs with trouble, obviously unintentionally, and it seems to happen to the same group. We have that now and another problem happened today. Again, I know from the years of experience these things just happen sometimes and if you are lucky you can get through the bad period by incredible customer service and follow up. If not, you lose the customer.

Jack and I spoke with our new patent attorney and he gave us an 8.5-9 chance our new composite patent application would get some type of approval. This was great news, so I gave them go ahead to send us final prices and begin. We hope to be patent pending by the end of September, which will give us some breathing room regarding being able to manufacture without worry. It is the late part the summer and it seems most people are on vacation, which is very frustrating when you are trying to sell. I will persevere. We sent a letter of intent to the potential customer who may want us to be their contract manufacturer to build, redesign, test, stock, ship, release, repair and support their product. It will be a big piece of business if it happens, but we have to be sure we will make enough money before we go too far.

No Road Is Ever Straight

Wendy, Barbara, Kayla, Barry and Alex went on their annual pilgrimage to the restaurant called Nobu in New York City. They said the food was amazing. I am both glad they enjoyed themselves and that I did not have to go. For me, food is mostly fuel and going into the city just to eat is not something I normally like to do. We sent Ghani the rendering for his dream idea. I hope he likes it enough to push our projectile project ahead quickly so we can get started with something.

8/19/10
4:48 PM EST
My office, NJ

We sent the rendering to Ghani, whose response was we moved very fast and he found the concept interesting. I followed up with asking if he had any changes and have not heard back yet. In the meantime, we are working on the fire suppression idea and will have a rendering for him by Monday. Zamri will follow up with him tomorrow regarding our housing idea to get moving in a section of Malaysia where he is involved with housing. I am using the time to follow up with people regarding our new composite technology all over the world and I am getting some responses. I had lunch with Kayla, which is always a pleasure, and started researching the nano technology company that MIGHT wants us to partner with. Their product may fit very well with our technologies and I will push on the NDA tomorrow if there is no word before then. Jack and Brett leave tomorrow for the National Guard show in Texas. They are loaded with all types of commercial and military applications. I never count on trade shows for anything worthwhile, but maybe this one will be different. If not, it will probably be our last for a long time.

There is more bad unemployment news and the Dow Jones Industrial went down again.

8/20/10
4:44 PM EST
My office, NJ

There was an accident last night at my tennis club and a piece of heavy equipment and a trailer slammed into the clubhouse, affecting the structural integrity of the building. Luckily, no one was injured. I met one of my partners there this morning and the water had been turned off. The place does not look good and I am figuring at least one million dollars in damage. Happily, the tennis courts were still in great shape and we had a really good time. Even if the clubhouse has to be remade, I think the indoor play area will be fine. I still feel very badly for the owners. I was taking my partner home to use my shower, since they were off at the club when we ran into one of the people in charge. Still in shock, he joked that I should tell Wendy that more people would be coming. Not to be undone, my amazing wife, upon hearing that when I got home, told me sarcastically to tell him there would be a towel charge for those who came. When I called him back with the retort, he loved it.

AUGUST

8/21/10
5:17 PM EST
Home, NJ

I met Elana at my office this morning at 8:30 AM and she put me through the usual highly vigorous band workout, leaving me tired but happy. She is a tough taskmaster and does not allow anything except the maximum effort, so I have to be at my best when I see her. From there, it was a race home to help pack Kayla's car, which was mostly already done when I got there. We said our goodbyes because she was going back to school, which is always tough. She is such a positive element in my life and I love having her around. She is scheduled back within a month, which is a very good thing. I met Dave and Howard at the usual spot at 11:30 and the ride was spirited. Whenever you have three printers in the same pack, there is lively conversation and this ride was no different. Howard and I made plans to play tennis tomorrow since Ira is away on vacation. I went back home to lunch and took a long bath to try to soothe my aching muscles. I have been in contact with Brett and Jack at the National Guard show in Texas. We got the two leads yesterday concerning potential uses for the forced air launcher, so I am in an upbeat mood about their participation.

8/21/10
7:49 PM EST
Our porch, NJ

It is a beautiful late summer night. There is a small wind blowing through the trees in our backyard. I sit here in our enclosed porch, mostly free from insects, and it is a calm, idyllic setting. The tree frogs and crickets are calling, mixed softly with the rock music coming from our neighbor's house. We heard from Kayla earlier. She got to school, but none of her friends were around so she had to unpack herself. She did not sound happy, so I just called her. Her friends are back now and she sounded fine, a very good thing for a dad to hear. We had dinner and Wendy is now upstairs watching a movie on the Hallmark Channel, which means it is a love story that will have a lot of conflict until the very end when everything will be fine. Believe it or not, I have seen most of the movie and see no reason to watch it again, so I am writing downstairs for now. I wrote a proposal for Ben's review regarding our partnership and potential takeover of a printing company in China. He wants to either set up a second manufacturing site ourselves or partner, so I wrote and sent a proposal. I have not heard back yet.

It is late summer and the remembrances of school never seem to fade. I still feel like I should be practicing for soccer and getting ready to go back to high school or college. Not that I miss that time or want to go back, but it is the feeling I get when I have forgotten to do something. The rock music from next door seems to be getting louder, so it may be time for me to go inside. It is not worth asking them to be quiet. They are good neighbors and I can't hear them from inside the house.

No Road Is Ever Straight

8/22/10
4:40 PM EST
Home, NJ

It rained last night and only four tennis courts were open early this morning. Howard and I got one and spent about 75 minutes playing in the humid outdoor conditions. I think he got a good workout as did I, and since it was raining off and on, I decided to forgo bicycle riding in favor of working out in my basement. After lunch, I went to see my parents and then ran some errands. I got a call from Brett with an update from the trade show in Texas. The attendance was not great, but they were getting attention from the other companies showing their products. The trade show ends tomorrow, then our guys will follow up on their leads and we can assess if it was worthwhile. We heard from Kayla who is still missing some of her stuff the university stored for her over the summer. Otherwise, she is very good. Alex is due home tonight for a week before going back to school. Myrna's brother-in-law Saul passed away; he almost had his perfect ending, which would have been to die at his desk. In his mid-80s, he loved his business and his job. He fell on some stairs last week. He was in a coma for awhile, but once off life support, he passed quickly without regaining consciousness. I hope his family is okay. The funeral is tomorrow. It is sad when anyone dies, but less so when they had a long, full, really good life. At that point, you are hoping for a good ending, which is something I think about more as time goes on. Since I almost totally believe in an afterlife, I am a lot less concerned about dying than many others. To me, it is mostly just a new phase to move into. On the other hand, I believe that the score is kept and what you do, both good and bad, counts moving forward. I try to be as good a person as I can because I want to be an example for my family and to have a reason to look forward to what comes next.

8/23/10
4:25 PM EST
My office, NJ

Today was the funeral for Saul. It was well attended and the energy level was high. It is not often you go to a service for someone who was respected, loved by all and lived into his 80s and have a great time. I hope they can say the same for me when I go. Barry was there as was his girlfriend, Claire. Normally bringing a girlfriend to a family funeral is the precursor to marriage. My first impression of her was good. I think they make a good match. Jessica was also there with Joe. She is due to deliver in December and she looks wonderful. Most of the family from Wendy's side, who were local, were there. It was a great show of support.

We finally got the PO for the hand washing monitors that Don prototyped a few months ago. It is for a pilot project for the Veterans Administration in Nebraska and the potential is huge. The first step is to get them into the field and make sure they function correctly. Don is amazing and I am glad he is working on it for us. A deal has been struck at our tennis club. Since the men's shower room was rendered inoperable by the accident, we can now use the women's facilities until 8:00. This works out fine for me; their locker room is nicer anyway. Alex is enjoying his few days of relaxation before he leaves on Friday. We heard from Kayla, who is happy to be back at school.

8/24/10
4:42 PM EST
My office, NJ

Brett and Jack are on their way back from the National Guard show in Texas. We found out today that the wonderful people at the Veterans Administration in Nebraska gave our contact information to a lot of other potential customers. The first called today and we are following up. The rains of the past few days have been great for our lawn and flowers. I may do some transplanting tonight. I spoke with Jeroen. He is coming here next month and I will go to Europe in October.

8/25/10
4:32 PM EST
My office, NJ

We have more inventions working. Again, who knows if one or any will be of use. It doesn't matter; we will keep going. I interviewed a young man who is graduating with a mechanical engineering degree in December and has no job prospects. As long as things stay good, we will hire him for January. He looks ready and very willing to work and that is the kind of person I like. Kayla called me today and except for some lost boxes with her bedding, she is fine. She got the package I sent her with various things to make her smile, including a ball made of rubber bands and some ketchup. I miss her a lot. The gift for the general went out last night. It is nothing grand, just some American made foods and a cutting board, but I hope he likes it. My brother is back from vacation. I am glad; I missed him.

More Tea Party candidates won in yesterday's midterm primaries. I have no idea what will happen in November, but change is in the air.

8/26/10
5:44 PM EST
My office, NJ

I interviewed a friend's son for an internship this summer. I really like being able to offer them and the young adults we take on are generally very smart, capable and want to work and learn. Kayla has been having trouble getting some of her clothes/room boxes from the college storage. She went to talk to the local people in charge. They ignored her, so she went up the chain of command and her stuff should be delivered tonight. I would not want my daughter mad at me. She is a very tough person, like my other children and especially my wife.

8/27/10
4:25 PM EST
My office, NJ

I finished going through our database and spoke or emailed almost everyone, which amounted to about 5000 people and took me approximately 18 months to finish. The next thing to do is start over again. Sales is the relentless pursuit of increasing the percentages by making calls, putting out new products and getting enough attention to be noticed, remembered and utilized. We are making great progress on the technical aspects of our fire suppression system and are hopeful we can attract U.S. based fire companies in its use for breaking down doors, going through windows and even buildings to help cut down the danger of explosions for entering firemen. We can then send in a fire suppression system of chemicals or foam so no one has to get too close at the initial stages. There is a meeting scheduled next week with the NDUM to go over the proposal for a grant for the system. I am hoping it is our first successful endeavor there. So far, sales for the month are fine. It is very calming to be in this position at least until next Wednesday when a new month begins.

I spoke to Uncle Dave, who had a bicycle accident. I thought he was joking when he said he only had a few broken bones, but he wasn't. He needed stitches and has a broken finger and two broken ribs. He is already talking about when he can go back riding. I admire his fortitude and hope to see him tomorrow.

It has been five years since Hurricane Katrina and from what I can see, they are still vulnerable to another big storm. Our global warming floating house systems would safeguard them. Maybe we can start the process in Malaysia and move it back.

8/29/10
3:16 PM EST
Home, NJ
Our porch

It has been an amazing day. The weather was perfect this morning, in the mid 60°s, and the sky was cobalt blue. I rode alone and was back in time to get ready to have lunch with my mom. It was calm and very pleasant. We talked about family and I gave her an update on what was happening with the business. Then it was off to town to visit Uncle Dave. He was wounded from his fall, but not beaten and we had a nice time at tea talking about business and life. He was very interested in our progress about going public, which should be now entering the final stages with some specific dates as to when I am due back in Malaysia. I got a call last night from Paul Warth. I was not surprised to hear he had been let go from his company, but he was not surprised either. We spoke about the potential for a four part alliance between his old company, another company in California that wanted to represent our product lines and Paul himself. I will follow up on Monday to see what is possible. If everyone keeps their head and what is in their best interest, it could be great for all of us, especially since Ben has wanted a West Coast presence representing us. Opportunities abound, the trick is filtering out the best one with the highest chances for success and that is mostly up to me.

8/30/10
4:25 PM EST
My office, NJ

Titan and Paul are in from Asia and they are at Jack's house learning about the composites and making samples. I spoke to one of the fire fighting suppliers today and they can supply us with the new DSPA dry sprinkler powder aerosol, which is a device you throw into a fire that puts it out. By combining the ability of our forced air launcher to shoot a projectile through a door, window or wall and the DSPA, we can put out fires from a long way away. There is virtually no danger to the fire fighters and much less equipment and manpower will be needed. This could be great news for townships and states who need to cut down costs for fire suppression. It is not a great deal, however, for the firefighters who would not be needed.

8/31/10
11:24 AM EST
Newark/Liberty Airport New Jersey

My computer just shut down and I lost my last entry for the day, so I am figuring that based on fate, I should change course in what I wrote. It was a good morning of tennis, getting my car in for a dent repair and getting through airport security. There are a lot big deals pending and my stomach is reflecting the pressure. I may also have a bug of some kind, so I will try to take it easy in the food area.

8/31/10
8:47 PM EST
East Brookstreet Hotel Ottawa Canada

We landed on time and as fate would have it, the driver I had for the day had been switched at the last minute and I ended up with the owner of the company. Frederick, definitely not Fred, was your typical entrepreneur, like me, with multiple interests that extend beyond car service. As I previously mentioned, drivers either say nothing or like to talk, and Frederick definitely liked to find out who was in his car. As I explained what I did, including the new ballistic armor project, he immediately became interested because another of his partners might have a use for us. That led to a whole discussion of what was possible, brought in another potential partner and by the time we got to Alcatel Lucent, we were already getting ready to exchange non-disclosure agreements so I could send him data sheets and leave a sample. It is strange how these things happen.

My stomach had been feeling badly and I had a headache, but both were improving by this time. Charity Nunn, the new head of labels, was an extremely bright, knowledgeable woman and we got along well. In addition to going over what we did and our new lines, she offered to help with referrals to others while I was here. I am back to AL again tomorrow morning and I hope to see her again. She is sending a requisition in the next month for all of the labels we make to get prices ready for 2011.

After that, Frederick and I spoke to the second referral for the armor he had given me and Rich from our office sent him some files of examples of the products. Eventually, he decided it would be best to wait to sign an NDA and exchange materials and samples before an actual meeting, which was fine for me. By that time, I was already in my hotel room and not seeing him in person in downtown Ottawa meant my next mission was dinner. I had heard about a mall and a shopping center about 20 minutes away and I set out to find it. I spoke with Al and Wendy on the way and both are great. Finally, after about 30 minutes, I saw the row of stores the hotel counter man had mentioned before the actual mall. It as getting late and as I scanned the strip mall, I saw a sign for salad and decided that would be fine. Walking into the pizzeria was like entering into another world and the only thing I was 99% sure of was that the family running it was not Italian. I told them I wanted a very big salad with grilled chicken and that is exactly what I got, plus some feta cheese, two bottles of water and a diet coke. They were very pleasant and I enjoyed my time talking to them. I love being around small business owners who work hard and have a passion for the business, their families and their lives.

Back at the hotel room, I ate my salad, my last pack of granola bars and some of the oatmeal mix I had brought. It is about 9:00 PM and I am going to sleep soon. What a treat to go to sleep early during the week and get up a little later. I hope my car is ready when I get home tomorrow.

SEPTEMBER

9/1/10
3:28 PM EST
In flight to Ottowa, Canada

After a great night's sleep of eight hours, I exercised, ate a big breakfast and was at Alcatel-Lucent by 9:00 AM via Paul, my driver for the day. The meetings there went well and afterward it was off to Gibson Design Company to meet the owner Scott Gibson. He is an industrial designer and has decades of experience in telecom that parallels ours. We spoke about design and marketing in general and agreed to work together. He has an application we hope to prototype within the next few weeks.

I was worried about the flight home because of possible delays, but so far so good and I can be at my car repair place by 5:00 PM. I called the owner Brad and he said it would be ready.

9/3/10
4:54 PM EST
My office, NJ

I got the news this morning that I had to be in Kuala Lumpur on October first at the final signing meeting for going public. Since I was already scheduled to leave for Europe on October 4th, it meant a lot of scrambling to change my plans. As it stands, I will leave on Tuesday, Sept. 28th, get to KL on Sept 30th, make calls, go to the meeting on October 1st, either leave that night or the next day for Amsterdam and then fly home the next Wednesday. It will be my longest business related trip to date and I am interested to see how well I hold up. This morning, Vinnie and I met Mike at Jack's house where Titan and Paul have been studying the new composite system all week. They have learned a great deal and we spent a few hours talking about production and sales. They are preparing, along with Brett, to go to the composites show in Beijing in a few weeks times. Today starts the Labor Day weekend here in the U.S., the final big holiday of the summer. Time has gone quickly and well. Wendy and I are staying local since my son Ben and his friends are using the Berkshire house. It is not a problem not to be traveling. I like it here and it is relaxing to have some time. Another Tea Party candidate has won a primary, this time for the senate race in Alaska. Big changes seem to be brewing in politics.

No Road Is Ever Straight

After riding and lunch, I worked in our garden, preparing it for winter by transplanting and planting for next year. It was a beautiful day here and not too hot, so it was wonderful being outside. Wendy and I went to a movie and then got dinner to bring home. It is a calm evening and very nice.

It is looking more like the Democrats will lose some of their seats in both houses. My hope is for a gridlock, so nothing more can be done, giving the system a chance to work to right itself without any more government interference.

9/5/10
3:48 PM EST
Home, NJ

It has been an amazingly beautiful summer day here in NJ. I played tennis with my brother and went riding with Uncle Dave. He is recovering quickly from his accident, but still looks a bit shaky. He told me that right after the accident, he got his bike into the shop before he went to the hospital emergency room to get himself taken care of. I can only imagine what Wendy would have said to me if I had been in the accident and I told her to go to the bike store first. Regardless, it was a pleasant time. I went back home and read some more of the Bible and the Qur'an. I am almost done with it and it has given me some understanding regarding Islam. It is a good basis to learn more. I will go back to the proposal for the Malaysian army now and then Cliff and Barbara are coming over for dinner. It has been a very calm day. I needed it.

9/6/10
5:04 PM EST
Home, NJ

It is Labor Day here in the U.S. I was listening to a radio program where some organized union leaders were proclaiming their pure intentions for the betterment of the workers and how they were the light to look up to as opposed to the horrible business owners and Wall Street. I guess they have a narrow, selective memory, considering the trouble labor unions have caused this country and are one of the prime reasons for the decay in our manufacturing sector. Unions have outgrown their usefulness and have been a drag on our economy for almost 100 years. I hope this time they are truly stamped down so that general business has some chance to come back. It is no accident that Labor Day is a day for idleness here in the U.S. and not one for work. We have to transform ourselves into a new economy. My companies are working towards it and the President and his liberal allies are working to destroy it. I relish the challenge.

9/7/10
8:02 PM EST
Home, NJ

Going public has once again created a new level of challenge and anxiety. Unknowingly, I did not give all the information necessary to our consultants in Malaysia, which caused a problem with the security commission. After a day with back and forth emails, faxes and phone calls with Gary and Howard and with the able assistance from Mike, I think we have everything as it should be. I am glad you normally only do this one time and then use the initial information as a base to go to other exchanges. My trip to Malaysia is now almost set and I am working on the appointments for the day before the formal signing on October 2nd. I hope to be solid with the appointments by Monday. I already emailed Jeroen about getting to Amsterdam earlier than planned, which will give me chance to see Igor, who is moving there. The formal political season has started here in the U.S. The gloves are off and the politicians are tasting blood already. Election night should be exceedingly interesting.

9/8/10
4:15 PM EST
My office, NJ

The information back and forth between all of us to get ready for the private offering continued into last night and throughout today. It is amazing how much detail is involved. We have more information going tomorrow. I had lunch with Nathaniel today, a tennis partner and friend. He is also a successful entrepreneur and nearing the time to jump off the cliff to go for his dreams. We have more inventions in work for the composite and air cannon areas. It is not boring. Tonight marks the beginning for the Jewish New Year and I leave for our synagogue soon to help usher. The head of a Florida church is threatening to burn Qur'ans to remember 9/11. He is obviously an idiot who is out to glorify himself and get publicity. I would no sooner justify burning the Qur'an than the Old Testament or an American flag. The ill will that clergyman has already caused will be felt by those who travel the world. We are fools to allow him to do it. He has crossed the line.

9/9/10
8:11 PM EST
Home, NJ

The High Holy Days began last night with our New Year celebration. The services were calm with no problems, as were today's. I started a new tradition with the formal turning over of some of the services to my friend Peter, a very experienced usher, which allowed me to leave the synagogue midday for a while to eat lunch at home and ride my bike. I am working on the new cancer detection system. We had our holiday dinner at my sister's house, which was very pleasant, though I ate too much. Tomorrow, Wendy leaves to spend a few days in the Berkshires with her mom. I will miss her.

It is possible that with the balance of the emails today, we have most if not all of the information to Malaysia for the public offering. I will believe it when they say we are done. As of now, we also have a meeting with the press in Malaysia on the 30th where I am also to give a short speech which I need to start work on.

9/10/10
9:20 AM EST
Home, NJ

I had a reaction to the two vaccine shots I received yesterday. Obviously, the combination of the flu, H1N1 and pneumonia all together was a not a good idea. I think I am feeling better and hope I can ride tomorrow morning with Uncle Dave. Wendy is in the Berkshires, so it is just Bailey and me until Sunday. I am working on lots of new ideas. We better hit on one of them soon. I can't keep justifying this massive R&D expenditure forever.

9/11/10
9:04 PM EST
Home, NJ

Today is the 9th anniversary of the 9/11 attacks. I hope we are better prepared to protect ourselves from a military standpoint worldwide. However, from a moral and justifiable standpoint, I have to wonder where we are when people like the minister in Florida can threaten to burn the Qur'an, knowing it will jeopardize not only our troops but all Americans trying to live in peace. Why does mankind think they can do anything in the name of religion, using God as their justification? Why does the constitutional right to burn the Qur'an, old or new testaments, flags of various countries or sacred symbols give people the actual okay to do these horrific things knowing they will cause great harm? Our country really needs to learn tolerance if we expect to be an example to the rest of the world and foster our system on others. We cannot throw stones at other governments if we are not perfect. Perhaps getting along, although seemingly an alien concept to many groups in the U.S., makes a great deal of sense, especially for the benefit of all, as opposed to domination and the use of force. Memories do not go away. If we lose our dominate position in the world, people will not forget how we treated them and it will come back to haunt us and our children. The Golden Rule was never truer than it is today; treat others as you would like to be treated. I hope I do that in my life and it is a good example for the people I work with and my family. I will work harder to be so.

It was a very nice day here in New Jersey with a beautiful blue sky and about 80°F. I rode with Uncle Dave this morning and he is feeling much better from his accident. After bringing my clothes to the office, it was off to Jack's house for his annual wine tasting party. Although I do not drink alcohol, I still had a great time and saw Mike, his wife and young son as well and Al and Mel. I also got a chance to talk with a guy who worked at Jack's old company. They make military communications devices and they might be interested in our new mobile delivery system, utilizing our air cannon to send their modules long distances to set up mobile communications networks.

SEPTEMBER

Afterward, Bailey and I had to go to the office since the alarm there had gone off. There was no security breach. Kayla called after dinner to say her housing plans had changed for next year. She and twelve other students, including eight boys, were all moving into a big house. Since they were all friends, the boys added an extra level of security, and she checked the place out to make sure it was safe and in good shape, I gave my okay. I also called Wendy to let her know and she was okay with the decision. Wendy is due home tomorrow and I will watch a little television before going to sleep. I have also been editing my new book today. My goal is to have the first six months to Katie by the end of October.

9/12/10
1:31 PM EST
Home, NJ

I have been wrestling with an invention idea for weeks. Stemming from my own fear of prostate cancer, the big question is how you can get an accurate scan of cancerous cells on a molecular level. You can get screened showing hot areas of potential problems now, but I want an exact, cell by cell depiction of what is going on inside the body and the question is how to get there. I am going to see Dr. Browne tomorrow. I am wondering if, in theory, you could take a million x-rays from every position on your body and put them all together to know where the good cells stop and the cancer cells start. Hopefully, he will not think I am crazy and maybe he has an idea of how to do it.

I was reading in the newspaper that the solution dropped from airplanes to fight forest fires might be toxic to the inhabitants they attempting to save. I then had the idea that the new material we are about to work on with our new Malaysian partners is supposed to absorb 70% of the heat from something. What if we dropped that from a plane? Would the particle cloud that was created be able to take out enough of the heat from a fire to stop it? It is another area we will check as soon as we get information and samples from the inventor.

Wendy is home from the Berkshires and is already out again visiting one of her friends who is going back home to California. It is raining here, which is a very good thing since it has been dry. Sunday afternoons are usually good times for reflection. They give me a chance to slow down a little and think.

Yesterday when Uncle Dave and I were biking, we stopped off at the bike store so I could get one of my hand brakes tightened. He spoke to a woman there who turned out to be someone that I dated for a short time when I was in college. I have seen her a few times since and we all got to talking about if we would like to be young again. They both said they would like to relive their twenties with the knowledge they have now. I, however, have no wish to go back and possibly make much worse mistakes than I originally did. I am happy to move forward and am glad I do not know what the future holds. That way, the decisions and responsibility are mine and the chances for new adventures will never stop.

9/13/10
3:55 PM EST
My office, NJ

The global price pressure on products continues. While the world does not pull out of the economic slump it is in, everyone, including us, has little compunction in trying to get the lowest prices possible. The downward spiral on being able to charge makes it extremely difficult to fund R&D and to get raises and bonuses to our people. My view has not changed. We need to move into more profitable areas, as we have been trying to do for the last 18 months. If they do not break soon then we may have to go to other new areas.

9/14/10
4:33 PM EST
My office, NJ

It was an amazing pre-dinner time last night. As I sat on our porch inventing, a thunder storm came in and everything grew so dark I had to move indoors. It was a rush from the inside of me to the outside. I came up with a new type of projectile towing spear that could be launched to distant places while trailing a cable that can be used to move supplies back and forth. It would be especially good to move materials over swollen rivers or other areas of devastation. I was supposed to play tennis this morning, but my partner and I got our signals crossed so I ended up biking outside, which was fantastic in the clear cool pre-autumn weather. The marketplace is ripe for new inventions and ideas. The trick, as always, is to get them to the right people who have the money to pay for them. I got an email from one of our contacts at CTRM. They have a potential customer for the global warming floating house project. I gave the go ahead for hurricane and tornado testing here, as we will need the rating to prove we can resist cyclones.

9/15/10
7:54 PM EST
Home, NJ

My new book is done. Now we begin the next step; signing, sending and giving them out. I am already editing this year's edition. It is good to stay ahead.

We hired a chemist today. He is the son of a man who worked at Jack's old company. He will be based at Jack's house and will do various types of research on everything we are or will be working on. His future is in his own hands, which is the best situation one could ask for. I had lunch with Dave Robinson, an old friend and surfing buddy. He has a home at the Jersey Shore and has been enjoying a wonderful summer. After I got back, I went to see the deputy fire chief at our local fire station. I wanted his input on our inventions and see if we were missing any areas where we could be of help. As it turned out, they liked what we were doing, but said the fire laws in building in the U.S. were so stringent he was not sure if our ability to launch projectiles to put out fires would be of use. However, in other parts of the world the fire precautions may not be so stringent and our equipment might be of use. We also agreed that in many small towns throughout the country there were places with no fire department and our fire suppression system might be of great use to them, something for us to consider. We are slowly refining our markets and will continue to do so to zero in on our best chances for success.

I have been emailing with Ben in China and the two days I am spending in Kuala Lumpur are filling up rapidly. It sounds like it could be a really fun time. There has not been much word from Brett in China, though I heard he had food poisoning. Being sick is bad, but being ill in another country away from home is much worse. I hope he is okay.

More Tea Party candidates are winning here in the U.S. primaries. Both Republicans and Democrats are worried as to what their influence will be in the midterm elections in November. I plan to vote for few if any candidates currently in office. A clean sweep would be good and I think I am not alone in my sentiments.

9/16/10
4:45 PM EST
My office, NJ

We have come up with a possible cure for cancer. Granted, we are not scientists, doctors or part of any other field you might normally figure would be suitable to figure out the solution to this horrible disease. However, it has been my experience that those who are not trained are often best for new and innovative ideas. That, combined with our mechanical capabilities for design and innovation and viewing the human body as a machine versus living organism led us to this possible solution. We have a partner who has connections into DARPA, the Defense Advanced Research Projects Agency, for a preliminary research grant. After he read the proposal, he did not say we were crazy to my surprise and then asked to show it to a few others. If the reactions are positive, he will submit it to the agency. He said they have a large area for medical advancement.

We spoke to a potential customer today regarding a new type of fire suppression system to help soldiers get out of burning vehicles. Jack and I worked on a plan and Eric should have a rendering ready for Monday. It is a product we can make ourselves and it would be great to finally sell something in one of our new areas. I spoke to Brett today, who is sick but able to work. Tomorrow is the last day of the show. The good news is they are getting a great response at the trade show and the potential is huge from all over the world.

9/17/10
3:52 PM EST
My office, NJ

I saw my brother today for tennis and, as always, he was a joy to be around. Tonight starts the Jewish holiday of Yom Kippur, our Day of Atonement. I will usher the early service tonight and tomorrow and then go back in the afternoon until 5:00 PM.

9/18/10
10:16 PM EST
Home, NJ

Last night and today went well at the synagogue. I have an incredible staff and co-captain and they all did well. We moved a lot of people in and out in short periods of time and the custodial staff was also excellent, as usual. This was our day to remember our sins and it also gave me a chance to talk to some of my fellow congregants. It made me all the more grateful for the incredible life I have and the chances to do more. I told some people, including Katie and Ben who were out for dinner tonight, about my idea for a cancer treatment and others my idea for global peace. They have an expected skepticism in their eyes, but all doubt me much less than a decade ago. It spurs me forward with more energy. I have laid my ego open for negative responses since I am trying to invent as quickly and as widely as possible. In doing so, many of my ideas will be shot down, ridiculed, ignored and considered foolish, but I must be willing to accept it all if I am to let the creative energy surge through me. The negative responses become harder to take over time, in that they are going at me personally. They are less so in others because I have an increasingly bigger worldwide team behind me giving credence to our ideas and ability to perform. I am hopeful my team and I have the drive and determination to bring my ideas to fruition. This will not only help us to succeed and profit, but help many others in the process. Both Ben and Katie look wonderful and seem very happy both in their lives apart and together. I heard from Kayla and Alex today and both sounded fine. Next week, everyone is home for Jeff's birthday party and I greatly look forward to us all being together.

9/19/10
6:58 PM EST
Home, NJ

I played tennis with my brother, who is well, and then I bicycled with Uncle Dave. It was a gorgeous late summer day here in New Jersey. We stalked the building I have been after for almost a decade and it still looks as good as ever. I brought my clothes to the office for the week and then went to see my parents. I told them about my idea for curing cancer and asked my dad, who has had four different types, if he would participate in the experiments if we got a grant to go ahead. Since it is minimally destructive to noncancer cells, he said he would. My father is truly an amazing man.

I bought some autumn flowers, chrysanthemums and planted them. I got some extra dirt and planted the balance of my Black Eyed Susan seeds. I hope they all grow again next year. It is Sunday night and the normal feelings of worry are starting to creep into my brain. Fall is coming here soon, temperatures will continue to drop and it will be nice to have sweaters on again. I look forward to the ice cold nights, incredibly clear night skies to see the stars and the various holidays leading up to and including the New Year.

9/20/10
5:45 PM EST
Home, NJ

Jeroen arrived from the Netherlands and we spent a good part of the afternoon working on strategy for expanding Ideal Jacobs Europe..

9/21/01
4:43 PM EST
My office, NJ

We started company reviews today. It has been a better year business wise and we were able to give out raises. Our team here in the U.S. has been fantastic and I want to be able to show them our appreciation and support. We had a cookout in Jeroen's honor. It was a beautiful early autumn day and everyone had a great time. Great news: our armor passed some very difficult shooting tests. It will be great to be able to share this with potential customers. Jeroen and I went to see a fire safety specialist today. We are going to work on a shoulder based compression cannon.

Ira's brother-in-law Herb passed away today. He was a good man. The Republicans and Democrats are battling it out harder, trying to gain or retain dominance after the midterm elections. The Tea Party group is building ever increasing power and the Democrats are not sure if this is good or not. I love American politics.

9/22/10
5:03 PM EST
My office, NJ

The employee reviews continue. It is good to go over how everyone is doing with them, what can be better and suggestions they have for the future. Our people have excellent, practical minds and their solutions to various problems are invaluable in streamlining our business. Jeroen, Jack, Vinnie, James and Mike got more samples ready for the hurricane, tornado, cyclone and ballistic armor testing for next week. On the heels of successful tests yesterday, I am hopeful they will prove our theories about time for production, strength of our finished materials and actual costs for the whole product. Just when I think things are done for going public, more issues come up. It is maddening at times and I wonder if we will ever finish. I am sure there will be more emails about it tonight. Meanwhile, I am trying to solidify our appointments in Kuala Lumpur next week as well as getting the flights ready for Europe.

9/23/10
4:37 PM EST
My office, NJ

Our export attorney John came in to give a talk about ITAR regulations. Our system seems to be in good shape for military related exports and he seemed pleased with the level of understanding of our team. At lunch, our guys hit him with questions from all sides of what is proper regarding moving information around the world and John was extremely helpful. We did some more reviews today and are continuing work with Jeroen regarding formalizing the new IJ Europe system and his role within it. We have a small amount of additional information to send to Malaysia regarding the public offering. I doubt that we are finished.

I spoke to Kayla last night. She is coming home this weekend with Alex and Ben and I can't wait to see them all. Jeroen is coming to our house for dinner tonight. He has already met and likes Wendy, but this will be his first exposure to Bailey and we never know how he will act. I also get to show Jeroen my flowers, which have been reacting well to the generally cooler and wetter weather. Alice is leaving tomorrow for England. She is very excited to see the "English Muffin," her new granddaughter. It is nice to see her in such high anticipation.

9/24/10
4:30 PM EST
My office, NJ

Jeroen and I booked airline seats and hotels for the trip and we have one more hotel to go. It turns out we are going to Spain. I have never been there. Almost all of the employees reviews are done with one more to go. It will be good to be done.

We are starting to get responses from the book mailings. It is nice that people like it. I am working on two new fire suppression inventions with Brett. One is to start a fire line to stop a forest fire and the other is to coat houses with foam so they won't burn in front of a fire. Both can be utilized from a quarter to a half mile away with our cannon. I wonder if anyone will buy it.

9/25/10
8:09 PM EST
Home, NJ

Last night was a pre-birthday dinner celebration for Jeff at Barbara and Cliff's. Kayla came in and looked wonderful. Her friend Alexa was with her, but they left early to take Alexa to the train station to go into Manhattan.

SEPTEMBER

Some of the people coming were stuck in traffic and by 9:00 when a few were still not down from the Boston area, Wendy and I gave up and came home. I biked early with Uncle Dave and we had a pleasant time. Then it was off to Jeff's party, which was exceptionally fun with all of the grand nieces and nephews except for Alex, who had too much work and stayed in St. Louis. I told him I understood when I spoke to him last night. He obviously knows how to take responsibility for the work that is needed of him and I am proud of him for sticking to his guns and getting things done. It is unfortunate he could not be here today. The party had good food and lots of happy people. Some reminisced about Jeff when he was a young man and he seemed very happy.

Afterward, it was back home where I started packing for Tuesday and signed books. I want to try to get a few hundred more signed before I leave. It is always interesting seeing my brother-in-law Buzz from the Boston area. He is an account/attorney and is a specialist in tax law. He has a different view of life from me and Cliff, who was also there. It is fun to get together.

9/26/10
4:09 PM EST
Home, NJ

I am finding that I am self-editing what I choose to write about. Going public has some wonderful implications, but troubling ones as well. As the " non-executive" chairman, which means I am not involved in the day to day running of the company, what I say or write is scrutinized with ever increasing detail so I have to be more careful. While this may be better for our stockholders and the price of our stock, it does create an increasing level of disservice to my readers who want to hear about all of the stuff going on, not just the good things. Unfortunately or fortunately, with more expansion and success comes scrutiny, so I will bow somewhat to reality and try to keep my comments toward what is acceptable. On the other hand, I do own the majority interest in our companies in Asia, so to heck with it. I will talk about what I think is important.

Throughout the last decade, I have gone to a series of therapists regarding various aspects of my life. In fact, our family sometimes refers to them as "trainers." We have trainers for sports and for teaching new subjects in school, so why not trainers to help mentally? As the pressures mount up, it is often good to speak to someone who is off to the sidelines with no agenda and able to give an unbiased opinion. I find them helpful, usually for a few months at a time, to give a reality check regarding what I am thinking and the various courses I am on. I find no stigma about therapists, just like I have no problem asking for help with my tennis game or if I wanted to learn a new language.

Another area I have been avoiding talking about in detail is the process of taking our companies in Asia public. I have never, ever, gone through the detailed scrutiny as that of consultants paving the way for the public offering.

Even so near the end, after a lot of the paperwork has been signed, both Ben and I have found areas, to our horror that we unintentionally did not disclose that should have been. It does not even occur to any of us from either our Asian or U.S. teams it needed to be done and now we have to make it right. That is what this week's trip to Asia is about. Sometimes when you are looking at so much small bits of information, the big stuff can shuffle past it. I hope we can work it out so there is no delay in our schedule, but I am also glad everything is now disclosed and we can move forward. I will have much more tolerance for someone in a similar position who says they simply forgot to mention something. With the avalanche of data, it is very easy for things to go unnoticed. We have found it now and I am hoping to be back on track by next weekend.

9/28/10
3:43 PM EST
JFK Airport, NY

The last two days have been spent in preparation for this trip. There are issues to resolve once I get to Kuala Lumpur (KL) in addition to various meetings, some of which still need to be formalized. As always, it was very difficult saying goodbye to Wendy. However, we are meeting in Paris the end of next week so that is something for us both to look forward to. I was a little hesitant this morning, playing a new partner in tennis. I was worried he would not show up, be late, be a lousy player or generally difficult to be around. None of the above occurred and we had a rousing game that left me tired out and ready for the flight. The trip from New Jersey via Mike the driver was filled with traffic and delays but he made it with time to spare. As has been the case for the last year, the public offering in Malaysia has me concerned and also incredibly excited. I feel it in my bones that if we can get through it then the other side of "being public" will put us into position to expand to many new levels. We just have to get there first.

I spoke to Kayla this morning. She is working for one of her professors, cataloging some special trees growing at her school and she found out this morning that she will be in charge of the computer program to chronicle all of the data and the results. The fact that there is no one to teach her the system and they basically handed her a manual and told her she is on her own is a testament to her wonderful abilities. There is a tornado watch for the entire area around here and there is talk we are delayed a little. I have a long layover in Turkey so as long as we take off within a decent time I should be fine.

There is a whole group of people next to me who seem to be traveling together. I cannot tell if they are work related or are part of a pleasure trip, but they seemed very happy about traveling and that works for me. The aircrew of the Turkish airlines plane I am on cut in front of the man in front of me on the security line. The guy got really mad and tried to block the captain from getting a box for his valuables and a ruckus almost ensued. I stayed back because if there is ever an altercation with a crewmember and a passenger, then the passenger will definitely lose. I try to keep to myself when possible; it usually works well when traveling alone. I should have eaten something sooner as I am getting a headache. I am going to eat, move to the gate and decide what to do from there.

9/28/10
4:47 PM EST
JFK Airport, NY

As you can tell by my entry, we are still on the ground. So far it is an hour delay, nothing major. Airports can be some of the loneliest places imaginable, which is why I am so careful to have music, movies and things to edit so my time is well spent and I can forget about where I am. It is that time in the trip when I dream about the best that can happen.

If all goes well:

1. The next stage of going public will be done and the end will truly be in sight.
2. We will enter into a new partnership with a group in Malaysia that has close ties to their military.
3. We will meet with a group from CTRM and their customer who is interested in our global warming floating houses.
4. We will meet with the two heads of CTRM to discuss future projects and collaborations.
5. The meeting with NDUM will not only begin an actual project, but they will agree to the Technical Assistance Agreement I already sent them that will enable us to trade actual information and samples for commercial/military projects.
6. Igor will get settled into IJ Europe, his new home, get along with everyone there and be happy.
7. I will play squash for the first time.
8. I will make sales calls with Jeroen and set up more potential business plus visit his software specialist to help create programs to measure our new plastic products for blast results.
9. The next stage in moving our new customer in Germany from buying prototypes to buying mass runs.
10. We will meet with the people from Trelleborg in Europe and create an alliance to joint develop and sell.
11. I will meet Wendy in Paris and we will have a fantastic time.
12. Everyone travels safely and with little delays. It is a lot to hope for; let's see what happens.

No Road Is Ever Straight

9/29/10
4:16 AM Istanbul time, 9:16 PM EST
In flight

Meanwhile, we got a proposal from a company in Malaysia today through Hing who wants to represent us for defense work in that country. If they have the sales contacts and the agreement is not too confining and will not hinder our other efforts, I am interested. Jack, Vinnie and James went to Westlake today to run the prototypes with our new plastic and cloth configurations. If they work then we will send them for hurricane/tornado/typhoon/cyclone testing and we can market it worldwide. If not, we have a big problem because we will have a composite product line we can't manufacture. I am hoping I have a report in my email when we land. My new book, The Ideal Adventure, is done and being distributed along with some sales materials. The response back has been positive and we probably have almost a thousand in the field already.

9/29/10
10:32 PM Turkey time, 3:32 AM EST
Millennium Lounge, Istanbul Airport

I do not know how they did it but even though we left late we arrived about on time. I made my way through the airport and actually found the correct transfer desk for Malaysia Airlines, got my ticket and I am now in the lounge. It is cool here though it is pretty warm in the airport itself. I love to watch people and every airport has its own flavor and look of people. Here, it is definitely a European/African mix.

I have been emailing with Ben and Hing and the schedule is firming up for the next two days. I can't seem to get on the internet with my laptop. We have an electrical engineer here in the U.S. who has been utilizing our facility for some printing research. We have become friendly, his name is Bob and he and I are trying to team together for two potential military projects. I read the presentation he gave about solar energy. It was fascinating and is spawning some ideas on how we might work together in a third area. I love inventing; it is like the ultimate crossword puzzle and the thrill of exploration into new areas is like a continuous injection of pure adrenaline. I need to walk before getting on the next plane but I have to be careful not to become overheated and too sweaty. It is a delicate balance.

Rham Emanuel, President Obama's Chief of Staff, may be leaving to run for the Mayoral Seat of Chicago. For a strong willed man like him, it must be very difficult not to be the boss. He would probably make a descent mayor. As for the President, I look increasingly forward to the November elections here in the U.S. blocking Mr. Obama's ability to create more legislation and put us more into debt is the best thing that could happen. As is typical with my former political party (Republican), with the incredible chance to take control of both houses of Congress, the Tea Party movement has emerged and all bets are off as to who will win or not. I am glad I am not in or running for political office.

166

SEPTEMBER

9/29/10
9:43 PM Malaysia time, 9:43 AM EST
In flight, 35002 feet, 601 miles per hour, -52°C outside

We are flying over Iran. This flight took off on time, good food was served and we have about 7 hours to go. I left New Jersey for the airport about 20.75 hours ago and sleep deprivation has set in. I know that because I am reacting emotionally to movies, which is a sure sign that I should take a nap soon. I have been going over my strategy for the next few days, the meeting with the underwriters in particular. They are having an open house the day before which is technically tomorrow and I think their top people will be there. Always trying for a win/win situation, I know that we are a mixed bag for them. We are the first Chinese/American company they are taking public and almost everything we have done has been great, but we have had a few problems in the last week. My guess is they will be happy with us, especially at the open house and also if we can potentially steer other companies to them to go public. That would benefit all of us as we might get a piece of that offering. I am viewing this as a selling situation and we will need each other in the future. If the bosses want us treated well then it is a good chance everyone will follow their lead. If our company can help others go public, we all win. Especially since our people will be invaluable regarding helping others to avoid some of the pitfalls we have fallen into.

I hope that the threat of that idiot preacher in the U.S. to burn Qur'ans will not have any lingering effects on me and other Americans traveling. Freedom of speech is a wonderful thing and people like that preacher use it to justify their attempts at getting five minutes of fame. Unfortunately, their idiocy, hypocrisy, fear and irrationality affects others and not him. I do, however, believe in Karma and the negative force that man has put out has probably already been paid back to him in spades. My head is starting to hurt, so it is time to try for a nap.

9/30/10
6:45 PM Malaysian time, 6:45 AM EST
Crowne Plaza Hotel Kuala Lumpur

Our flight was early this morning and I had my luggage, was in a cab and here to the hotel by 6:30 AM. Since I was so early, the hotel nicely gave me a temporary room until mine was ready and after quickly changing I went to the gym. I was feeling okay right up until I hit minute 35 on the elliptical and that was it for the day. I went back, had a wonderful shower, changed, called Wendy, who sounds great, and then went to meet Ben. He stays here so much they put him on the special services floor, which means he can use their dining room for breakfast, and he got me in also. I did not realize how hungry I was until I started eating. In between mouthfuls, Ben and I went over what had been going on for the last few weeks, the incredible strain and pressure we were both under and to finalize our strategy with the underwriters tomorrow. It sounded like things were better than I had thought and problems linked to the company were probably going to be taken care of at tomorrow's meeting. If so, we can go on with the offering on the same schedule. If not, we deal with what happens.

Then we switched to marketing and sales regarding the composite products. Ben wanted to be able to offer panels for five different applications like cyclone and typhoon buildings so his team would have something to sell. He also wanted to be able to offer customer parts that customers could incorporate into their products. After the successful Westlake tests yesterday I was able to say yes to everything and we would begin working on it when I got back. We also plan to put a prototyping plant into IJT like the one at Jack's so we could develop here and make samples.

Afterward, I switched back to my original hotel room and then Hing came by to go to the annual open house for our underwriters. It was very important for us to be there to support them. As we walked into the banquet hall there were two rows of company employees to greet all of the guests. Once inside, we met Mei and Yap our two principal intermediaries for the underwriting group and they in turn introduced us to their senior management. It was fascinating to sample the incredible variety of foods, many so spicy I dared not try them. There was a band playing with mostly Asian instruments and singing songs in Malay, the national language. It was a very festive, happy atmosphere.

Afterward, Hing left us until dinner tonight, and Abul picked us up to go to NDUM. He had been worried that we had no concrete products to work on with NDUM and I assured him we were going to move into specific areas at the meeting. I slept most of the way and once there, we sat down with Ghani and Jesbil, as well as Zamri and his associate.

The discussion went and we covered the following areas.
1. We would start work immediately on a new type of box and/or container that would be blast, rifle, fire and maybe blast wave resistant. We will need Trelleborg's help with the last part. We will check how much it will cost to test various types of samples in the U.S. and here and the time schedule to see what is possible. There is an immediate need to ensure that transported munitions don't blow up their containers and that terrorists can't stop the vehicle and walk away with their armaments.
2. We need to get the Technical Assitance Agreement (TAA) issued so that we can work on the item above and Jesbil and Ghani are supposed to get back to us in the morning with any changes so I can get them to our export attorney and then into the U.S. government for approval.
3. The compressed air device: they would center specifically on the contents for the spherical balls. They loved the idea for use with fire suppression and also wanted to use it for oil spills. I am hoping they will put out an immediate call for a grant; they have already assigned one of their professors to coordinate the project from their side.
4. For the global warming houses, we will work on prices for row houses and also check the heat movement material to see if it is relevant.

OCTOBER

10/1/10
12:21 AM Malaysian time, 12:21 PM EST
Crown Plaza Hotel Kuala Lumpur

I had time for a short nap, which was very hard to wake up from, and met Hing and Ben downstairs. Since the hotel was reasonably close Hing decided we should walk and luckily it was not too hot. Once there, we met up with the people from the Nickel and Dimed Company. Don't let the name fool you. They are extremely well connected into the Malaysian defense sector and they want to represent our composite and other products. The head of the company had a total of seven other people with him including the man who will become our main contact. By the time we finished, we had worked out some details of working together. I am ready for sleep.

10/1/10
10:47 PM Malaysia time, 10:47 AM EST
Kuala Lumpur Airport

I was woken up this morning by an announcement through the hotel address system. I could not understand the message, so I grabbed my laptop bag, passport and phone, threw on some clothes and went downstairs to the lobby. I subsequently found out it was a test alarm for the employees only, so I trudged back upstairs and turned off my alarm clock. I had lost about twenty minutes of sleep, but it could have been much worse. I went outside for my normal exercise, walking and phone call regime and all is well with the office and Wendy. I had breakfast and then met Ben and Hing in the lobby. This was it, the big meeting where we were to iron out the final problems for the public offering and seeing if there were any potential penalties for the information we had mistakenly failed to disclose. When we arrived, I met our two other directors, then Ku. Our attorney came in and we entered the meeting. I was initially hopeful since the people handling the offering were informally dressed, which was unusual for meetings here. As we sat down, their attorney read all of the potential penalties and fines if the SC decided they did not like our explanations for the lack of information. Our company, since my grandfather, has been run as an entrepreneur enterprise. We do things quickly, often without prior assessments and run by what feels right. While our systems for money control, purchasing and overall governance are tight, they are not to the exacting standards of this government and it was this clash of corporate cultures that created the problems. When the short meeting was over their decision was to stop our progress until we addressed all of the questions. We held the first board of directors meeting of Ideal Jacobs Malaysia. As we sat round the table and went through the various problems and our solutions, it became evident that our directors were all high grade people who would service our company well. In less than two hours, we had our plan of attack, everyone knew what was needed and we adjourned. As soon as we supplied our information, the underwriters would go to the SC, find out if they were acceptable and move on from there.

After lunch, I was dropped off at the hotel and the idea of a second work-out quickly faded when I ended up taking a two hour, much needed nap. Ben and I then rode to a dinner meeting hosted by our contact with the MIGHT Corporation. I was specifically looking forward to this time to meet the inventor of a new type of heat absorbing powder that could revolutionize the tele-com and building industry. The inventor and her husband were fascinating and I highly enjoyed hearing about how she discovered the process and their plans for increased production. They were all happy to hear about our plans to utilize the power for two major areas and we agreed to supply a quick marketing plan showing the potential if the product worked for our applications. The final step was to decide to send Paul Jordan from Thailand to here, get some samples of the material and hand deliver them to the U.S. where he, Vinnie and Jack could begin immediate tests. It was an excellent meeting and would have been worth the trip by itself. I said goodbye to Ben and our regular taxi driver, who we have known from previous trips, got me right over here to KL airport. Now through passport control and security, I am sitting in the Malaysia Air lounge, one of the best and I will go to the gate soon.

10/2/10
9:56 PM Turkey time, 2:56 AM EST
In flight to Istanbul, less than 8 hours to go.

So far we are on schedule and I don't have a long layover so I hope not to be delayed. I did it again. I had diet soda with caffeine with dinner and it was totally my fault, but the chicken was hot and spicy, so now I am not tired. On the other hand, I need to convert to Amsterdam time anyway so if I can get a few hours on this flight I should be fine. Editing on my new book is going well, I am up to 8/7/10. Happily, it seems I can edit even on long flights when my eyes are tired. I am listening to a singing group from the 1960s called the Fifth Dimension. Their songs bring me back to a time when I was a preteen and slowly developing the many habits, rituals, obsessions, drives, passions and belief that I can change the world. It is true, we are a combination of our experiences, our genes and that inside essence that drives us to go in a prede-termined path we set for ourselves. The older I get the more unusual I appear to be. I have no interest in dining, long vacations, smoking, drugs, relaxing and being contented with what is. I want to make my mark in the world, do good things, help people, be incredibly successful and watch my kids be the best they can be. I also want my ideas to be legitimized to have worth and impact. Unfortunately, that often means I am not contented unless I am so tired that I cannot move or be in constant motion where there is the potential for change. I also know that without my wife I would never stop working and would go all out indefinitely until I self destructed. She keeps me grounded enough so I can continue to soar on a day-by-day basis and enjoy the incredible journey as it is happening. She is and has always been my home base, which is the reason for my meeting her in Paris for the weekend. Given a choice, I would have gone home right after Spain, but she deserves to be able to go to the places she loves and yes, see a museum with me and even go to an expensive, long dinner which she knows is totally of no interest to me. However, a partnership is a team where everyone involved benefits and part of my job is to give her what she wants. I can easily view it that way. I will enjoy our weekend in Paris, the visit to the museum and dinner, even though I never would have done it alone.

I count my blessings continually and I believe in reincarnation. I also believe that the score is kept, call it Karma, and the good or bad things you do in a past life will either hurt or help you in your position in your next one. For the life I have now, which is more than I could have hoped for so far, I must have done something really good and must do better now to go further the next time. I have been given the chance to do something great in this world, to help the safety, security and bring a better life to large groups of people. It is my job to push my teams and myself as hard as possible to achieve what is within our realms, all while having a fantastic time along the way.

10/2/10
5:25 PM Amsterdam time, 11:25 AM EST
NH Hotel

We landed a little early in Istanbul and I got through the transit desk for my new ticket and up into the main airport area in good time. I wrote the IJ October newsletter and after boarding and settling in for the plane, I did some more editing but was soon too tired to move. We landed early. I picked up my suitcase, some food for tonight and lunch in case I wanted to stay in. I found a really nice young cab driver that drove me here to the hotel. I was a little apprehensive about this facility, but it turned out to be a good choice. Jeroen actually got me a small apartment for a few days, which is great since it has a small kitchen. I exercised in the gym and then rented a bicycle and toured the town of Naarden. It is very beautiful and filled with very old buildings and an arsenal that has been turned into a museum. Believe it or not, I was actually going to go in on my own, except the nice man there wanted euros and I did not have any with me. Speaking of pleasant people, the town was full of them and I spent time going up and down cobblestone streets and looking through shop windows, all the while trying to be careful because it seemed that cars had the right of way over pedestrians. After I got back, I ate dinner and now I am trying to stay up for a little while longer before going to sleep to try to get onto Amsterdam time. I emailed with Jeroen, who is picking me up tomorrow at 1:00 for biking and then dinner. I spoke to Wendy, who is doing well and we both miss each other. I look forward to a good, long night of rest.

10/3/10
11:42 AM Netherlands time, 5:42 AM EST
Sunday morning

I got about 12 hours of sleep last night and did not even have bad dreams. I am not sure I have ever slept that much before. When I awoke my stomach was in turmoil as it has stayed all morning. Regardless, I got up and exercised in the gym and went for a 30-minute walk. I was following a pathway and suddenly saw sailboats. Elated, I moved forward to reveal some type of large lake or inland waterway. It was beautiful. Once inside the parking lot, I noticed some red colored bushes and realized they were the same type as I used to see down at the New Jersey Shore when I was a kid. That time was a definite mixture of good and bad memories, one of which was being an overweight child and having to be seen in a bathing suit. Once you have been ridiculed for being overweight, no matter how many extra pounds you had (and I did not have that much), you never forget it. I look back at the time with a mixture of hate and fondness since that feeling of being fat has never left me and I look with great satisfaction with others of my age who once had perfect bodies and have been thickened by the passage of time. Being obsessive and compulsive has some definite advantages and one of which is if you are always concerned with gaining weight you monitor everything and generally don't.

My stomach feels like I am being punched continually in a kick boxing match. I asked Jeroen if we could walk instead of ride bikes. As long as I don't feel worse I am fine, this has happened many times before and I generally don't give in to it. Maybe he and I can stop for tea.

Meanwhile, I edited and send out the October newsletter to Rich and Al. I wrote them a note that if I was too hard on President Obama then they could modify it; they are both great fans of his. I also got in a report from Paul Jordan regarding affirmation of the need for cyclone and typhoon resistant buildings in Asia, I will use it to support the two projects that will go through MIGHT to the Malaysian Prime Minister. I will now go back through the proposal to get it ready to send to our people for review. It is a beautiful day here.

10/3/10
8:19 PM Netherlands time, 2:19 PM EST
NE Hotel

Jeroen and his eldest son Daniel picked me up and off we went for a wonderful tour of the Dutch countryside. One of the interesting things about this area and all of the Netherlands is their mixture of farm/homes and business all mixed together. It is common to see a factory with a field in the back with sheep or horses. We went for a walk by a large lake and then to the town of Maarden that I visited yesterday, which is three centuries old. Daniel had lots of energy and the two times I raced him and I lost. We stopped at two cafés, Daniel had a wonderful time loading up on sweets and Jeroen enjoyed a beer. We then went back to his house and picked up his wonderful wife Tamara and their young son Michael. We were off to visit a garden which was just after the peak of summer but still very beautiful. We went to their house for dinner and all during the time I got to speak with Jeroen and Tamara about our plans for the future and my and their dreams for Jeroen and Ideal Jacobs Europe.

Jeroen and Daniel dropped me back off at the hotel with the clothes and supplies I had sent from the U.S. and I will incorporate them into what I have and send the used clothes back via air. I got confirmation from Ben that Suwaleerat will be formally in charge of IJT once we go public, I think it is a good move.

10/4/10
NE Hotel
7:29 PM Amsterdam time, 1:29 PM EST

I spent most of last night sick and unable to sleep. My stomach felt like I was in a second, much worse kickboxing match. I tried to workout this morning but I only made it 30 minutes into my walk before my stomach pains were so bad I had to stop. Worrying about everything, especially sales calls for the day, I was able to take a quick nap before Jeroen picked me up and I decided it was time to break out the Amoxicillin that I carry for emergencies. That plus a few antacid tablets, Advils and some tea and I was in decent enough shape after we picked up Igor to work at his hotel. He looked well and excited. We had time for brief chat about what I expected, the faith I had in him, and our hopes for the future.

The sales call were to a carbon composite designer and manufacturer and a software specialist. The carbon manufacturer wanted to talk about teaming up with our composites and various potential projects, we got along very well and worked on some plans for the future. The software developer had the ability to show how our various materials would react against various types of firearms and bombs both in and out of water. He could save us a fortune in prototypes, getting rid of potential options that won't work and let us settle on those with the best chances. We left with the agreement to share various documents so we could link together and transfer information.

10/5/10
2:22 PM Netherlands time, 8:22 AM EST
Lencon Headquarters

I slept well last night, my stomach was steadily improving and got up at 4:30 to talk to Wendy; it was 10:30 PM her time. She sounds fine, misses me as I do her and is ready to leave Wednesday night for Paris. I was able to work out for my normal routine and eat breakfast; two wonderful things I have a new appreciation of after the last few days. Jeroen picked me up and it was off to Lencon headquarters, where Jeroen works when he is not working for IJE.

10/6/10
11:50 AM German time, 5:50 AM EST
On our way to Munich
Haufbrau House Transition Resort

I got up this morning, did my band workout then walked along the resort boundaries, which, under the early morning cloudy, cool sky was fantastic. I had my iPod and was listening to an eclectic group of some of my favorite music and enjoyed myself immensely. After breakfast Jeroen and I went to Rosenberger Corp. with the hope of increasing our business both in getting more parts and getting bigger orders for the one we had already made. Jeroen did a great job during the various conversations and the potential there for increased future business seemed good. I was happy with him and the calls, the people were very pleasant and all seemed to get along. As usual I had no problem when they broke away to speak to Jeroen in German, they were more comfortable in their native tongue and I wanted them to be able to speak freely. I was able to get the gist of what they were saying by their pointing to drawings, showing samples, watching their body movements and recognizing occasional words.

We stopped at this place for lunch and while Jeroen was on his cell phone I heard a vibration noise and I though his other phone was ringing. It turned out to be a cow in a nearby field, funny things you could never make up on your own.

10/6/10
4:37 PM German time, 10:37 AM EST
Munich Airport

On the way to the airport I got an email from Gary that we needed to talk about what to do next regarding information requests from Malaysia for going public. I keep thinking this will end, but it seems to go on. My teams and I are past frustrated, but we have to see it through. We are running out of options in how we can answer the inquiries. I hope this last attempt by Gary will work.

Jeroen is on his way upstairs to see if we can get our bags checked in and through security early. It should be about a 2-hour flight and I am hoping to be at the hotel by 11:00 PM. If , I will decide whether to exercise again or sleep for a few hours and get up and do it in the morning. The good news is that it is a hotel airport and I am making the assumption they are close to each other. If so, the flight is at 7:30 AM tomorrow which means we need to be there by 5:45 at the latest. I will need to get up by 3:00 to exercise normally. As you can see, it is a little tight from all directions. It will probably depend on how tired I am when I finally get to the room.

OCTOBER

10/7/10
6:06 AM Spanish time, 12:06 AM EST
Madrid Airport

We arrived in Madrid last night, about 30 minutes late and the baggage took an additional thirty minutes. It is now just before midnight and after we hailed a taxi we found out that the "Airport" hotel is not all that near the airport. So after a 25 euro cab ride, we got to the hotel to find that I had screwed up the booking and there is only one room that we had to share and it is smoking room at that. Jeroen, being the veteran, great traveler he is said no problem and after I got ready to work out he went to sleep. Finding a place to exercise in the hotel was not easy since nothing was open. I finally found an entrance to a bunch of meeting rooms, put on the film "The Curious Case of Benjamin Button" on my iPod and circled the room for about an hour. I have downloaded movies in case of times like these and instead of getting upset at the room situation I focused on the uniqueness of my situation and was able to enjoy my time alone. At 1:30 I went up to the room. A few hours of sleep later, I received my wake up call from the front desk and my alarm clock almost made me jump to the ceiling. We got through airport security quickly and are now waiting at the McDonald's restaurant for our gate. Jeroen is happy; he is on his second cup of coffee already and got a free beer last night because he got there at closing and there was no way to take his money. This is life on the road and lots of interesting times. I look forward to Paris.

10/8/10
6:16 AM Spanish time, 12:16 AM EST
La Caruna Airport

Bottom gate area - I am alone.

We were up early yesterday morning and got to La Caruna on schedule. Jeroen had not been able to get a rental car in advance, but he was finally able to secure one and off we went to find the Panador Hotel. Within an hour, passing the Spanish countryside and a few towns we were in the town of Ferrol. There was a large naval shipyard and military presence there.

Unfortunately we did not know where to meet the people from Trelleborg but I declared it a vacation day, which meant whatever happened was fine and worst case we would go sight seeing so there was no pressure on either of us. After some wonderful help from the people at the shipyard visitor office we were off to find the convention center for the naval show. Incredibly after getting lost Jeroen, as usual found where we were going and as we walked into the trade show we were struck by how small it was. It had less than 25 booths and a small conference area. This had been sponsored by few companies and was centered on a specific area of naval procurement.

We met the two representatives from Trelleborg, one was an oil and gas specialist the other defense and we spoke briefly about utilizing their syntactic foam with our armor to create a new material that will stop projectiles like sniper bullets, blasts from bombs and also force waves. Unfortunately they had not been kept up to date of any of it, which meant no one had been help-ing to sell our combined product in Europe. We agreed they would call later if they wanted to have a drink together and after we left I emailed their boss in the U.S. about a proposal for mutual research and selling in the U.S., Europe and Asia. We had briefly spoken about it before but now I had a clearer idea of how we could really help each other.

Jeroen and I then went back to the hotel, changed and went out to lunch. There were no more sales calls and unless the two Trelleborg people called we were done with meetings. We found a very nice restaurant and my halting Spanish was good enough to get us an excellent lunch. Afterward it was back to the hotel where I had nap and then went for a second walk in search of a scissors and some bottled water. My stomach had been getting progressively better but the antibiotics I was on were having some side ef-fects so I decided later in the day to stop taking them. I met back with Jeroen and after taking a taxi to a restaurant that was supposed to be open and wasn't and back to the hotel, I worked out in the hotel basement and then we met for dinner upstairs.

Amazingly the food was excellent, the service fast and it wasn't incred-ibly expensive. Jeroen and I spoke about world strategy, sales and psychol-ogy. So much of business in general and sales in particular is trying to figure out what people want we spend a lot of time working on trying to figure out the best ways to find out. It is good when we get together talking face to face and, in many circumstances, is best. I was back in my room by 11:00 PM.

The four hours of sleep felt great and Jeroen and I were on the road by 5:00 AM. With his GPS and excellent driving skills we got here to the airport before 6:00 AM. Wendy should already be in Paris. I have my two plane tick-ets and am ready to go.

10/8/10
1:48 PM French time, 7:48 AM EST
Orly Airport

The flights went well, the first one was an extremely small prop plane and the second was a little late but not a problem. Now we are all waiting for our luggage. I was able to work through the second flight but I am quickly burning out. I hope the luggage is here and comes out soon.

10/8/10
10:09 PM French time, 4:10 PM EST
Best Western Victor Hugo Hotel Paris

By the time I got to the hotel the effects of the trip came tumbling down on my shoulders and I was mentally done. Wendy was there and we went out for some food, but I was in no shape to speak coherently so she went for a nap and I took a walk down to the Eiffel Tower and over to been Franklin Rue, a short street dedicated to that great man. I got back and exercised a little in my room, by the time I had a shower my mental health was back and I was able to enjoy seeing my wonderful wife again. After a great dinner we watched some old family movies I had on DVD and then part of another movie and it was soon time for sleep. After an energy-depleting trip it is not unusual to need some time to decompress to get back to normal, something I should always remember and plan for.

10/9/10
5:47 PM French time, 11:47 AM EST
Best Western Victor Hugo Hotel Paris

After nine hours of needed sleep and a good breakfast downstairs Wendy and I ventured forth to a farmer's market recommended by Bunny from a previous trip. It turned out to be a wonderful adventure. The market was about a full city block long; narrow with just enough room for the stalls on either side and two rows of people going up and down each way. There were every kind of fruit, vegetable, cheese, flow, nuts and meats imaginable. There were even some clothes and jewelry vendors. Wendy and I started from one end and went all the way down to the other side. The sights and smells of the foods were like rapid fire water balloons. As we moved forward we were bombarded with new sensory signals every few feet. At the other end, I suggested we buy food so we could have lunch at the hotel and we ended up with chicken, bread, cheese and vegetables. After we finished at the market and dropped the food back here it was off to the Rodin Museum. Rodin is the artist famous for his sculpture "The Thinker," which was there along with many of his other works and one painting from his friend and equally famous artist, Monet. Although I am not a big museum aficionado, it was interesting and I am glad I went. There was an amazing garden and its upkeep must be a formidable task.

Afterward, it was back here for a picnic lunch on the floor (thank you Financial Times newspaper for being our protective covering) and then we split up. Wendy went out shopping and I went for another walk down by Benjamin Franklin Rue to pay my respects to that great man again and onto the Eiffel Tower. While walking I was on email and as of this morning we are at a crossroads regarding the public offering. If Gary can't answer their final questions satisfactorily the deal is off, it is up to him and his response this week. Ben seems to think it will be okay and is already looking ahead, I am not so sure.

Meanwhile, Paul is in the U.S. with the new material from the Malaysian scientist and we begin testing today.

While walking I heard a group of South American Indian musicians and liked their music so much I bought two of their CDs. It has a rather haunting quality, which I enjoy listening to when I am thinking, writing and or relaxing.

Then it was back here, I did my band workout, spent some time with Wendy and we will soon get ready to go to a French restaurant tonight for dinner. It is supposed to be very good and I hope Wendy enjoys it.

No Road Is Ever Straight

10/10/10
8:51 PM Paris time, 3:51 PM EST
Best Western Victor Hugo Hotel

We got to the restaurant at 7:00 PM and the first thing I liked about it was that the service was fantastic while not being intrusive. We were the first ones there, so Hubert, the Maitre'd, came to our table to chat. We went over the menu and my numerous dietary restrictions and he came back with what he thought would work best. As it turned out, the food was very good. The numerous types of bread were fantastic and I even ate desert. They had a selection on the menu that was called "the Trolley" that had ice cream, sorbet, macaroons, rice pudding, chocolate soufflé and many more. Suffice it to say that by the time I finished my tea I was totally full as was Wendy and we were both very happy. I rarely go to expensive dinners, I find them long and onerous, but in this case, besides doing it for my lovely wife, it was an extremely pleasant experience with a top-notch organization and I would go back. An amusing side note I had fish for dinner and asked Hubert to make sure there were no bones in it. He promised to check and if there were any he would lock the chef up in the freezer for a while as his penalty, of course there were none.

Afterward it was back to the hotel roof, where we hoped to see the sparkling light show of the Eiffel Tower but unfortunately, we missed it. As with the Rodin Museum, the dinner tonight and many other things in life, I would never have experienced this had my wife not strongly suggested I do it. She knows how far she can push me while keeping it a pleasant experience and so I will continue to take her advice. She is a very smart woman.

10/11/10
11:59 AM Paris time, 5:59 AM EST
Orly Airport ICARE Lounge

A very cool day it is, date wise, an even more so since it is my sister's birthday. I had a decent night's sleep considering I am still not sure if I have a cold or just allergies. I got up at 5:30, exercised in the room and went walking. It was still dark out and a little eerie down by the Eiffel Tower, but there was a lot happening there. Some type of marathon was going on and the police and organizers were setting up barriers and all types of sound equipment. I paid my last respects to the statue of Ben Franklin and his road by taking a picture on my phone. I did not go to the tower itself, but went down along the river and crossed over the David Ben Gurion Bridge.

Once back to the hotel I went up to the roof a few more times because the view of Paris is so magnificent. Realizing that the marathon could mess up the traffic we got underway a little earlier than planned and sure enough the traffic was backing up and roads were being cut off.

There are rare moments in life when you are in the presence of a genius, someone who had an incredible talent and had found an outlet to express it. Our cabdriver was one of those elite. Seeing we were going to be gridlocked he backed down a one way street and proceed through an amazing maze of various sized pathways to get us out of the city and to the airport early, we actually gave him a round of applause for his efforts which he greatly appreciated. Check-in was fine as was security, my bag and I got searched again, Wendy mentioned she was never the one to slow us down, which I readily agreed she is a fine traveling companion. She is out looking at the shops and we are due to board within the hour.

It is a good time to look back almost two weeks ago at what I had hoped to achieve for the trip and see what actually happened.

If all goes well:

1. The next stage of going public will be done and the end will truly be in sight. We have been stopped because of a problem with getting our Underwriter in Asia the information they require. We have one more chance and if we fail the project is probably dead. Update: This has not worked out at all well and it continues to be a giant knife cutting into my gut every time I think about it. I am quickly coming to the point where I just want it over one way or the other.

2. We will enter into a new partnership with a group in Malaysia that has close ties to their Military. Update: We have moved forward on this, in fact Paul has already gotten a sample of the material is in New Jersey, tests have already started and I am optimistic as to what can happen. It may be possible to set up licensing agreements not only in our areas but perhaps join others as well.

3. We will meet with a group from CTRM and their customer who is interested in our global warming floating houses. Update: This did not happen.

4. We will meet with the two heads of CTRM to discuss future projects and collaborations. Update: This did not happen although we were in contact and everything there seems okay for the moment.

5. The meeting with NDUM will not only begin an actual project but they will agree to the export agreement with us and the U.S. government. Update: Progress was made here we have an actual project to work on as well as joint testing so that is moving fine. We are going ahead with the export agreement.

6. Igor will get settled into IJ Europe and his new home and get along with everyone there and be happy. Update: So far so good here.

7. I will play squash for the first time. Update: I got sick and could not play.

8. We will make other calls with Jeroen and set-up more potential business and visit his software specialist to help create software to measure our new plastic products for blast results. Update: The calls went very well as did the meeting with the software specialist and another composite firm whom I hope to set up TAAs.

9. The next stage in moving our new customer in Germany from buying

prototypes to buying mass runs. Update: That is going well. Mass runs should hopeful start the beginning of the year and we got more new parts to quote on.

10. We will meet with the people from Trelleborg in Europe and create an alliance to joint develop and sell throughout Europe. Update: That happened, I have been in contact with their head man in the U.S. and I will pursue it when I get back.

11. I will meet Wendy in Paris and we will have a fantastic time. Update: This happened and was great.

12. Everyone gets to and from safely and with little delays. A lot to hope for; let's see what happens. Update: So far so good.

10/12/10
4:27 PM EST
My office, NJ

We got home on Sunday about 5:00 PM to a joyous reunion with our wonderful daughter. Bailey was also very happy to see us and we him. We spend the remainder of the day unpacking and relaxing. Yesterday was a great day; I got a great deal done and even slept last night. I picked up Paul this morning and on to the office. We are experimenting with the new powder from Malaysia. Elsewhere with the effects of jet lag and I am very tired and somewhat grouchy. I had lunch with Kayla, she should be on her way back to college now and I already miss her.

10/14/10
4:45 PM EST
My office, NJ

It has been a day of paperwork and getting a lot done. This is Paul's last day, he leaves tonight. Unfortunately the powder sample he brought has failed every test we put it through so we have no idea how to utilize it. It is a new type of silica, maybe we just don't know what to do with it. I am waiting for guidance from the inventor in Malaysia.

10/15/10
10:36 PM EST
The Berkshires

I played tennis with my wonderful brother this morning. It has been a few weeks and it was great to see him. The news about his daughter, Rachel being pregnant, is now okay to spread the word. We got an inquiry from the Picatinny Arsenal and sent back our solution. Now we wait. We are up in the Berkshires at our second home and Carla and Mitch are with us. They are wonderful, caring, really good people and we are having a wonderful time.

OCTOBER

10/16/10
5:28 PM EST
Our house in the Berkshires

I slept well last night and after a great breakfast with Wendy, Mitch and Carla, Mitch and I set out mountain biking. The long route here in Lenox starts out on a long gradual incline, which was interrupted this morning by a quick stop at the hardware store to buy some chain lubricating oil. Mitch had mentioned yesterday his bike might need some and I said that the hardware store oil was not the right kind for his bike, gently mocking the notion of using multi-purpose non-specific oil. As is normal when I do that, I eat my words and had to actually buy the same oil for my bike to stop the squeaking, which worked well for the rest of the journey. It was a mixture of high winds, cool temperatures and occasional very light rain, none of which darkened our spirits or our ride. We had a wonderful time over the next two and half hours. Although Mitch had not biked much, he did extremely well and even took the lead as we ended the route.

Once back at the house, I cleaned my bike and put it in the basement and then heard something that made me extremely unhappy. It was a slight squeak and I knew right away that our caretaker had put down adhesive strips to catch the field mice that had decided to take up residence in our house. Although I don't like having the mice around, I prefer the traps that kill immediately as opposed to ones that just catch and hold them via adhesive. I tried to save the mouse, but could not so I took him outside and killed him quickly to put him out of his misery. It was highly unpleasant and I hope there is another way to take care of the problem. I fear there is not. I will caution our caretaker to make sure he checks the traps frequently, killing any caught mice quickly so they do not suffer. In the meantime, I am not sure if I should check the basement again to make sure no more live ones are there or not, since my checking might be scaring them into the traps. It is a dilemma I have not worked out, but it is one reason I will be glad to go home tomorrow morning. Otherwise, I like it a lot here.

The girls came home soon afterward with lunch and then we went into Stockbridge to walk around. It is a very quaint, beautiful small New England town and we had a nice stroll while the ladies went in and out of various shops. Mitch just came back from traveling last Friday and leaves again this Monday. We have had a great time comparing notes on business. We think alike in many ways and I enjoy his and Carla's company. I have no idea what is happening in the world as I am not checking and after the great nap I just had I do not really have a need to know at this moment.

10/17/10
7:30 PM EST
Home, NJ

After a breakfast with Bunny this morning, Jeffrey was not feeling well; we said our goodbyes and Wendy, Barbara and I were off to the highway and home about 12:30 PM. It was really good to see Bailey. I then went biking. It was a beautiful, warm, fall day here in New Jersey and I had a fun time riding through my long route and enjoying being home and alone. Afterward it was dinner with my lovely wife and we watched the latest edition of Iron Chef, a program on the Food Network which is a contest for the best chefs in the country. The reason I mention it is because Barry's boss is on the show and doing well, so we have a vested interest in how it works out. If he survives the competition and wins, then it will probably be a boom for his business and a help to Barry.

I heard from Ben that Hing and Ku are meeting with our consultants who spoke to the SC last Friday. We will see what they say regarding our public offering. I spoke with Bunny before. Jeffrey's health is declining and she needs help with him on a daily basis. Things will probably not get better and the options are becoming more limited. The only great thing is that they have enough money to get any help needed on a long term basis. It is extremely sad and disheartening to see his decline and the effect it is having on everyone close to him.

I spoke to my parents and except for some pain that my mom has been battling and my dad's chronic teeth problems, they seem relatively okay. My dad is always interested in what is happening in Asia. It gives us some good areas to talk about.

10/18/10
4:13 PM EST
My office, NJ

Gary was in today. Our company is in good shape and as I expected we have spent virtually all of the profits on R&D, which is fine for now but not in the indefinite future. I had lunch with Elana, which is always a pleasant time and she made me more muffins. I also spoke with Mark from WOR. His daughter is doing well at Cornell as is he and his wife as empty nesters. He is still looking for a good spot for me on his station. When it is right, it will happen. I am continuing on the next run-through of the database regarding mining for new business. It will take at least a few months; it is a lot of work.

10/19/10
4:52 PM EST
My office, NJ

I went to see Dr. Mesnard today for my semi-annual checkup. He is a fantastic doctor as well as a very calm, nice, intelligent man. My checkup went fine, the blood work comes back in a few days and we discussed prostate cancer and the new ways of viewing it through the medical community. I am paranoid about getting it especially via my family history but he advised me that my family history was not much different than anyone else's and caution should be the road for any treatment thought needed.

OCTOBER

10/20/10
3:55 PM EST
My office, NJ

The wind is out of my sails. We have a mistake on our billing screen and I thought we had more sales for the month than we do. Couple that with increased problems with the Malaysia offering, scrambling to get them final information which I don't think we can do, huge amounts of additional R&D expenses and I feel like I am being crushed in from all sides.

10/22/10
4:50 PM EST
My office, NJ

It has been a very hectic two days. We have been moving quickly to get additional information regarding IJ Mexico and IJUS for the consultants in Malaysia and I am hoping that we are finally done as of this afternoon. Of course, I have said that many times over the last six months so I will hold judgment until later next week. My father-in-law has been in the hospital for a few days with a urinary tract infection the doctors can't seem to stop. It has brought on other problems and he may have to go to a halfway facility for a few days until his system is balanced again. Poor Bunny was supposed to come down here today for a reunion, but she is staying up in the Berkshires instead. Wendy and Barbara will probably go to see them next week.

The pressure on my crew from going public is showing, I am yelling a lot more than usual and they are reacting with emotion as well.

Kayla wants to go to Australia for vacation. I tried to book some flights, but when I went to order them online the prices suddenly shifted way up, which meant I would wait.

I got a tetanus shot today.

There are more growing pains for IJ Europe. I have been working with Jeroen for about four years. He is on the cusp of exploding in business and I hope for all of us, he soars.

10/23/10
3:57 PM EST
Home, NJ

It has been a gorgeous day here in NJ. Temperatures this morning were cool and Uncle Dave and I had a fine ride. The leaves on the trees are about at their autumn peak and it is dazzling to watch them as they shake with the wind and fall in multitudes onto the ground. Wendy left early for her camp reunion in New York City and I should hear from her soon about how it went and when she is coming home. After riding, I went to see my parents, who look reasonably well. My dad is concerned that his prostate cancer is coming back, but there is a chance that the PSA screen test was altered by an infection. He is setting up a protocol for antibiotics and being retested. He and his friend probably have the best combined information and history on prostate cancer than anyone in the nation. They have both been survivors for over 20 years and one reason is that they had studied extensively and have dictated their own care. Their various physicians have not always agreed with their choices. However, this allowed them to have a productive tunnel vision of cause and effect and a combined experience that I want access if the disease ever hits me.

My tetanus shot from yesterday has been hurting a bit, but nothing the technician did not warn me about. Except for not getting the Shingles shot, which you have to be sixty years old for, I think I am pretty well covered.

Bailey likes it out here on the porch. We share the single couch; he gets the front and I get the back. He does not like to be touched, so there are at least two inches between us. He pops up his head or perks his ears whenever someone like the mailman or some wildlife runs by, and otherwise he prefers to relax. I am listening to one of my favorite musicians Michael Gettel and his San Juan Suite. Some artists seem to speak to me and he is definitely one of them.

10/24/10
3:10 PM EST
Home, NJ

I feel a little like waiting for a baby to be born. There is no more word from Ben regarding the SC meeting, which starts his Monday morning and my tonight.

My brother was away for tennis. He and Eve went to Brown University's White Coat ceremony for their newest group of doctors to be. Lisa has been in the class a few months and although it is very difficult, she seems to be thriving there. I went biking instead, watered my plants, had lunch and went for a walk with Wendy. I am making chicken shish-kabobs for dinner. I have never done that before but had the sudden urge to try. Jeff came back home yesterday and he seems to be better. For now, we wait to hear from Malaysia. I do not expect to get any information until I wake up tomorrow morning.

10/25/10
4:40 PM EST
My office, NJ

I did sleep last night but the dreams were understandably more strange than usual. I woke up to some emails from Ben, which I was hesitant about reading. The SC wanted clarification on some issues, which we will take care of immediately. Ben feels we are in pretty good shape, but I will be assured when it is done. I am pretty confident we are not finished yet. I have spent a great deal of time worrying about this project, as has Ben and members of or worldwide team, and my intake of antacid pills has gone up accordingly. The day stayed positive from there. Tennis went well and I worked on marketing and sales. I am hoping for a calm evening and a good night's sleep.

OCTOBER

10/26/10
5:06 PM EST
My office, NJ

The day was spent in more marketing and sales. It can get frustrating, but it has to be done. The Trelleborg alliance is moving along. The more I sell, the more that happens. The equation has stayed consistent my entire career.

10/28/10
4:51 PM EST
My office, NJ

I set up a trip for Alice to go Texas. We get the double advantage of me contacting everyone first and then her going to see them in person. She is extremely good on the road and I need to utilize her more. More composite tests are out and people are starting to get the possibilities of what we can do. It is a long road.

10/29/10
2:43 PM EST
My office, NJ

I think I can empathize with the bomb squad people in Iraq and Afghanistan. Their worlds are filled with incredible rushes of adrenaline on a daily basis. Being on the edge gives them a feeling of being alive like an electric current running through their bodies. It is a small wonder many miss it so much that they choose to keep going back so they can once again tap into that huge flow of energy within themselves. I too have that access, although not in the danger area. The thrill of building a multi-national company and the potential of going public in Malaysia sends my being into constant waves of intense emotion most often accompanied by massive levels of adrenaline. Sometimes it is so potent, I can barely sit down for long periods of time.

The problem occurs when the situation slows down and the highs are not there. The influx of boredom comes in like a freight train and even when I have important things to do, time starts to drag and I get fidgety. I have been in one of those periods this week. I am doing what is necessary for the company. The day-to-day actions of basic sales and marketing are more than a requirement. They are the lifeblood of all of our companies and I know it. However, it does not give the same rush and surges as the big decisions on the top levels of moving our company globally, dealing with the large possibilities, problems, huge amounts of frustrations and exhaustion. I miss it, I crave it and I want more. But to get there I have to continually keep earning the right of admission and that means the day-to-day, normal stuff must go on.

10/30/10
3:29 PM EST
Home, NJ

I called my mom yesterday and asked if she wanted to have lunch today which meant I needed to get out early to bike. Wendy left at 9:00 to pick up Barbara and go to the Berkshires to have a one day visit with their parents. By that time I was already on the road. It was about 44°F when I started and I had multiple layers of clothes which protected me well against the cold and the wind. By the time I got back home mid morning, the temperatures had risen and the sky was partly cloudy and beautiful. It was a fine ride and I thought about very little, a sure sign I needed to relax.

Lunch with my mom was calm and enjoyable as usual. We spoke about family and what was happening in business. After dropping her off and picking up some food, I got home to see the end of the Rally for Sanity hosted by John Stewart and Stephen Colbert. It was an extremely well done event and the ending keynote speech by Mr. Stewart was both inspiring and thought provoking. The discussion of what an American is as opposed to what the media portrays was insightful and an accurate gauge of the truth. From traveling the world, I can attest to the idea that the world really likes individual Americans and the vast majority would live in the U.S. if given the chance. He was also right that although we are all strongly individualistic, it all seems to work in getting along in our everyday lives. The problems are the media in general and the emphasis on the fringe elements in our society. If I did not know better, I would say he was getting ready to run for public office. I hope he does; I would vote for him based on what I saw today.

I am due to go pick up Ira and Eve and go see a play that our tennis partner is in. It is good to support our friends and if it is lousy, we will leave at the intermission. It is rare for me to be out late on a Saturday night and I probably won't get home until 11:00 PM, but once in a while it is okay. As Wendy says, I will be living on the wild side. My kids often don't start going out before 10:00 PM. Life is all perspective.

10/31/10
2:06 PM EST
Home, NJ

It is Halloween here in the U.S., a tradition where children (and some adults) dress in costumes, go door to door and say trick or treat, which normally results in getting a piece or two of candy. The general rules of a homeowner are that if your front light is off, then you are not participating. Since it is Sunday afternoon, I am expecting some younger kids out with their parents before dark. Wendy got home from the Berkshires a little after I returned from biking. It was an uneventful trip and she was happy that she and her sister went to support her mom and see her dad. After tennis this morning, the bike ride in the beautiful, cool autumn air was grand. It was fun to see people of all ages in various costumes walking around.

I heard from Alex, who wants to get his own credit card so he can build a credit history. Since he is a student and does not work it is not that easy. We are trying to work it out now. While out riding, I was planning to look at the building I have wanted to buy for the last decade. Unfortunately, today I saw a vacant sign on it by a realtor and after some digging, I found out the tenant was vacating and they were trying to rent the whole building. Since I won't be ready to go after it for at least 15 months, one year before our lease is up, this puts me into an interesting position. If they are unable to rent it for the next year then the price will probably go down. However, if they are able to rent it all out within the next 12 months, they will never sell it to me, besides which I don't want it with tenants. It poses an interesting "what-if" scenario, so we will sit and watch for a while to see what happens. It would be nice to have the building but it is not a necessity. Things often have a way of turning out okay.

I may go sit outside on the porch; the weather is amazing. If I do, a nap will probably ensue whether I plan it or not. It actually sounds like a good idea.

November

11/1/10
4:50 PM EST
My office, NJ
　　More paperwork.

11/2/10
4:15 PM EST
My office, NJ
　　Today is the big day here in New Jersey and the U.S. as a whole; the midterm elections have arrived. I voted this morning after a close tennis match and now I am eagerly awaiting the results when I get up tomorrow morning. The polls close at 8:00 PM here and some of the local races will be called by the news stations before I go to sleep, but the bulk will be tomorrow morning. So far, it seems that the Republicans will take the House and make inroads to the Senate, picking up some additional governorships. I am hoping for a gridlock and maybe even some turning back of the most recent legislation. I had lunch with my mentor John today. It is good to get another view on what we are doing. Some of my actions he agrees with and others he does not. Mentors are used as sounding boards, not judges with the power to veto pathways.

11/3/10
4:20 PM EST
My office, NJ
　　The Republicans will take over the House of Representatives with a substantial majority in January. Coupled with conservative Democrats they should be a formidable force. There are still some Senate races in contention; the Democrats hold a slim majority, but since many are conservative Democrats, I am not sure the president has an ally there. In other words, unless the president can forge a new coalition or the Republicans join the conservative Democrats, nothing will happen. On the other hand, if either does happen, then some major changes could take place in the next two years. Otherwise, we will have a gridlock and nothing will change.
　　Business continues to be moderate, but we are still spending all profits on R&D and going public. As you can tell from my tone, I am nearing my end on both and if we don't succeed in at least one soon, then both will be stopped within the next six months. We can't keep up this level of spending.

NOVEMBER

It is not fiscally responsible on my part and the wear and tear on my teams worldwide is too great to continue much longer.

The weather has turned cooler; in fact, we have had frost the last two days, which means the bulk of my beautiful flowers have died. I plan to clear them out this weekend and get ready for next year. It is sad to see them go, but good to be getting into the colder season. Reviews on my latest book are good and it is nice to hear that people like it. Most authors (and artists in general) have very fragile egos when it comes to displaying their art. You are baring your soul and it is easy for people to do real, everlasting damage. It is a real gamble putting your work out there. I, for one, have had my writing destroyed in public and it is not fun.

11/4/10
4:57 PM EST
Home, NJ

As always happens with new projects, there comes a time when they live or die. Our composite material passed for hurricane window and door coverings but failed for construction panels and tornado. In other words, we have nothing to sell and I have already shut down that part of the business. We will attempt the military and defense area for another few months and if we cannot sell anything, we will shut down the entire area. It will be a big blow since I have put a fortune into it, but we will move into new areas. If I wasn't willing to fail, I would not have done it.

With yesterday's testing failures, I emailed Ben to stop the prototype composite plant in IJT. Ben and I also discussed modifying our marketing and sales plans to reflect where we now think business will come and go and how it will all be affected by the Republican gains this week, the devaluation of the U.S. dollar and the increase in the Chinese RMB. Running a small multinational business is complicated and all of the interrelating economies have to be taken into consideration. It is both invigorating and frustrating, but extremely necessary and today was spent in contemplation of it all. Our people know that big changes are in the wind and those at risk know they have to surge with energy and intelligence to survive. Small businesses are like small families. In our case, if someone is not pulling their weight or doing what is in the best interest for the whole, then they are watched carefully and then fed to the sharks. It makes for an interesting cultural environment and as long as people are looking out for the benefit of all, then it is a smooth running positive machine. When this is not the case, it can get difficult for those who don't measure up. I have abandoned all sales for the commercial composites and am now centering on military, defense and our other proven product lines. It is definitely not boring and an incredible challenge. Happily, I like the atmosphere of striving for what can be and pushing myself and my teams to get there. This is not the place for most people to work.

No Road Is Ever Straight

11/6/10
5:55 PM EST
Home, NJ

There has been no word yet from DARPA on the White Paper we coauthored to locate enemy soldiers hiding in trenches. I am redoing our White Paper on locating and eradicating fast growing cancers originating from military related substances. We are working on a new invention to identify the sunken tripwires for IEDs. Our proposal will go out next week and two groups are interested.

11/7/10
4:43 PM EST
Home, NJ

I am listening to a very old Simon and Garfunkel song called "Scarborough Fair." It was popular during the 1970s and I remember singing it when I was in music class during middle school. It is amazing what memories music can bring back. Middle school was not a horrible time for me, but one of intense change and I was very happy to go to high school and college.

This morning marked the end of Daylight Saving Time, which meant an extra hour of sleep. It will now get dark much earlier until next month when the days start to lengthen again. We are moving into winter; many of the leaves have fallen from the trees and most of the plants in my garden have died. I spent part of yesterday pulling some of them up and preparing the ground to sleep for the winter. I played tennis with my wonderful brother this morning after I worked out in our cellar and then it was off biking. The weather is chilly but not too bad and I tried out my new thermal boots. They worked so well that I am allocating them to weather of less than 40°F before I use them again.

Wendy came with me to see my parents this afternoon and they seem okay. Wendy's new car suddenly stopped working and we called the roadside service to which we are subscribed. A very nice young man came by and gave us a jump. Fortunately, it started but something still does not feel right, so Wendy will take it in to be checked at the Lexus dealer tomorrow. She will get a loaner until a thorough inspection can be done.

I got more email from Ben in China. The public offering is not going well and I am getting the feeling that it may need to be stopped. If so it is no great problem, true we will have lost a lot of money but it will put in good stead for the future and go to a different exchange.

Sometimes I have trouble sleeping on the Sunday night after a time change. Actually, I sometimes have trouble on Sunday nights in general, so I am hoping for the best. I switched out almost all of my summer and spring clothes for winter this week, which is a sure sign that colder weather will be coming.

NOVEMBER

11/8/10
4:18 PM EST
My office, NJ

It is already starting to get dark outside; the shorter days are definitely here. It was a crazy day getting ready for a major presentation for Irving Oil. We came up with a great idea to utilize their company history and products to advertise on their pump labels. At least we thought so, until I called the person in charge who was less than thrilled with my plan to help his company. No worries; I will not give up easily. If this man does not want to talk with me, it gives me the excuse to go higher up in the command. Being passive, easy going and non-aggressive is not the Ideal Jacobs style and it rarely works, so I will stay with being me.

One of our former employees Peter Pidgursky called. He left us about eight years ago to pursue his dream to go into law enforcement in Georgia. He is now a sergeant, has a southern accent, carries at least two guns at all times and sounds incredibly happy. It is amazing what happens when you go for your dreams and achieve them. He is a testament to doing that.

It started sleeting today outside; winter is definitely coming.

11/9/10
4:33 PM EST
My office, NJ

I have decided to get the new PCA3 tests for prostate cancer. The disease runs in my family. Actually, it runs in everyone's families and most men will get it if they live long enough. While prostate cancer itself can stay dormant for decades, the real fear is that it will spread. Therefore, I am getting the test to put my mind at ease (I hope) or, in the worst case, figure out if something needs to be done.

We had an ISO 91001/2008 quality audit today. Our system seems tight and the auditor agreed. There were no negative comments, which is always a great thing to hear after an audit conclusion. I have overloaded my incoming email with more rejections from outdated addresses that I have sent out for various products. I am sending to addresses that I received up to five years ago and many people have left their companies. I can't tell before I send them. I will leave soon and not take the chance of adding too many more in case I cause a systems failure. We have passed some new shooting tests, but still have no definite customers or projects. Passing all of the tests in the world will do nothing if you can't sell the systems and products. We are now on a time line for mid-January. If we have no armor orders, then we will have to make some changes in our staff and structure, which will not be pleasant. Lots more selling and paperwork; I will stay on it until it is finished or we get busy enough that additional marketing will need to wait for awhile.

No Road Is Ever Straight

11/10/10
4:25 PM EST
My office, NJ

One of the toughest parts about running a company is deciding what information to tell to whom. If you told everyone everything, it would be a disaster and nothing would get done. On the other hand, if you forget or neglect to tell someone something they feel they should know it also creates problems. Right now I am in charge of Ideal Jacobs worldwide, Ben is in charge of Ideal Jacobs Asia and we both filter what we tell each other. With something as detail oriented as going public, it is bound to cause problems when not everything gets transmitted. Normally, he and I are extremely good about keeping each other in the loop, but the recent events have dwarfed our abilities to cover everything and the resulting strain is showing. Of course, the strain is showing from the overall process and its cumulative effects. Over the past year, both Ben and I have seriously wondered why we are doing this and if we should continue. I have given up guessing when and if this project will be completed. But if it does, knowing me, this experience will immediately begin to recede in my memory so I will forget how much effort it actually took. Without knowing it, we went past the date required to cancel our space in Millburn. I don't mind since I showed some of the space to two entrepreneurs who are starting a new business. We are giving them free space to help get them started. More paperwork and selling; the effects are indirect, but they show. By the law of percentages it will happen, so I will keep going.

11/11/10
4:00 PM EST
Home, NJ

The public offering has gone from a remote possibility to suddenly much more real and Ben emailed me to get ready to possibly be in Kuala Lumpur on Monday, December 1st. We are checking flights now and I may try to stop in at Ideal Jacobs Xiamen and possibly South Korea on the way back. I won't know for certain for a few days and it means leaving over the Thanksgiving weekend. As long as I have Thursday and Friday at home, I should be fine. We found out that DARPA rejected our proposal to find enemy soldiers in trenches utilizing a new type of visual guidance system. So it goes, maybe we will try to market the idea somewhere else. We Skyped with Igor in the Netherlands yesterday. The combination of a good job, a girlfriend and a nice place to live has made his transition much easier than normal and he will probably want to make it permanent. Mr. Obama is in Asia trying to get business between the U.S. and Middle Eastern countries jump-started. I am hopeful for his efforts, but am not sure what he can really accomplish in a few days. Our potential partners at Trelleborg are setting up some new locations in South Korea and Australia. I will try to visit both during my next two trips and coordinate with Kayla while she is in Sydney so we can have lunch.

NOVEMBER

11/12/10
4:43 PM EST
My office, NJ

I went to Picatinny Arsenal this morning to go over our ideas for identifying wires connect to IED explosive devices on roadways. Happily, our basic ideas were acceptable and with some modification, which should be ready next week, we are hopeful of a workable solution. It is early on in the process and a lot of work and money will be needed, but it would be great both for our business and to help safeguard our troops and allies throughout the world. I emailed with the Colonel and he is also interested in the invention in addition to our immobilizing device. It is always fun going to the Arsenal. I got to see a real tank.

Alex is due home tonight from school. He needs to buy fabric for his spring clothes collection tomorrow after he, Wendy and I have breakfast. He has already won $5000 for continuing education with a chance for $20,000 more. He is extremely industrious and I have full confidence that he can do anything he wishes. He leaves again tomorrow afternoon for school but will back soon for the Thanksgiving holidays.

Mr. Obama and the feds are planning to pump $600 billion into the U.S. economy by simply printing money. In effect, they are devaluing the currency and the rest of the world is extremely upset with us, as they should be. People here don't understand that if we print more money it will be worth less, but Mr. Obama has his plan and nothing will deter him except being voted out of office. He tried to get the rest of the world to force the Chinese government to let their currency rise and they refused. The Chinese are too powerful to be forced to do much. We need to rebuild our economy, as does Europe, and in a few years when that happens we can start playing hardball again or at least act in parity worldwide. The time for one country to dominate the world has passed and I think it is a good plan for everyone to try to work together.

I have been doing a lot of emailing to people throughout our database and it is fun to reconnect after years have gone by. One of the great parts about business is the reach you can have worldwide with those good people whom you can create a mutually beneficial relationship.

11/13/10
1:14 PM EST
Home, NJ

It is a beautiful fall afternoon here in New Jersey. The temperature is mild enough for Bailey and me to be out here on the porch. Many of the autumn leaves have already fallen but enough are left to provide an intermittent panorama of incredible sequences of greens, oranges, reds and browns. I love this time of year. It is almost Thanksgiving, the calm before the cold winter winds and snow. The kids are home in less than two weeks. Alex came in late last night and I saw him around midnight for a brief moment. He, Wendy and I had breakfast this morning. He looks wonderful and the main discussion was his plans for the future. He goes before a final board hearing in January for the large scholarship he is after and he will then apply to a design school in London he hopes to attend in the fall. He will "sell" me back his car to pay for his living expenses. Yes, I know, Wendy and I bought it for him in the first place, but it is his to do with as he pleases. I like the idea of having a 4-wheel-drive Jeep around for bad weather and transporting stuff, so I am sure we can come to an agreement.

In retrospect, yesterday's trip to the Arsenal was fantastic and we are already working on revisions for the IED spotting device. I am confident we can come up with a working model, enough to prove the concept and then go for funding by the government, a private company or ourselves if it is necessary to get to a working model. I have always loved the idea of being able to make a change for the better and this would be a major achievement, not to mention opening up avenues for other projects.

I went biking with Uncle Dave this morning and I was probably not the best company. I am under a lot of pressure with going public and the military inventions, which are both taking gigantic amounts of time and money. I think the stress I am under is both for the actual projects themselves and also the overall question of whether I am on the right path or not. We are where we are because I chose it; the responsibility and blame is mine alone. If it is successful, it is a team effort. The nice part is that all of these areas have time lines so there will be a definite conclusion as to whether they worked, failed or were partially successful. That is not bad. It gives the chance for closure and the ability to accept whatever happens and move onto the next path. I love that about my life, I can accept the conclusion either way and move on. The pain is usually temporary even if it is deep, but we can always move forward. It is a good reason never to bet the farm on any one project so there is always a tomorrow. My aversion to debt is both an advantage and disadvantage. It is good that I probably will not go bankrupt, but bad that the chance for really big money will probably never happen because I won't go all in and take the risk of ending up with nothing. In the end, the paranoia of total defeat is good to have, as is the unbridled optimism of what can be. It is amazing for me to watch, my mind working from these two different poles to come up with workable solutions. As I tell people, my life is usually broken up this way: 90 percent great, 5 percent good and 5 percent mediocre or bad. I will not risk anything to change those odds. Whatever I am doing to get it broken down that way, I want to continue.

11/14/10
5:11 PM EST
Home, NJ

Dinner last night with our friends John and Susan was excellent. They are intelligent and extremely nice and the conversation was stimulating, current and a lot of fun. I look forward to seeing them again. I woke up earlier than usual for a Sunday via my alarm clocks to exercise before seeing Uncle

Ira for tennis. Afterward, Mike the driver took us to see Ben at his new apartment in Brooklyn. We saw his girlfriend and my editor Katie for a few minutes and both of them look well and happy. We then had lunch with Ben, as Katie was headed to a music rehearsal, and then Wendy and I went home. It was a beautiful day here so I went for a short bike ride to check out my building, which now has two "available" signs on it. Uncle Dave had spoken to the broker who said it was not for sale, which is fine for me. Now we wait 11 months and see if anyone rents it. If not, we attack. I did some more work on my flower beds to get them ready for next year. I am about to order and go out to get turkey burgers for Wendy and I for dinner. As always, it is Sunday night and we shall see if I exercised enough to sleep – I never know. There has been no more word from Ben or anyone else from Asia. We have our tasks and we will be on them tomorrow and Tuesday.

11/15/10
4:47 PM EST
Home, NJ

Al is in Texas, so the pressure increases on all of us to take her place. It is doable, but a little more stress. On the other hand, it gives us a chance to see how the systems are working when she is not there, so it has a good side.

Incredible news: Chef Forgione of Forge Restaurant in Manhattan has made it to the finals of the Next Iron Chef competition on the Food Network. Why is this big? Because my nephew Barry is his sous chef and both he and Barry are going to be on television this Sunday for the final competition. It is very exciting and if they win, it could mean Barry's boss will start another restaurant, which Barry will run.

It has been a crazy day of more work on going public. I had a 6:00 AM phone call with Ku from Malaysia, numerous emails with everyone and a day of more marketing worldwide. Sometimes I think we are crazy in trying to grow the entire corporation with the size of the sales staff we have. Then again, by wringing every ounce of energy out of myself it is amazing what can be done. We will continue until we can't go on or decide to grow that area with more people. Most of the time it is fun for me and I get a chance to interact with lots of people, which I enjoy.

11/16/10
4:51 PM EST
My office, NJ

I had breakfast with one of my tennis partners Nathaniel this morning. He seems destined for stardom in the business area. It is fun watching him soar and hopefully adding some fuel to his journey. Who knows, we may actually work together one day. Back in the office, it was a crazy day of continual action including a large block of time in a phone conference with Al in Texas with two customers. Things seemed to go well. It is strange having our people out selling instead of me. Once you get to your 50s, it becomes less acceptable to make sales calls. It is fine to make deals and high-level meetings, especially going around the world, but day-to-day sales are not necessary unless it is unusual or extremely important. I have warned my people that mid-January is the cutoff date for the ballistics area. Either we have a pending sale or we make big changes.

The world is laughing at our government's monetary policy. While we devalue our currency we are telling others to raise or keep theirs the same. They must think we are naïve, which is worse than being arrogant.

11/17/10
4:15 PM EST

I wrote this for Kayla's college newspaper regarding the murder of one of the teaching assistants:

My name is Andrew Jacobs and I am the extremely proud parent of a Cornell sophomore. With the recent murder of a teaching assistant, I would like to explain a few things about parents and the positive, unintended consequence of his tragic death. First of all, I would like to deeply thank him for the interest he took in my daughter and for helping her to switch to her current major of environmental biology last year. She spoke highly of him as a man of character, good will and intelligence. As I have read, he was in Nicaragua to further his research and career in natural resources. This unintended consequence I mentioned lies not in what he was studying, but where. Let me preface this by saying I routinely travel throughout the U.S., Asia and Europe, have met scores of incredibly great people and have a huge love for humanity as a whole. However, I also have had some close calls regarding safety and have learned a few things about being outside the U.S. Due to his untimely death, perhaps students might be willing to listen to this advice.

Many people in the world love Americans and hate our government. Some have decided individuals should pay for whatever crimes we have committed as a country and will go after anyone as a consequence. Others will see Americans as a target for ransom and rightly so, since we are known for wealth and being willing to pay. Still others want to come to the U.S. and are willing to do almost anything to find a way to get here, including luring students like yourselves with drugs, sex, intimidation or force. In other words, like it or not, we are all vulnerable and as young people, you are much more vulnerable than others. Since you also tend to want to travel on lower budgets and see the real side of most countries, you will often be put into circumstances that regular tourists and business people avoid. My point is that often the only thing separating you from potential harm or even death is your brain and your common sense.

My advice is that if you are in a situation where your brain is telling you not to do something, then don't do it. If a situation seems too good to be true, then it probably is. If people are paying unusual attention to you, then it should be a warning to get out. If something just doesn't feel right, then pay attention to your gut and leave. If your friends want to stay, that it is their problem. Like it or not, your main and only actual responsibility is to yourself.

I cannot imagine how horrible it must be for the teaching assistant's family. The only solace that could matter is to prevent other students potentially at risk from ending up with the same fate. If this tragedy gets even one person to think twice before doing something potentially fatal, then something good would have come from it.

The best path is not to get into trouble in the first place, but the second best course is to realize the danger and get out before it is too late, no matter what the financial or possible emotional consequences, like being called a coward. I know you are young and you feel invincible and that nothing will happen to you. This is true for most of you, but as a parent and remembering what potential this wonderful young man once had, I urge you, with all of my heart, to be aware of danger. To his family, I offer my sympathy and the knowledge that he made a positive difference in my daughter's life and will for all of Cornell's future students.

11/18/10
4:45 PM EST
My office, NJ

Winter is coming; it is already almost dark.

I heard back from the people at Cornell and they might want to print my article with some changes. I told them their editing was fine. If it goes in, I hope it does some good. I spoke to Kayla last night and she was happy I wrote it, which was good enough for me with nothing else.

We spent the day getting more paperwork ready for the public offering. I heard from Ben in China. If we don't make it by December 31st, then the government will demand a whole additional year of operation before they grant approval and that will not be acceptable to us. From our side, if we have all of the requests, we will probably be done early next week. If not, it could go on indefinitely.

I went to the urologist yesterday and had a new test for prostate cancer. I am concerned but been formulating various plans depending on the results. It is not a pleasant thing to think about, but I always feel better when I am well prepared. I started marketing our two new inventions today. The first is the Immobilizer, a new type of shotgun shell that will shoot a substance instead of metal balls that will render the victims incapable of action in a very short time. The other is the ability to locate IED explosive devices even if they are buried up to a foot in dirt and sand. We have two really good products to sell. If they aren't accepted, then that will probably kill our efforts since the self imposed mid- January deadline is fast approaching. I am cautiously optimistic. In retrospect, if the public offering doesn't go and the composite and other areas don't either, then that will mean a cash, material and time outlay of over three million dollars over the past 18 months. If that happens, then that is okay. I would not have changed what we did. I was prepared for it not to work and if it fails, it was still a path we needed to take on the way to wherever we will go from here. Failure is part of the adventure. Accept it or don't start the journey.

11/19/10
4:08 PM EST
My office, NJ

I hired a young man as of January 3rd. He will have his mechanical engineering degree and there are very few jobs available. We do not need him, but I am always looking for good people and I remember what it was like when I got out of college and could not get a job in my chosen field. He will have a few months trial and if he works hard and we have the business, we will keep him. If not, it is much easier to get a job if you already have one, so we are giving him a big boost no matter what and he realizes it. It is good to do something nice.

Today was the day we distributed turkeys and hams to our people here in New Jersey. Again, it is nice to do something for our team, which has been phenomenal.

There has been more back and forth from Malaysia. It feels like dealing with the Yin and the Yang. Sometimes the news is great and other times it is horrible. I never have a 100% grasp as to exactly where the process is. It is no one's fault. There is too much information going through right now and I am leaving it up to Ben and our team in Asia to sort through what is needed and push forward.

I am waiting now for the video to give a simulation for our IED detection device. I will send it to our contact at the Picatinny Arsenal and to the Colonel. I have also started to sell the idea. Jack and James have been working on the 12- gauge immobilizer prototype. As seems normal, the successful final design may end up being a printing related construction. So much of what we develop springs from what we have learned through the many decades in the printing business, which is an extremely fortunate base of information.

11/20/10
Aprox. 3:00 PM EST
Home, NJ

My brother told me yesterday that my dad's cancer has spread to his pelvis. His choices of treatment will be down to radiation or nothing if what my brother told me turns out to be accurate. His options are limited and he may just decide to ride it out to the end. He has seemingly been so close to death so many times that it will be hard to adjust to the fact that the end is actually happening. Deep down, we are all figuring he will astound the doctors again and rebound for a while longer. In the meantime, I put in a call to my sister to see what she knows and I will plan on seeing him tomorrow. What do you say to someone whose time here might be ending? Since I believe in life after death, I don't have a great foreboding or fear about death. I think it is a transition to another phase, but I will be very sad not to see my family and friends and be out of the game of life, no longer trying to make things better and having a great time. But for my father, who does not believe in that, it is much harder. Years ago, when I asked him what he feared most when he got older, he replied being cooped up in an old age home or losing his mind or eventually being in a hospital bed full of tubes. If the prognosis is correct and he does not have that long, then I can at least offer him the great part of what has not happened and knowing him as I do, he will be able to see it. Not having Alzheimer's disease or Parkinson's disease is a big plus. Having the potential to be at home until the end and even dying in his own bed are wonderful alternatives to what could have happened. He is strong willed and can force himself to see these advantages and I will try to offer them if the time is right. As for what happens after you die, that is such a personal point in life, I would not try to change his mind at this late date. I think he is at peace with the way he has lived his life and has few regrets. In the end, that is an amazing thing to be able to claim. He lived his life the way he wanted, which is not bad to be able to say at 86 years old. Wendy and I are going to an early movie; I will not think about this for a while.

11/21/10
3:31 PM EST
Home, NJ

It has been a very nice day so far. I played tennis with my wonderful brother, biked my normal Sunday route and checked on the building I want to buy. Nothing different there; the signs are the same and Uncle Dave says they still have a tenant and are trying to rent the rest. It is all the better if they have lots of time with no takers. We have a year before we can move. After lunch, I worked on the new IED invention. I have an idea for a secondary use for the same system and our new intern who starts in January sparked a potential idea, so we will try it out. I also worked on the immobilizer invention and will send it to Jack and James tomorrow. My nephew Barry and his boss are on the Food Network tonight for the Next Iron Chef finals. It is over at 10:00 PM and I have a feeling I will stay up to see it.

11/22/10
9:51 PM EST
Home, NJ

Having a father who had prostate cancer two decades ago marked our family for life. For over twenty years, he has been drilling into us that the odds of us getting the disease are likely with our family history. I have become so paranoid that I started seeing a urologist much earlier than most men and that led me to a false scare five years ago. From that day forward, I do not think I have passed a day without thinking about some potential problems. Today was the day when I had to deal with reality. I am fortunate to have my dad, who has become an expert in his own right regarding various treatments and protocols. Without him I would not have known the potential dangers and cures and probably would have sailed along in good natured and ignorant bliss. Regardless if it was worth the twenty years of concern and last five years of paranoia, I now know what to do. After getting the first reply from the urologist I had the normal reaction of total fear and panic that I would die within a year, which is hardly a likely outcome since I did not even have any confirmation I had the disease to begin with.

I went to see my medical intuitive Nancy who is also a therapist and a member of my team. My team members are those who not only watch out for my well being but also keep me in line and on the right path. There is virtually no chance I will begin drinking, doing drugs, carousing with women or doing anything against my strong rules of conduct with them around. They all have unique abilities and Nancy can amazingly "see" what is happening inside my body.

Before I got to see her, I had some time to think and realized that there was probably no chance I could have passed the test I just failed at the urologist. Here is what happened. Five years ago, I had two prostate biopsies and both proved inconclusive. In other words, there were areas that could not be fully declared as cancer. Barring a miracle, that condition could not have improved. There was no way this new test would have showed me completely clean. The results I got were an incredibly small percentage above the number that was a cause for potential concern. That was it, but the urologist wanted me to have the next level of testing done, which, by the way, is probably equally as unpleasant as the test I just took. Of course, it has been five years, so maybe it will be worse and the memory just dimmed.

Regardless, Nancy and I spoke and now that I feel much better, I have a plan of attack. I love plans of attack; they give me power, direction and some control. I will email the doctor tomorrow with my questions, concerns, the protocol I would like to follow and make sure he and I are on the same page. Happily, through my dad and research, I know a lot about this disease. If I have it, I know the ways to treat it, the short and long term consequences, the costs, what insurance will probably not cover and what to do in general. This is a major piece of comforting knowledge and I am confident that if I do have it, the disease can be either controlled or killed depending on what I want to do. Therefore, I feel much better and will hopefully sleep tonight.

11/23/10
9:43 PM EST
Home, NJ

I made an appointment with my urologist for the biopsy. The good news is that they now use an anesthetic during the procedure so it should not be nearly as uncomfortable as last time. Kayla and Alex came home from college today for the Thanksgiving holiday and they both look great. It is wonderful to have them home. Jack and James worked on the new immobilizer invention, but unfortunately the initial tests have failed. I am not sure if there is a chance for success there. I have my trip booked to Malaysia for the first full week of December, but there is more trouble with the under-writers so I am not sure if my trip will be worthwhile from that standpoint. More tension and pressure; just what I need at the moment. The trick now is to try to stop thinking about my biopsy for more than an hour at a time, which probably won't happen until the next test is done and the results are favorable. It certainly reminds me of how great a life I have and to try to enjoy every minute of it.

11/25/10
11:07 PM EST
Home, NJ

The day before a big holiday is usually very slow or crazy and yesterday was good crazy. This morning was Thanksgiving morning and Uncle Dave and I biked through the cold weather. I was dressed well for the condition and it caused me little trouble. As the afternoon progressed, more people came over to our house, including my parents, who were on their way to my sisters for dinner. We had a wonderful celebration; I ate too much and it went well. Wendy and I have these holidays down to a science: she takes care of the preparations and I take care of the cleanup. After everyone went home, Wendy, Ben, Kayla, Katie and I celebrated "pre-Chanukah" since we would not be together on the actual holiday. The kids loved the presents that Wendy spent a lot of thought and time putting together.

Tomorrow I will bike alone unless it is pouring rain outside and then I have to decide whether to exchange my Blackberry mobile phone or not. I am having some intermittent keyboard problems and I don't want to be in trouble when I leave for Asia next week. I am setting up the schedule now and working it out with our people there. I am trying to utilize my time as efficiently and productively as possible. It has been a great day, one I always look forward to. It is a chance to be with my family, feel thankful for the won-derful lives we have, hope they continue and realize we have a responsibility to try to keep it that way for ourselves and help others.

11/26/10
10:33 PM EST
Home, NJ

I went biking alone this morning. Fortunately, the rain ended and I did not get wet. We had lunch here with the kids and Bunny came over, as Jeffrey wasn't feeling well. Later we went over to Barbara and Cliff's and had a sec-ond Thanksgiving dinner, this time with Jessica and Joe. Barry and Cliff deep fried a turkey at Kayla's request, which was very good. It was a lot of fun and I was very tired, which is common when I have a few days off. After dinner, Barry, Ben and Katie went back home. The last few days have been very fun.

No Road Is Ever Straight

11/27/10
4:48 PM EST
Home, NJ

The weather turned colder here and when I woke up it was down in the 30s with a 27°F wind chill factor. Happily, I was dressed well and the wind caused me little discomfort. A lot of the ride was spent in quiet thinking about various topics including next week's trip to Malaysia. The time has come for a decision from our underwriters about whether we go public or not and additional action on our part no matter what their decision. I have been emailing with Paul getting ready to go to IJT and will have dinner with Pk the Saturday I arrive in Kuala Lumpur. My main thrust with our sales and marketing people will be that I don't care how many estimates they get, I only count actual profitable sales.

I started packing for the trip and most of it is now done. I had lunch with Kayla after biking and then we went to Cliff's house to get the oil from the turkey fry from yesterday. I was able to dispose of it in our garbage area at work. It has been quiet, peaceful and pleasant day. Wendy, Kay and I are planning to go out to dinner after I feed Bailey. We had our first snow sprinkle yesterday and now the holiday season is definitely upon us; a wonderful time of year.

11/28/10
5:14 PM EST
Home, NJ

It was a cold day here in New Jersey but with lots of sunshine, which made biking after tennis with my brother a delight. Alex flew back to St. Louis this morning and Kay is now stuck on the highway in the Thanksgiving traffic trying to get back to Ithaca, NY. It has become quiet again here in New Jersey; just Wendy, me and Bailey, which is not a bad thing. I just finished the December newsletter. I am sure that Rich and Al will modify my right/conservative leaning rhetoric more towards the middle. It is good to have people with multiple viewpoints check my work before it goes out. Sometimes I come off a little too strong and do not want to offend people with my viewpoints. Strong will is good, but a strident view is not. It is back to work tomorrow and I look forward to being back in my routine. I am almost ready to leave on Thursday and it will be good to be back on the road.

11/29/10
4:54 PM EST
My office, NJ

It is very good to be back in the office. Four days is a lot of time to be away. Unfortunately, I had been thinking about laying off Jack's assistant and today I decided to do it. We have to start reducing monetary and time efforts into the composite. There are no orders in sight and the time has come. Jan. 15th is the cut off. Laying people off is the part of my job that I hate most, both for them and for the fact I misjudged the market and brought them on in the first place. Sometimes I do it for optimism, sometimes I miscalculate and sometimes I just want to give someone a temporary chance, a first job to get them started knowing that their time is limited and that they then have the stepping stone to move from.

Other than that, it has been a good day and I even heard from Miss Rose regarding her accommodations for the first part of her trip in Australia. I am reticent about her going but am very hopeful that things will be fine. She has a very good head of her shoulders sand will stand up for herself, still I worry. The house will be quiet again when I go home, just Wendy and Bailey. I like our "empty nest" routine and have no fear of it continuing. I saw Jessica over the holiday and she is due very soon with her first child. Another generation begins, which means a whole new group of youngsters who have not heard my stories, my singing or dancing. What a treat; a whole new audience to try to dazzle.

11/30/10
4:55 PM EST
My office, NJ

The day started with more problems with the public offering and did not stop until late morning. There is a lot to go over when I get there this weekend and there may be some pressured moments between me, our people and the underwriters. Actually, there is probably no doubt that will happen, so I will prepare mentally. I do know that the pressure is building to such a point that the end is near one way or another because too many people are under too much stress. I checked sales for North America and Europe and as far as I can tell, we are on par with last year and our groups in Asia are doing much better. However, we have spent virtually all of the profits on R&D from this side, which will stop next month. Either way, major decisions are coming and I look forward to some closure.

DECEMBER

12/1/10
4:14 PM EST
My office, NJ

More work with going public. After lunch, my stomach went haywire; something like what happened in the Netherlands the last time I was there. I am hoping this will not last long because I travel tomorrow and I am going to be on the plane unless I cannot walk. November sales ended up being okay; not great and not bad. I have no complaints. However, our overhead is still too high and unfortunately, that could mean a layoff or two in the new year. One of the groups we were doing research with for the composites just had a big business reversal, so they are out of the research market for now, in survival mode and will probably stay there for at least 6 months to build back up on their standard pieces of business. I keep feeling I have just not found the right way to sell this new product line. We went from base materials to specific applications and maybe that is the wrong path. Luckily, there is no crisis. We are fine, we just have to get to the realization that maybe it is time to change direction; a tough decision.

12/2/10
5:26 PM EST
LaGuardia Airport Queens, NY

My stomach went crazy yesterday after lunch until early evening when it started to improve. I loaded up on all types of medications and happily I was able to sleep after I finished packing. I woke up this morning a little better and was able to work out in my basement, have my usual breakfast and play tennis. As is normal in this situation, being sick has no relevance to tennis and if you can walk, then "Guy Code" dictates that you go. I did and happily, I ended up playing my best and had a great workout. After that, it was a morning of paperwork in the office. My people are always happy when I eventually leave on the day of a trip because I tend to be a bit hyperactive. I went home and spent some time with Wendy and Bailey until Mike the driver picked me up at 3:30.

Going from New Jersey to Queens during rush hour is always a gamble so I scheduled a lot of extra time to get to the airport. I was prepared for virtually anything regarding security, scans or pat-downs, since I have to get to Malaysia, but it turned out to be easy and swift. I had to check my suitcase. I had thought it might be small enough to carry on, but no such luck.

DECEMBER

I am hopeful it will be in Toronto with me when I arrive. I do not know the procedure in that airport regarding transit flights and since I have no boarding pass, I will need to get one there. It may mean going out of security and going back in, but I hope to have lots of time and will try not to dwell on the potential for problems.

Meanwhile, my stomach is not great but not bad and I have eaten little today so I will eat some of the food I brought. I have 2 ½ hours before boarding, so I may even watch a movie or some television programs I am carrying with me. Unfortunately, there are no lounges, but I gladly trade them to get on my next flight with my bags on time. It is not strange how the basics become so important; you can do a lot to me as long as I make my flights. There are a lot of tired looking people around here, all seemingly looking to get home. The holidays are approaching here in the States and they, like me, are probably planning to get off the road until January. Kayla and Alex are due home in about two weeks for their winter vacations and it will be good to have them back.

12/2/10
11:19 PM EST
Toronto Airport, Canada

I got my suitcase back! It came through with no problem and it was a good, calm flight with a very nice staff. I was first in line at immigration and got to the Cathay Pacific ticket counter swiftly and easily. I was excited at the prospect of being able to carry on my suitcase, but again the attendant dashed that hope, so now I will rely on this great airline to get my bag to KL the same time I do. I started eating again and will keep reintroducing food until either I am fine or a repeat rebellion occurs.

My goals for this trip:
1. To make sure that the relationships between all IJ companies are beneficial
2. To redefine my role as chairman and the details involved
3. To go public profitably
4. To get commitments regarding loan payments
5. To work with our sales forces in Malaysia and Thailand, see who has potential, who doesn't and what changes should to be made
6. To bring the Malaysian Distributor Nickel and Dime firmly into our group
7. To work on the possibility of revitalizing IJ India

12/3/10
11:05 PM China time, 10:05 AM EST
Approx. 6:13 minutes to arrival

It was a little tough to stay awake before boarding, but we were on our way before 2:00 AM Toronto time. I boarded to an extremely welcomed sight, which was a flat seat, meaning I could actually get some real sleep. I slept about seven hours, which is pretty amazing for me on a plane. While eating dinner, my stomach was feeling better, I was reading my favorite newspaper, The Financial Times, and was trying to formulate a new global opinion as to what is going on. It is obvious from the U.S. side that the rush of business out of here and Europe is continuing and that customers in all parts of the world will keep pressuring us for Chinese prices no matter where it is made. While I think we can maintain our niche markets in the U.S. and Europe for the temporary higher priced areas, I see little chance for major growth in our core business of labels, gaskets, metal and plastic parts and other product lines. The trend will continue to produce in Asia and distribute throughout the rest of the world. Happily, we already have that in position and they are growing at a very healthy rate. As always, with change there are growing pains.

I know that our people in Asia think we are crazy for producing in the U.S. at all and we should move everything to them. However, they are currently unable to get the initial projects here and in Europe. In other words, the team we have is the team we need and we have to keep the balance, maximize all of our areas and try to have peace and good teamwork between all involved. With the various experience, fears, cultural differences, and goals our company has, that is going to be a continual struggle. Actually, the next few days will be critical in that process.

Another reason for my trip is to check the IJT sales force. There is a new salesman there who has promised, in my mind, improbable amounts of sales in a short time. While I admire his confidence, I think the likelihood of his promised success is doubtful. I will know better once I meet him in person. I am hearing a lot about the large amount of RFQs that IJT has submitted to customers and how great that is, but as my dad always said, you can't eat estimates. I am only interested in actual sales and the rest is irrelevant.

Peace has descended on this airplane. For all involved, it is a time of transition to a new country, culture and time zone. If things go normally, it will start to alter again about one hour before landing. As for now, it is very calm and pleasant.

12/4/10
6:41 AM China time, 5:41 PM EST
Hong Kong Airport

The flight ended well and was about 50 minutes early. Getting through the transfer area and going through security was happily not a problem. I now sit in the Cathay Pacific Lounge, which is very nice and has a great fruit assortment of which I have already indulged. Since they will most likely feed us on the plane, I will refrain from eating anything else. I spoke to Wendy, who is doing fine, though both she and Bailey miss me, as I do them. There has been no word on the Jessica front, meaning no new baby yet. She is due within the next ten days.

I like the feel of Asia, the rapid pulse, high energy and need to move quickly. I heard from my brother wishing me good luck on this trip. It is Friday evening at home and I normally would have seen him this morning for tennis.

DECEMBER

He is a kind and very decent man. I am very lucky to have him as my brother.

12/4/10
9:53 PM Malaysian time, 8:53 AM EST
Crowne Plaza Hotel Kuala Lumpur

The plane to KL was on time and well run and I inwardly celebrated as my suitcase came around on the luggage carousel. I got to the hotel about 3:00 PM and was out doing my band workout by 4:00. My body was not into it at first, but I mostly got through it and then lasted about 30 minutes on the elliptical machine. Thank goodness I had my iPod with the latest Star Trek movie to keep my mind occupied or I never would have made it working out that long. After a badly needed shower and shave, I went to meet Hing and Ku. We worked on a variety of issues related to going public. The meeting lasted about an hour and we got through a lot of details. Afterward, I headed back to my room.

12/5/10
10:51 AM Malaysian time, 9:51 PM EST
Crowne Plaza Hotel

I was fortunate enough to get about ten hours of badly needed sleep last night. After my band workout on the tennis court, I called Wendy, who had just gotten back from seeing a movie. She sounded fine and it was great to hear her voice.

I have always wanted to be in a position like this; a big deal with the chance to get much bigger. If we can get through this process and grow the company, then there is potential for big money for all of us. You don't get many opportunities like this in life and I want this work.

12/5/10
8:44 PM Malaysian time, 7:44 AM EST
Crowne Plaza Hotel KL

Ben emailed me at about 3:45 PM and said he had just landed and was coming to the hotel now. While I waited, I fell asleep and when I woke up he had emailed me he was at the hotel and asked me to meet at the lounge on his floor.

As for going public, our underwriters are now doing everything they can to get us listed, but the securities commission did not get back with a certain approval and may not this week, which means we cannot be listed before the end of the year. If we are not listed by the end of the year, then we have to stop the process because we cannot legally transfer money from IJ Xiamen to fund IJ Malaysia and Thailand.

We have reached the end of process and either the government gives their approval of the last piece of information and the underwriters agree we have covered all of their questions in time to list this year or we are done.

It is odd, coming down to the end and having it be the last minute, but that is probably the nature of these things. Ben and I talked about both scenarios if we go public and if we don't and each has benefits and negatives. I would still like for it to happen and when we go in tomorrow for the last meeting, we will push to get it done.

Regarding expansion, Geri Lee, our head of Asian sales (excluding IJX), has contacts with Dell in India and they want us to put a small plant there. Ben also wants to put a small plant in China and another one in Malaysia, but nothing will be decided until after we go public or not. We need help there, which is one of the reasons I am going later this week to see what I can offer.

We then spoke about IJ Thailand. While the plant is in good shape (thank you, Vinnie), there are virtually no sales and Ben hired a new salesman who is promising big things.

As Ben said, with the amount of restrictions in going public, we cannot operate as we did before. Our decision making would be slowed down. Now, depending on the scope and amount of money involved, the project has to go before the board for approval. Granted, Ben and I own more than 50% of the company, but we still have to call a board meeting, explain things to the other members and vote. Things in general will be delayed especially for change. If we go forward, I am planning a streamlined version of directors meetings via email, but that has to be worked out afterward. As I said, there are pros and cons to being public, but one of the great parts is that it will put us in a better position for much bigger projects and to grow more quickly and profitably.

12/6/10
6:03 PM Malaysian time, 5:03 AM EST
Crowne Plaza Hotel KL

I woke at 2:00 AM this morning and had trouble going back to sleep, which is highly unusual for me. I got up at 6:00 and went out to the tennis court to do my band workout. I noticed a giant rainbow and thought it was a good sign. The only issue was I was not sure if it meant it was better to go public or not. After a hearty breakfast, I met Ben and Hing downstairs. Hing had delayed his family vacation for the evening so he could be with us. We spent the morning with our underwriters going through some issues, but it was nothing that could not be handled quickly. At lunch, Ben was getting visibly more upset since we could not get an answer about the timing for our listing. After a while, we realized that we could not be listed this year and the best chance would be the second quarter of 2010. Hearing that news, both Ben and I knew that there was no chance of going forward simply because through Chinese regulations, we could not move enough cash over from IJX to continue to fund both IJT and IJM and he and I were not going to loan them any more money.

We immediately stopped the meeting and left. We were all pretty upset when we got back to the hotel. While sitting there, Ku, Ben, Jossie, Pk and I slowly began to talk.

As I had wanted, we decided to keep the systems in place that were created for going public. Once we agreed on that, we began discussing where to go from here and the potential to go public in 2-3 years when we would have had a chance to grow more, open one or two more factories and make some needed personnel changes. The more we spoke, the more excited we became realizing that the freedom of not being public now would give us the chance to make the decisions for changes that would put us into a much better position immediately, which we have not been able to do for the last 12 months.

Still, it was a great shock and our people will be disappointed for the short term, but I truly believe it is for the best, especially if we do go public in three years when we would be worth much more than we are now. I find it fascinating how the conversation went from nothing to dull interest to intense excitement. I love the minds of people who will not be stopped even after being slapped down. I will have dinner with Ben later and we can talk about more options, but this is what we came up with so far:

1. Create a new holding company in Hong Kong, Singapore, Bermuda or the Cayman Islands because of their excellent tax structures in case we want to replace IJ Malaysia as the main corporate entity.
2. Put in a plant in India and an additional plant into China in the next 12 months.
3. Keep IJT as it is now, but if it doesn't break even in 6 months, then stop the plant, ship the equipment to China and make IJT a sales office. The advantage is that we could move it to a tax free zone, which could possibly save us from being killed with a 20% tax on everything now.
4. The other IJT option is to set up a small secondary plant in a tax free zone in Bangkok, which would potentially make the whole operation temporarily tax free.
5. Close the corporate headquarters in KL and move IJ Malaysia to Penang, create a sales office there. PK and Geri, our sales manager, will actually live there.
6. Keep the structure that we set up for going public so we are ready for the future.
7. Have IJUS deal directly with IJT or IJM and have them sub-contract the work to IJX. This way, the money will flow directly into them, help pay for their overhead and lessen the problem of moving money from IJ to supply them with capital.

There will be more coming in the next few weeks, but for now we need a few days to get used to what is not happening and that life will be much easier without the underwriters making continuous document requests with ridiculous time schedules. We learned a lot this time and it will pave the way for a much easier journey for the future.

12/7/10
12:05 AM Malaysian time, 11:05 PM EST
Kuala Lumpur International Airport

As it turned out, when I went back to meet Ben for dinner he was still meeting with Jossie, Pk and Ku. We met for about a half hour more then we all split up. I went outside to the pool to look at the Twin Towers, had dinner and then went back to my room to go to bed. Again I did not sleep that well and got up this morning and went back to the tennis court to do my band workout and walk. As I did, I spoke to Al, Mike and Brett. Besides the fact they were all worried about me, as per not going public, which was very nice, they wanted to hear about what else as going on. Brett and I were working on a new invention. I also spoke to my wonderful wife, who was a wall of support as always and then it was in to change, pack and go see Ben at the lounge. Geri, our head of sales for Malaysia, was already there and it gave us a chance to talk and plan. She is a dynamo; she started off her career cold-calling for sales like I did and I liked her right away. After she gave her report about her views of what to do for Malaysia, we spoke about Singapore and Thailand. I think she will be good and she is very pleased we are moving the office here from Kuala Lumpur to Penang where she now lives.

Afterward, Ben and I had a final quick meeting regarding yesterday and both reaffirmed our plans to go public in the next few years and the critical needs to keep up the systems we had installed for this aborted first try. We are in sync and ready to push forward to grow and move to multiple new levels. It is good to be having fun again and not have the weight of the underwriters always on our shoulders. Then it was here to the airport. There is a lot to do at IJT and it starts when I land. I am hoping for a good nap on the plane, as it promises to be a long afternoon and early evening. I am not sure how Pasin, Suwaleerat and Paul will react to Geri's promotion. Suwaleerat already emailed congratulations. I believe Geri could be a big help to her for sales. I hope I am right.

12/7/10
7:58 PM Thai time, 7:58 AM EST
Intercontinental Hotel Bangkok

Our flight was early. Paul picked me up and we were at IJT by 3:00 PM. I wanted to talk with Suwaleerat, Pasin and Paul separately and then together to try to get a feeling of the dynamic between them and where the strengths and weaknesses fell. I chose Suwaleerat to lead because she is very pleasant, tries hard and I like her. As we talked about how she divided her time and what she worked on, it turned out that 50% of her efforts were spent in calculating costs and selling prices for the massive amount of RFQs they received weekly. Since they also got prices from IJX, this seemed like a redundancy in effort. I got all three of them together and suggested that she no longer cost anything. By utilizing IJX prices and adding on for the various import taxes, she could get a selling price based on shipping from Bangkok, which is what most of our customers wanted. If IJT did get business on this basis, then they could decide afterward if they wanted to produce it in Thailand or import from IJX. It would save a mountain of time, which we decided would be evenly split between going after new accounts and learning more about the workings of the plant, so that she could take over full time as General Manager. They all liked the idea.

Next, I spoke to Paul which was actually a continuation from the car. He needs to be outside more talking to prospects. With the extra 25% of Suwaleerat's time, he will teach her about the balance of the basics of the business, freeing him to go after composite sales and working on various engineering needs for different products.

Next, I spoke to Pasin. He has given some very high estimates of how much he can sell and I gave him the chance to reduce them, but he thinks he can do it. More power to him, I said, everyone would support him trying. He mentioned that he was only trying to sell what IJT produces since the customers wanted a local supplier. I told him I had been through this before and the customers only wanted the lowest price shipped from a local supplier. They did not care where a product was produced, only it was of adequate quality, in the demanded time and the proper price. I hope he agreed with my thinking, though I am not sure.

We all had a pleasant dinner and I am hoping a new ground has been laid for a much better chance for new and increased sales, everyone working together and each having more to do of the things they liked.

With the responsibility we gave Geri today, her neck is on the line for them so I am sure she will also be there for as much help and support as is needed. I am cautiously optimistic for the future of IJT. We will let them run for a few months and I will monitor them through Geri to see where they go. Paul drove me to this hotel we have stayed in before, which is excellent, and I have plans to work out in some manner after I finish here. It is relatively early and I hope to be asleep by 11:00.

12/8/10
9:29 PM Thai time, 9:29 AM EST
Intercontinental Hotel Bangkok

After a great workout and breakfast, Pasin picked me up at 8:30 this morning and it was off to Sanmina-SCI. This was really important because I would get the chance to see how he acted in front of a customer. Traffic was light and we got there about an hour early. Happily, the customer was able to see us. He was very pleasant, Pasin handled it well and we all got along. Often in Europe and Asia the buyer and our people go into their local language to make it easier to communicate. I have no problem with this and while they were talking I was moving our composite renderings on the table into the view of the customer. He liked what he saw. His family was into selling defense products to the Thai military, so not only was he interested in our regular products, but there was a chance for our other area too.

From there, we stopped at a coffee shop where Paul and Suwaleerat eventually joined us. While we waited, we spoke about selling techniques, starting an IJT newsletter and also designed a new product. Since the next potential customer was interested in disaster planning related products, we designed a new type of catcher to help slow down a mud slide before it takes out a town. Once we got to MTEC, which is the Thai version of MIGHT in Malaysia, we were ready to rumble. They listened to our information, saw our renderings and were excited to try to help match us to groups who might need our products in Thailand. We will see what happens, but it was worth the call.

Then we left Suwaleerat and Paul drove me to my hotel where we finished the design for the mud slide catcher and spoke more about sales and the functions for him, Suwaleerat, Pasin and Geri. Afterward, it was back to the room for more paperwork. I worked out again, had dinner and I will try to go to sleep soon. I need to be up early to go to the airport.

12/10/10
6:39 AM Malaysian time, 5:39 PM EST
In transit to KL Airport

I got up at 4:40 AM, which was not easy, exercised and spoke to Brett and Al. The waters have been churned here, which means more potential for success. I need to keep coming on a regular basis. I got to the Crowne Plaza at about 1:00 PM and ate lunch while speaking with Ku. He went over the possible options of going public later and where we may set up a new holding company. He would get us a formal proposal in a few weeks. Afterward, I went to my room to change and get my laptop to show Abul some of the new military inventions and realized I had left it at security in Bangkok this morning. Amazingly, Paul was able to get it for me, but it meant I could no longer write, which sent me into a panic.

Abul wanted to try to sell our new bullet proof vest product to his friend, a doctor who was interested in our new mud slide catcher. It was off to a meeting at MIGHT. By this time, I was getting pretty tired but revved up again when meeting with Major Zailani and Dr. Hali. We discussed why our experiments did not work and a new plan for tests and possible manufacture. She believes her product is much less expensive than what is on the market, not to mention organically based and will absorb heat at a much higher rate than synthetic versions, so we will pursue it further. When I get back, I will set up a phone meeting with her, Vinnie and Jack to see if there is potential.

Then it was back to the hotel, by which time I was exhausted, and I prepared to meet with Faiz from Nickel and Dime. He is a very interesting young man and after repeated texts back and forth, we were both tired. He suggested we go eat at a Subway fast food store, which was perfect for me especially after the large amount of local food I had eaten. It was a fascinating meeting. He not only works on the defense side of his company, but is also in charge of the model and marketing for their modeling agency. It was a lot of fun and his connections into the Malaysian military seem very strong. He wants to try to fulfill the requirement they have for 2000 bullet proof vests. I will check it when I get back.

12/10/10
8:20 AM Malaysian time, 7:20 PM EST
Kuala Lumpur International Airport

There was a minor problem at check-in. The computers were down and I could not get the boarding pass for my connection flight. I have less than an hour on the changeover and it would have been tight. They could not do it at the lounge, but they could at the gate, which meant I was now ready. It is a great feeling to be prepared. I felt naked without my computer.

12/10/10
9:32 AM EST
In flight - 8:04 to go currently headed towards the Aleutian Islands

Handwritten log – I am not sure if I have ever done it this way before.

Singapore Airlines is excellent. The flight has been fine so far, but I have only slept a little bit. The whole flight should be about 18 hours. I have been working on charting our sales, where they are coming from, where we can get more and what happens if we do or we don't. I am thinking of actually circulating my chart worldwide so that all of our teams can see what is expected of them and me. It may be the only way to truly motivate some of our people in productive action and what happens if they don't produce. A lot will be clear on 1/15, 4/1 and 7/1, which are the milestone days for review. If the numbers or the potential is not realized, then action will be taken. Ben is concerned about our Asian overhead, but I am more worried about building up our sales for now. Again, by 7/1/10, a lot will be clear and the actions need to be taken. The options we have are:

Staying private
Private investors
Going public

I prefer the option of going public, but it will mean extra expenses for the reporting needed. I think it is worth it. Ben and I will email more next week. Downsizing could affect all areas of the company and it all depends on the sales and where they are. Worldwide, we have about one million dollars in overhead we could cut quickly if needed. We will see soon.

12/10/10
3:38 PM EST
In flight - 1 ½ hours to go, currently over Canada

I slept about 5 ½ hours and feel pretty good. If all goes well, I will be home by 7:00 PM. Right now, I have plans to be in Europe in February and Asia again in March not to mention a few days in Florida with Bunny and Jeff for some tennis and rest. It will be great to get home.

12/11/10
4:40 PM EST
Home, NJ

I got back before 7:00 PM last night to the wonderful sight of my wife and Bailey. I got about 9 hours of sleep and was off to ride after breakfast. It was a chilly morning, but I was dressed well and it was fun. After lunch with Wendy, I had an appointment with one of my therapists who is also a medical intuitive. I have a test procedure scheduled for Monday and she gave her opinion that she thought I would be fine and the results would reflect it. It was good news and tonight we are going out with our friends Carla and Mitch. It has been awhile and it will be good to see them.

12/12/10
4:08 PM EST
Home, NJ

It was great to be back on my normal Sunday schedule. After tennis with my brother, who is doing well, I worked out in our basement due to the rain. I had lunch and went to the office to catch up. I got a lot done including speaking to Brett about the new 12-gauge shotgun shock project and working on my new worldwide sales project.

12/13/10
3:26 AM EST
Home, NJ

As you can tell from the time of the entry, I cannot sleep. It is probably a combination of delayed jet lag, allergies and concern about my doctor visit. It did, however, give me the chance to edit my log from the trip, which I can circulate this morning. This extra time means I am now mostly caught up and might get a chance for a nap this morning before our holiday part. I am excited to begin all of our new plans worldwide.

12/13/10
5:12 PM EST
My office, NJ

I had the prostate biopsy today, but will not get the results until Thursday or Friday – now I wait. Wendy was able to come to our holiday party today, which was great fun.

I spent the balance of the day doing paperwork. There is a lot to do to catch up from the trip and move forward. I sent Ben a spreadsheet for all salespeople worldwide for projections for the next three years. I await his okay to circulate it so everyone knows what is expected.

12/14/10
4:20 PM EST
Home, NJ

I love it when I have been away and have the chance to really catch up. It was a usual day of roller coaster highs and lows. The low was finding out that our shock shotgun cartridge had already been developed by another company. I stopped the project. The goods news is that we have new potential elsewhere. We are waiting for some more specifications on the bulletproof jacket from Faiz. The good news is that we can now make it lighter and more price competitive than what is in the marketplace. We are working on a new type of safety enclosure for our troops in Afghanistan and the TAA is finicky. It is getting close to being finished so we will be able to submit it to the government for approval and be able to export samples and drawings to our selected partners overseas. The new head of military from Trelleborg is coming next week to see our prototype plant and discuss strategy and Igor has decided he wants to stay in the Netherlands, which will help speed the growth of IJ Europe. He wants to move in with his girlfriend, though she has to say yes first and nothing is definite until she gives a firm move-in date. I am working on the sales teams for IJT and IJM.

It was an especially good day after the doctor's visit of yesterday. The results have been weighing on my mind, but I am trying to dwell on the various scenarios and how I would handle them. In the worst case, I have cancer to some degree and through my research, family relations and business related contacts I have a lot of knowledge about various types of treatment and will deal with it. It is all very distracting and I would like to get to a point where I can stop thinking about it. That may or may not happen this week. I have been living with my dad's various cancers for decades. His constant updates can be grueling and they make it so I cannot stop thinking about it. It has me very thankful for the incredible life I have and I count my blessings all the time. I am extremely grateful and I try to take nothing for granted.

12/15/10
4:45 PM EST
My office, NJ

Today was the Briss (circumcision) for Jess and Joe's new little baby Cooper. I did not watch the event, but was present. It represents a new generation in our family and also meant that we (my generation) are moving one level up toward being the oldest. It is a somewhat uneasy feeling, but much better than the alternative of death.

12/16/10
4:35 PM EST
My office, NJ

I spoke with Ben last night and today. The public offering is now potentially back on again if the investor will stay with us until the first quarter of the year at the same stock price. I spoke with Wendy and we agreed we could wait for the loan payback until March if the offering went through.

No word from my urologist. I had lunch with John Rudder and by that time I was a bit panicked with worry, but he happily calmed me down. He is a good man as well as my mentor. He was the last person not to bless it, so I am confident we can go ahead now. I had called a friendly competitor two days ago to see if they were interested in a joint venture or wanted to buy part of IJ Malaysia as an investor since we were not going public. He did not call until today and by then the offering was back on, so I did not give him the option. I got the feeling he might have been interested, but if so he should not have waited. As I try to tell everyone who will listen, call back when you are supposed to, keep your promises, be on time and be honest and it will get you a long way toward building trust with others. Everyone makes mistakes, but it is the fabric of the person's moral fiber that you are bonding with and that cannot be faked for long. I am not bored and my stomach is starting to get nervous again about the medical test. But it looks like another day to wait.

12/17/10
2:40 PM EST
My office, NJ

My urologist emailed – I am fine. The happiness level is hard to define!

We heard from one of the Trelleborg agents from Italy and they want reinforced structures for cargo ships to be able to resist pirates. At the trade show in Texas that Brett and Jack attended, they met a company who makes non-armored versions and we are partnering with them to create a finished product. We also had an ISO 14001 Environmental Audit today, which went well with no bad findings. I am tired, but extremely good.

12/18/10
2:13 PM EST
Home, NJ

It is hard to express the incredible feeling of relief and exhilaration from the test results. Gone are the fears that my death might be imminent, that I may not see the many events I hope to be a part of like the marriage of my kids, grandchildren, going public or reaching the life goals I have like creating 10,000 jobs and maybe winning a Nobel Prize. It is like being given another chance and since I always count my blessings anyway, it just makes the coming journey that much sweeter. After I got the great news, I contacted all the people who knew, though I had not told many, and all have been incredibly supportive and filled with positive energy and good will.

We had my brother's annual Chanukah dinner last night, which was extremely pleasant as always. Later, the effects of the various pressures of the last few weeks seemed to all come about and sleep overtook me. After about 9 hours I got up, ate breakfast, did my band workout, walked on the treadmill and then also walked outside. It is a beautifully cold day here in NJ, too cold for me to bicycle but wonderful to be outdoors never the less. Alex's flight is due about 3:00 PM and I will pick him up. It will be wonderful to see him and it will give us some time to update each other as to what is going on.

I spoke with Faiz, our contact with Nickel and Dime Company in Malaysia. His work to get us an order for Bullet Proof Vests for the Malaysian Army is moving ahead and we need to be ready in case it comes through. Jack is working on our new process, which needs to be certified here by a formal testing house to prove to all potential customers and my team that our product works. None of us want the possibility of a faulty product that may result in injury or death. We want to be in the business, but want to make sure we meet or exceed the protection we are offering. We are meeting Monday in the office to work on the test samples we will build to mimic those in production and send those for formalized testing. It will not be cheap, but it is highly necessary. In the meantime, Jack is preparing the information for our contact in Afghanistan for the protective enclosures we are hoping to supply.

12/19/10
1:57 PM EST
Home, NJ

Wendy and I went out to dinner last night to celebrate our 26th wedding anniversary. It is hard to believe we have known each other 27 years, half of my life. It has been a fantastic journey that I hope will not slow down for a very long time. We spoke about life, our kids and what we hope for in the next year. It is wonderful to dream and plan. I am glad we are together.

I got a lot of needed sleep last night and this morning I had a quick phone meeting with Ben, who is back in China. The only issue left regarding going public is to get a commitment from our underwriters that if we decide to go ahead they will not stand in our way and will okay us to be finished before April 1st. If we get it, we go ahead and if not, we have to stop. We need to have enough funds on hand to be able to finance our multiple forays into new products like the bulletproof vest panels and fighting structures for Afghanistan without forcing Ben and me into more debt. When I thought I might have prostate cancer, I realized that the time to go public was not an open-ended window. If we were going to do it, I needed to grab the chance now because too many factors could be involved later. Now that the scare has passed, at least for now, I realized it was still a sign to move forward. We are making good progress on our new bulletproof vest panels. Faiz emailed me this morning that he is gathering specifications and the timing needed for the Malaysian Army's deployment to the Middle East.

I played tennis with my brother, did the band workout in my basement and went outside in the cold air. It was all very pleasant and I am now happily sore from the multiple endeavors.

This weekend the Senate passed the "Don't Ask, Don't Tell" repeal for our military, which means that gay people can serve without declaring their sexual orientation and they no longer have to cover it up. I am glad they did this. There are other bills up for consideration; ironically, this "Lame Duck" session of Congress may get more good legislation done than it has in the last two years.

12/20/10
4:29 PM EST
My office, NJ

I pulled something in my left lower leg this morning playing tennis. It is hurting a bit and I hope it heals before tomorrow's game. Otherwise, I am in for some pain. I spoke with Ben early this morning regarding sales procedures in Thailand. Happily, we are in agreement that all RFQs received at IJM and IJT should go to IJX immediately for pricing and can then be produced at IJT if we get the business. We will not have a chance at the big bulletproof vest order in Malaysia, which is unfortunate, but so it goes. We are still going to go ahead and find out if our panels are price competitive and if so, go through the necessary testing. We are continuing work on the defense structures for the U.S. Army in Afghanistan and should have a presentation ready in a few days. If they go for it, they will fund it and if not, hopefully someone else will want it.

I had lunch with two entrepreneurs to whom we are offering free space to launch their new company. I forced them to write a business plan and I got a copy of it today. It was well written and logical, so they may have a chance. They were also happy I made them do it because it gave them structure to their passion and helped to not only funnel their energy but to reduce their stress, at least part of the time. They plan to launch next month and embark on a frightening, wonderful adventure. The Christmas holiday starts this Friday and things seem to be slowing down in anticipation.

12/21/10
3:55 PM EST
My office, NJ

I was planning to hire a chemist intern for the summer. He is a son of a family friend. I invited him, while he was home from college, to a development meeting for the armor. I could tell from his last email to me he really did not want to go, so I gave him an easy excuse not to come. He did say he was not coming, as he wanted to stay home and see his sister who was also coming home from college. I emailed him later and told him that I could tell from his email what he was thinking and he missed out on a great chance for a unique experience. I have been on email for years and use it extensively. I can usually tell pretty accurately what a person is thinking by the way they word their responses. Those who think they can cover up their feelings by writing instead of phone calling are usually wrong. I emailed him this only because his father is a friend and it is a lesson he should learn early. Whether I actually hire him as an intern, which was solid before, is now in doubt. Perhaps it is the best lesson I could have taught him.

DECEMBER

I spoke with Ben this morning and green lighted going public. In anticipation, I have already emailed Ben about bringing a bunch of our people on the day we are formally listed so we can have a sales summit and hopefully get some world team spirit and cooperation going to a much higher degree.

12/22/10
5:41 PM EST
Home, NJ

Jack and I met with the new Trelleborg head of U.S. military sales today. We discussed a non-binding world alliance to joint market and develop and a good groundwork seems to have been laid. We will send more information back and forth and all of us will go sell as much as we can to see what people want to buy. It is good to have more people selling our product lines. The higher the attempts, the higher the chances for business. As always, sales is a numbers game.

12/23/10
4:30 PM EST
Home, NJ

It is the day before the Christmas holiday officially starts and the slowdown this week has been palatable. It is not a problem, as it has been a very good year and I have no complaints. We did hear from the LTC in Afghanistan regarding our proposal for an armored fighting hut and he liked it and will make changes. I am hopeful it can be submitted for approval to his command next week. We also got more renderings done from Eric regarding our new mudslide retarding devices and I sent out our plans for creating 40 foot safety containers for ships attacked by pirates. This device will allow a crew to safely hide for days until help arrives or equip them to attack back if desired. It has been a very productive week for inventions, new ideas and marketing. With that in mind, I submitted a plan for a new armor website to be utilized by Trelleborg personnel and agents for renderings, videos, white papers and other information to make it easy to entice potential customers into doing business.

Nothing has really changed since Guttenberg and his bibles. Something has to be created, sold, accepted and paid for. The actual items and services may change, but the systems remain the same. The basic economics are that simple, but are so hard to learn. Strip out the emotion and you are left with the rules of the marketplace, which is easy to say but very hard to do.

Jeroen spoke with his partner today and gave notice that he will be leaving Lencon to work for IJE full time during 2011. The discussion had it ups and downs, but in the end I think it will be a very beneficial move for Jeroen and us. There will be pain in the separation before it is done. Change is good and necessary, but it means immediate and often continual pain on some scale. Many people try to avoid it, but we try to run towards it. From our experience, the tide of constant movement means a reduction in the pain and an increase in the benefits. It is simple, like sales; the more that happens and the better chance for positive change, the more that will happen. It is like being tournament tough in sports. While you are in that state, the negatives hurt less and once you are out of training, the pain and the duration increase from all sides. It is a good reason to stay in shape.

12/25/10
1:32 PM EST
Home, NJ
Christmas Day

I did very little yesterday. I worked out and spent time with my family. It was wonderful.

This morning I decided to accept a personal challenge and I went biking out in the cold weather. With the 26°F wind chill, it was quite cold but I made it through. Although, I resolved not do it again if it gets any colder. I love to bike in the warm weather. The hotter, the better and this time of year often has a cutoff day signifying a halt until the spring. Today may have been it. In the meantime, I have been thinking in general about business and came up with an addition to our defensive hut design for our people in Afghanistan. The TAA went back to our export attorney, who has some more questions and I am hoping we can be done next week and get it submitted to our government for approval.

As with many Jews here in our area, we will be going to the movies this afternoon. Wendy, Kayla, Alex and I will be joined by Barbara and Cliff and then have Chinese food for dinner, another tradition. I spoke to my friend Jim Jensen, who is located in a suburb of Salt Lake City Utah. He and his wonderful wife Janet sound well. He is one of those people one is very fortunate in life to find, who would drop everything to help me or my family as I would do for him. That kind of trust takes decades to build and I am extremely fortunate to count him with me.

It is the time year for reflection, seeing where I am and how I am doing regarding my overall life plan. It has been an amazing year of getting into position for what will hopefully come. A lot of the preliminary research is done for our new armor material and we are scheduled to go public in April. We are setting up additional sales people, agents and other alliances which should all start producing results this year. If my overall plan is sound and my team's efforts are fruitful, then we should see a lot of activity for new customer's sales and products in 2011. There are a lot of interlocking deals all moving toward conclusion. By the odds, not all can work, but some should. The anticipation of not knowing and realizing that what should happen rarely does will make for a lot of thrilling moments.

I think the good potential of what can happen is what keeps a lot of life fresh and interesting. The idea that nothing is preordained and that possibilities flourish until just before the point in time where they are defined means that the chances for continual betterment are always there. As an optimist, I believe there is little that can't be made better and the potential to help others can always be increased. The paranoia in me wants to safeguard what we have, utilize insurance against the bad times that will eventually come and protect us against the idiocy of others who can't see what is in their own best interest. The push and pull within myself with these two combating tidal waves of force are sometimes monumental, which always generates an increased need for a physical release of energy to give me time to think and sort things out.

I truly look forward to helping create a lot more jobs, utilizing my relatives and friends who are having a hard time due to the current economy. I know that their talents are underutilized and if given the chance and the right spot, they can soar to incredible heights of success and fulfillment. But I can't get them their chances until we grow a lot more, which is another reason for us to move along the paths I have chartered as quickly as possible. It doesn't matter if I am wrong, the journey still has to be undertaken and unsuccessful steps have to be climbed to reach prosperity. It is all part of the same journey. The fear of failure is an avoidance of change. I can't let either ever slow me down, although they are useful vantage points to view the road and to be as sure as possible of its solidness. The pressure never totally leaves me; if you feel you have the ability to reach plateaus and make things better, you can never be satisfied until you are there. My wishes for 2011 are good health for my family and the continued chances to reach our capabilities in the various areas we choose. Being in the game is one of the greatest gifts because it means you have the chance to move forward. I would not trade it for regulated security that would prevent growth. It is the ability to absorb the change, the failures and the negativity and convert it to positive energy that lets you soar that is the real essence of life. It gives you the chance to truly taste the best that life has, to love, honor and cherish and make positive, lasting change.

12/26/10
4:22 PM EST
Home, NJ

The movie yesterday, "The King's Speech," turned out to be excellent and from there Barbara, Cliff, Kayla, Alex, Wendy and I went back to our house. We ordered Chinese food, but when Cliff and I got to the restaurant the place was going crazy with too much business and they were not telling when we would get our food. I canceled the order and on the way back home, Cliff noticed an open pizza takeout store so we got some food from there. Happily, our crew at home did not care either way and the pleasant gathering ended at about 9:15 PM.

I got up early and played tennis with Ira, then we took Alex for his birthday brunch celebration at a local restaurant. On the way, the snowstorm, well predicted in advance, began to come down in earnest. After we ate and had a very lovely time, we dropped him off at the train station to go into Manhattan to stay with his cousin Barry for the night and went home. I consider shoveling snow an art form, which my wife and daughter understand so they did not mind that I parked at the bottom of the driveway and cleaned it off before driving on it. The snow can become packed under my wheels and make ice paths along the surface. By that time, the blizzard had begun and as of an hour ago it is snowing at a rate of 1-2 inches per hour. I shoveled everything in the hopes of keeping ahead of the storm, but this could be a tough one.

I got out our snow blower and it is now stationed at the top of our driveway, ready to go if there is too much for me to handle by shovel. I have already canceled my tennis game for tomorrow, so I will get up and tackle what is out there before dawn. My real worry is that the storm will overwhelm the snow clearing equipment of the town and I won't be able to get out of my street onto the main road or the governor declares a snow emergency and the roads are closed. I can do nothing about either, so I will concentrate on things I can actually control. It is dusk outside our window and the snow seems to be going sideways with great intensity. Happily, my son Ben got one of the last planes out of Cleveland, Ohio, where he was visiting his girlfriend's family, back into Newark and he is now safely home in Brooklyn. None of us are planning to go out except Alex, who is in Manhattan, and things virtually never stop there. In the worst case, he can walk to where he needs to go.

12/27/10
4:40 PM EST
My office, NJ

As it got later last night, it became very evident that we were going to get slammed by this storm. I set my alarms for the normal 4:40 AM time and figured I would get up and shovel until I got myself out. Worst case, I figured I would use my snow blower, but I was hoping that would not be necessary. I got up to the roar of heavy winds outside and when I opened our garage door all I saw at first was snow. It must have been about 30 inches. Everything was engulfed and it looked like a hopeless task. I shoveled a little to get a feel for it, whether the snow was heavy or light. Happily, it was a perfect consistency for the snow blower, which was dry and easy to move. The temperature was also well below freezing, which meant it would stay that way for a while.

I made a path over to my fine machine, but could not get her started. Crestfallen, I started with a shovel, but then I decided to recheck all of the switches and sure enough, one was not in the correct position. I made the change and she purred to life. My apologies to my nearby neighbors for the loud noise so early in the morning, but I had little choice. I have never seen a snow like this and I have been shoveling for almost five decades. This was immense, but my snow blower and I were able to make great headway in an hour. By that time, my hands were freezing and aching from trying to control her huge amount of power, I had bought a very good machine. I spent the next hour cleaning everything up and getting a path for Bailey in the backyard. More than two hours later, I was back inside and changing for work. I had no idea how the roads were. Ours had just been plowed, but I was determined to try in case I had people waiting at the office who could not get in. Amazingly, I only saw a few other cars and was in my office in less than 30 minutes. There I met Vinnie and two others who had also made it, and we rejoiced at having made it safely. Al finally got in about two hours later. She and Mel had been stuck on a local highway and that was it for the day. Luckily, this is a vacation week for many and I was able to get a lot of paperwork done including work on our TAA agreement. I will leave soon to pick up Alex at the train and then head home for dinner. In lieu of trying to play tennis tomorrow, I will shovel more to clean up what wasn't done today and make a pathway to our front door. My body is sore now and will be a lot more tomorrow morning. The exercise is tough, fun and burns a lot of calories. I have no complaints.

12/28/10
4:30 PM EST
My office, NJ

I got up this morning and continued shoveling from the big storm. I got a lot more done and should be able to finish tomorrow morning before I play tennis. Life here in the office is mostly back to normal. Some people still could not get in because of bad road conditions and traffic. It is almost the end of the year and my normal time for final audits of our Quality, Environmental and Health and Safety Systems. Alex decided to stay in the city again last night because there were electrical problems with the trains. He should be home tonight. Kayla has been getting ready for her first solo vacation to Australia and I am getting progressively more nervous about her going alone, but have tried to mitigate my fears by finding emergency contacts down under who could help her if needed. Once a dad, always a dad. I want her to have a great time and I look forward to her getting back home safely. Of course, she leaves the next day to go back to college, so it will be a short visit. Alex will leave about the same time so the house will become quiet again. I leave for Florida in about three weeks for two nights to see Jeff and Nanny. It is a yearly event featuring seeing them, tennis, swimming and iced tea; a fun time. It also looks like I am going to Europe at the end of January to visit with Jeroen and the Trelleborg agents. We are working on a big project for him, but I fear the price will be more than he was hoping to pay. It was designed with total quality in mind and will probably have to be cost reduced to make it competitive. It is his call on what to do. We are making plans for Jeroen and Igor to be out of Lencon's office and on their own under IJE by May. If the sales come as I hope, they will be profitable immediately.

12/29/10
4:44 PM EST
My office, NJ

I finally finished the front walk and the shoveling is done! Now all I have to do is get my snow blower back into the shed, though the steps are still engulfed with snow. I guess I am not done yet. Rich has been working on the new IJ Armor website which will be for Trelleborg employees and agents to use as a resource for themselves and potential customers. I think it is going to be awesome. I modified a sales agreement we had with one of our reps and sent it to the Trelleborg agent in Italy, but there has been no word back. We will need to get them all under a commission agreement so that we can make sure they get paid. Kayla's friend Alexa came to visit last night and she will be here until tomorrow when Kayla leaves for Australia. She is a wonderful, great friend to Kayla and I like having her around. Alex's internship is going well. He is learning to make parts of dresses for actual garments being sold, which is a great experience for him. I wrote the January Newsletter. I wonder what next year will bring. It is probably better that I don't know.

12/30/10
4:30 PM EST
My office, NJ

It has been a good day. No shoveling to start, right to my band workout and then a rousing game of tough tennis. I spent the day doing marketing and sales. Rich finished the preliminary armor website and it looks great. I sent it out to our Trelleborg partner for review. Kayla called this afternoon and asked if she needed a visa to visit Australia. Neither Al nor I thought so, but after checking it turned out she did. Kayla did it on her own online and the way she handled it gave me great confidence in her ability to handle this trip. She texted Wendy that she is at JFK Airport and is going through ticketing and security. She is due to takeoff in less than an hour. I will try not to worry too much in general and will feel better when she is on the plane tonight. Things have quieted down and if our preliminary sales figures are correct, then next month is in good shape. Like being in a plane for a long ride, the day before a holiday usually quiets down and becomes peaceful the same way. It is a nice time to be in the office.

12/31/10
11:52 AM EST
Home, NJ

Kayla texted me from her layover in San Francisco and she should be in Sydney in about 4 to 5 hours. I got up this morning to read a note from Alex; it is the type you do not want to get. It seemed that a raccoon had gotten into our garage and he almost stepped on it. The good news is that he was not bitten and apparently he scared the animal away. The bad news was the raccoon left a mess. The additional good news was it gave me the push to clean the garage, which I took care of after doing my band workout and playing tennis with my wonderful brother. I also got the snow blower back into the shed, hopefully for the balance of the winter. I am now delightfully tired and plan to pick up the non-lethal raccoon trap from my brother this afternoon, just in case the animal is still hiding in my garage. I am also taking Wendy to lunch and may go see my parents.

Tonight is Wendy and my annual New Year's Eve dinner with Barbara and Cliff. I plan to be home early and hope to sleep by 11:00 PM. The year is ending well and I have extremely high hopes for all of us around the world. We have spent the last two years getting into position with manufacturing plants, distribution centers and personnel as well as new technology and product lines. I hope to have additions of agents and partnerships also in work by the second quarter and to help grow our sales in Malaysia, Thailand and Singapore. We all have a lot of work ahead of us, but it is the kind I love. Make enough intelligent attempts and a certain number will score. As for our country, I am afraid the unemployment level will not go below 9%, but I hope I am wrong. It would be good if the banks here in the U.S. loosened up on their credit loans to entrepreneurs so they can reach for their dreams. By the end of 2012, we will have to make a decision about where to move, as our lease is up in April 2013. I wonder if the building I have been watching will be available and if we will be able to buy it? I am also wondering if we will get another plant in China and new plants in Malaysia and India. There is so much potential and fun to be had. I have a lot to look forward to, but all along the way I will continually tell myself to remember how fantastic it is to be able to go after my dreams, help people along the way, both directly and indirectly, and to be a force in general. The ability to think you can make a positive impact on yourself and the people and world around you is one of the greatest gifts and responsibilities of all. I know that I owe back for what I have and I will be gladly repaying that debt for the rest of my life. To all of you, I wish the best of New Year and I hope we can meet somehow, someway in the near future. I won't be hard to spot. Like my grandfather, I am the one who always seems to be moving quickly, the way I like to be.

Glossary Of Terms

Assembly - a group of metal and plastic parts that are put together to form a new product like a circuit pack
ALU - Alcatel-Lucent

CTRM - Composites Technology Research Malaysia Sdn Bhd; a Malaysian-based company specializing in compoisite technology and aerospace

EMI Shield - a material that will stop the flow of electromagnetic interference (EMI) "noise"
EPA - Environmental Protection Agency

Flame Rating - a designation for a material that shows it is resistant to a certain level of heat and flame

High Holy Days - A combination of a New Year and The Day of Atonement in the Jewish faith

IJM - Ideal Jacobs Mexico
IJN - Ideal Jacobs Netherlands
IJX - Ideal Jacobs Xiamen, China
ITAR - International Traffic and Arms Regulations; a protocol set by the US Department of state to control the export of defense related goods and services

MTCA - Micro TCA; a telecommunications platform targeting requirements for communications equipment

NDUM - National Defence University of Malaysia

OSHA - Occupational Safety and Health Administration
OSHA SHARP - Regional group for those companies with excellent health and safety systems

Passover - Jewish holiday celebrating the freeing of the Jewish slaves from ancient Egypt

Tanglewood - a music resort located in Lenox, Massachusetts that features outdoor summer concerts and classes for students
Tea Party - A conservative political movement founded in 2009 to protest and respond to the actions of President Obama and Congress

WOR - A New York based talk radio station that featured radio shows by Andrew Jacobs

226

Name Locator

The chart below can be used to help determine the friends, family and associates that Andrew is talking about .

Jacobs Family

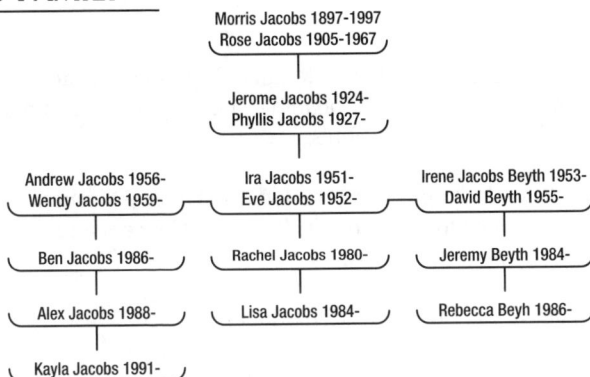

Morris Jacobs 1897-1997
Rose Jacobs 1905-1967

Jerome Jacobs 1924-
Phyllis Jacobs 1927-

Andrew Jacobs 1956-
Wendy Jacobs 1959-

Ira Jacobs 1951-
Eve Jacobs 1952-

Irene Jacobs Beyth 1953-
David Beyth 1955-

Ben Jacobs 1986-

Rachel Jacobs 1980-

Jeremy Beyth 1984-

Alex Jacobs 1988-

Lisa Jacobs 1984-

Rebecca Beyh 1986-

Kayla Jacobs 1991-

Aaron Family

Jeffrey Aaron 1930-
Bunny Aaron 1934-2011

Nathan Greenberg 1919-
Barbara Greenberg 1927-

Wendy Jacobs 1959-
Andrew Jacobs 1956-

Buz Aaron 1956-
Terry Willins 1955-

Barbara Frish 1954-
Clifford Frish 1952-

Hank Greenberg 1953-

Samual Aaron 1996-

Jessica Frish 1984-

Ruthann Greenberg 1956-

Barry Frish 1981-

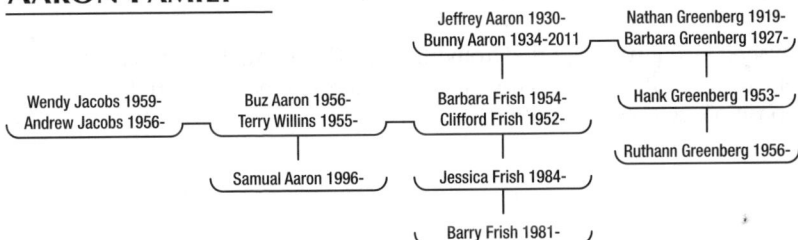

Business Associates

- **Ideal Jacobs US**
  - Brett Claydon, *VP of Product Development*
  - Jack Dispenza, *VP of Product Realization*
- **Ideal Jacobs Xiamen**
  - Ben Meng, *President*
  - Rina He, *Operations Manager*
  - Rosalyn Liu, *Customer Support Manager*
- **Ideal Jacobs Netherlands**
  - Jan-Willem Lucas, *Engineering Manager*
  - Jeroen Kuiper, *Managing Director*
  - Tamara Kuiper, *Jeroen's Wife*
- **Ideal Jacobs Mexico**
  - Paulina Vallejo, *General Manager*
- **WOR Radio**
  - Joe Bartlett, *Radio Host*
- Don Argintar, *Corporate Computer Specialist*
- Dan Gallagher, *Renewable Fuels*
- Candace Kelly, *ISO Auditor*
- Ed Weingram, *Patent Attorney*
- Douglas Macgregor, *Product Consultant*

Family Friends

- Dr. Kevin Browne, *Andy's Dentist*
- John Budish
- Rabbi Dan Cohen & Elana Cohen
  Family Friends; Radio Show Collaborators
- Howard Davis, *Corporate Attorney*
- Jeremy Gorin, *Friend of Ben Jacobs*
- Phoebe Greenfield, *Andy's Former Next-Door Neighbor*
- Paul Gross, *Tennis Coach*
- Katie Hannington, *Book Editor; Girlfriend to Ben Jacobs'*
- Alan Holzman
- Bailey Jacobs, *The Jacobs' Family Dog*
- Laurie Levey, *Andy's Childhood Friend*
- Gary Moscowitz, *Accountant; God Father to Kayla Jacobs*
- Marc Plotkin, *Entrepreneur; Muscian; Friend of Ben Jacobs*
- John Rudder
- Jean Shepard, *Radio Celebrity; Andrew's Mentor*
- Max Sussman, *Boyfriend to Kayla Jacobs*
- David Williams "Uncle Dave," *God Father to Ben Jacobs*

Colophon

This book was prepared using Adobe InDesign CS5 on an Apple iMac Intel Core Duo running OS X 10.6.7. The original text was supplied from the author as individual Microsoft Word files and was imported into Adobe InDesign CS5.

The body text is set in 9.5 point Optima Regular. Time stamp headings are in 10.5 point Optima Bold. The chapter headings are in 48 point Optima Bold. All body fonts are PostScript Type 1 fonts.

The front and back cover designs were created using Adobe Illustrator CS5 on an Apple iMac Intel Core Duo running OS X 10.6.7. Concept and designs by Richard Green III and Andrew Jacobs.

Layout and formatting were done by Richard Green III.

Editing was performed by Kate Hannington and Richard Green III. Proofreading corrections were entered into master Microsoft Word documents. Text was then imported and formatted in InDesign CS5.

The finished layout was exported from InDesign CS5 in Adobe Acrobat 9 format. The resulting PDF file was used to transfer the volume to the print facility for imposition, set-up and printing.

RG3

ALSO BY ANDREW JACOBS

BOOKS

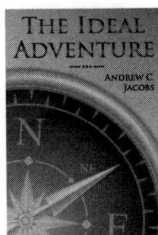

THE IDEAL ADVENTURE

The Ideal Adventure is the continuing story of eccentric, crazy, obsessive compulsive Andrew Jacobs who is leading his small mutli-national company into the 22 century. Why wait until this one is over?

THE IDEAL ERA

The Ideal Era chronicles the adventures in the life of global entrepreneur Andrew Jacobs. His diary picks up from his last book with the exploits of life on and off the road as he tries to build a small global empire. Come along for a truthful ride of world business from one man's perspective.

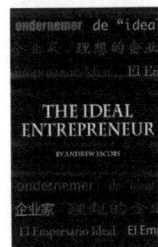

THE IDEAL ENTREPRENEUR

It became apparent that we needed additional locations worldwide. While manufacturing plants were not necessary we did put in distribution centers in Mexico, The Netherlands and China. Coordinating sites, people and various cultures was and continues to be a fascinating challenge. We had a window to get bigger, we knew it and tried to move as quickly as possible.

BEYOND THE ROAD TO CHINA

Ideal Jacobs Xiamen, China has been created and this book chronicles the adventures of transforming it into a profitable, vibrant young company. Also shared are various world voyages, Andrew's philosophies and how to continually have a good time while pursuing your life's dreams.

MY ROAD TO CHINA

I never planned to have a manufacturing plant in China but when one of our customers "suggested" it might be a good idea, we decided it was time to do it. My Road to China is a diary of the adventure from start-up to full-scale operation of Ideal Jacobs Corp. in Xiamen, China.

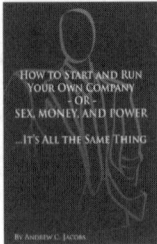

HOW TO START AND RUN YOUR OWN COMPANY -OR- SEX, MONEY AND POWER...IT'S ALL THE SAME THING

Have you ever felt that you could do a better job than your supervisor or the owner of the company you now work for? Have you wanted to make the decisions and live or die by your own wits? Most people, at one point in their life, have wondered what it would be like to own their own business.

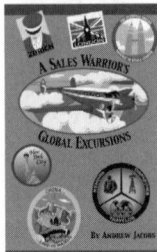

A SALES WARRIOR'S GLOBAL EXCURSIONS

Have you ever wondered what goes through the mind of a salesman when he is going after new customers, fixing trouble, and clawing his way to fame and/or fortune? A Sales Warrior's Global Excursions provides insight into this as well as contains the fictional novel by Andrew Jacobs about being the first "embedded" printer in the Iraq war.

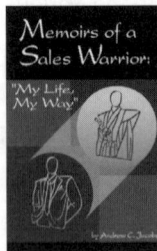

MEMOIRS OF A SALES WARRIOR: MY LIFE, MY WAY

Memoirs of a Sales Warrior covers many of Andrew Jacobs' life experiences and offers advice for dealing with the trials and tribulations that we all encounter during our journey through life. It also provides a blueprint for success, both within the working world and in our personal lives.

Audio CDs

On The Air

My dream of being a radio celebrity finally came true thirty-three years after I graduated college. I was finally in New York City and had two radio shows in the biggest media market in the country. The best part – I really loved doing it and the fact that I had to wait more than three decades only added to the joy.

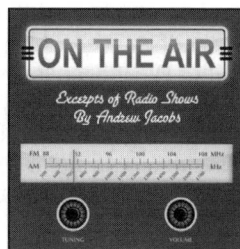

The Tao Of Andrew CD Box Set

In my life there have been turning points that have defined who I am. The four CD's in this box set have documented some of these moments, the people involved, how they have affected me and what I have learned. It is my hope that talking about some of my bumps and bruises will enable you to avoid them and allow you to move forward faster with a little less pain.

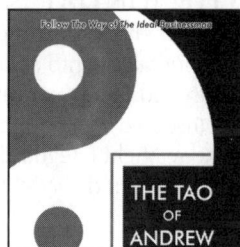

Hitting The Ideal Wall

It happens to all of us. The world closes in and there appears to be no way out. We have hit "the wall." Listen how you can keep that wall from crashing down in front of you and blocking your way. Turn it into the "Ideal Wall" by putting it behind you as a support to launch you toward success.

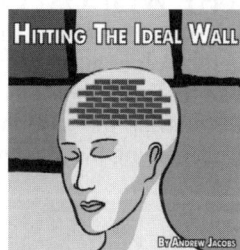

The Sunday Night Lifeguards: Living Through Tough Times

What happens when the economy slows down, unemployment skyrockets, retirements are pushed back and suddenly job security and the mental well being that goes with it are in jeopardy? How much money does it take to make us happy? Who decides and how do we know if we are doing it right? Our answers may surprise you.

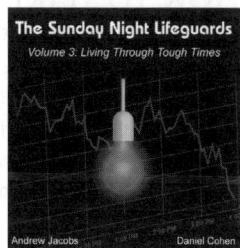

THE SUNDAY NIGHT LIFEGUARDS: CRISIS OF FAITH

Andrew Jacobs and Rabbi Daniel Cohen are back again, this time tackling the question of a "Crisis of Faith." What happens when your core religious beliefs don't seem to carry the same weight as before? Doubts begin to creep in and suddenly you are not sure what you believe and the best path to take. Is doubt a bad thing? Let the Lifeguards help you through the night.

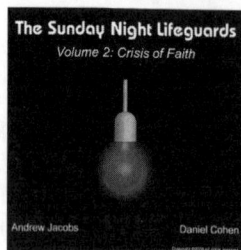

The Sunday Night Lifeguards
Volume 2: Crisis of Faith
Andrew Jacobs   Daniel Cohen

THE SUNDAY NIGHT LIFEGUARDS

It's hard enough getting to sleep on Sunday nights without taking into account such factors as life and death and family matters. Now, you can wade into the troubled waters of daily life with the help of The Sunday Night Lifeguards. Fear not the troubled waters... The Sunday Night Lifeguards are here to help.

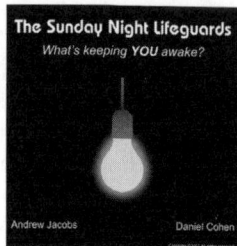

The Sunday Night Lifeguards
What's keeping YOU awake?
Andrew Jacobs   Daniel Cohen

THE WISDOM OF MY PARENTS

Like everyone else of my generation my parents are getting older and I wanted to record what life was like for them, their memories and advice. I believe the sum up the wisdom for their generation and it is something I wanted to keep forever.

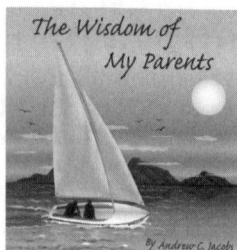

The Wisdom of My Parents
By Andrew C. Jacobs

HOW TO START AND RUN YOUR OWN COMPANY

As a companion to his book of the same title this CD brings a human side to starting and running your own business. Aided by his nephew and chef, Barry Frish, they explore some of the do's and don't of business and why most people should not own their own company.

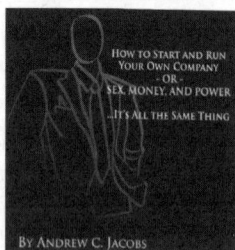

HOW TO START AND RUN
YOUR OWN COMPANY
- OR -
SEX, MONEY, AND POWER
...IT'S ALL THE SAME THING
BY ANDREW C. JACOBS